Women and Dance

Sylphs and Sirens

Christy Adair

Foreword by Janet Wolff

M
MACMILLAN

80387

First published 1992 by
THE MACMILLAN PRESS LTD
Houndmills, Basingstoke, Hampshire RG21 2XS
and London
Companies and representatives
throughout the world

ISBN 0–333–47625–5 hardcover
ISBN 0–333–47626–3 paperback

A catalogue record for this book is available
from the British Library.

Reprinted 1994

Printed in Hong Kong

Series Standing Order (Women in Society)

If you would like to receive future titles in this series as they are published, you can
make use of our standing order facility. To place a standing order please contact your
bookseller or, in case of difficulty,write to us at the address below with your name
and address and the name of the series. Please state with which title you wish to
begin your standing order. (If you live outside the United Kingdom we may not have
the rights for your area, in which case we will forward your order to the publisher
concerned.)

Customer Services Department, Macmillan Distribution Ltd
Houndmills, Basingstoke, Hampshire RG21 2XS, England

To Bonnie and Tansy

Contents

Illustrations

Foreword

Dance continues to be marginal to critical studies in the arts, and, as Christy Adair says in her introduction to this book, it is also marginal to feminist debates about culture. Social histories of the arts, including histories of dance, are for the most part descriptive and atheoretical; those social histories which are based on theoretical advances of the last twenty years are mainly limited to the visual arts. In the sociology of culture, dance only appears in small-scale, empirical studies of particular companies or groups of dancers, providing little in the way of a more complex understanding of how dance operates in the social sphere. European sociology of art, based in a neo-Marxist framework, has continued to privilege literature and the visual arts over the performing arts. And in the newer interdisciplinary arena of cultural studies, dance is only discussed (and this very infrequently) in the context of social dance as part of youth culture.

Now, it seems increasingly anomalous to ignore dance in critical cultural studies, at a time when the focus of the analysis of ideology, representation, and social relations is *the body*. Foucault has revolutionised the way in which we understand politics and culture, and the body now has to be seen as central to the operations of power and knowledge, across the realms of medicine, mental illness, correctional practices and institutions, and sexuality. This means not only that we have immediate access to a new analysis of what the dancing body might mean in contemporary culture, but also that the very marginalisation of dance (and dance studies) is cast in a new light. In a culture which depends in many ways on repressions of the body, the subversive possibilities of the moving body are safely contained by institutional and ideological strategies which render the dance harmless (construing it as effete, esoteric or highbrow, or containing it within the carnivalesque and the disco floor).

But dance has already been appearing on edges of critical theory. Christy Adair cites the few early attempts to talk about social dance in the framework of cultural studies. The metaphor of theory as 'choreography' has also recently been in play in literary studies, and the implications of this vocabulary might repay analysis. Most importantly, feminist cultural studies can begin from the insistence of some writers that we start from the body, and consider the role of dance, and the potential of dance, in the project of a feminist cultural politics. Here, I am thinking less of so-called French feminism, with its various calls to a politics of the body (with the dual risks, often pointed out, of essentialism or mysticism associated with this project), but rather of the more pragmatic formulations of those who work with Adrienne Rich's recommendation of a 'politics of location', firmly grounded in the corporeal experience. But bodies are not static. A feminist analysis of the dance can expand this work to demonstrate the nature and power of the moving body and the dancing body.

Christy Adair's study is valuable, first, because it introduces non-dancers to a history of dance – a history from the point of view of gender. Conversely, it introduces students of the dance to critical theory, and suggests ways in which dance studies can benefit from this work. Most importantly, and crucially, she brings dance into the centre of the study of gender and culture. Feminism, cultural studies, and dance analysis will all benefit from this reorientation, and from future work which I hope will take up this project.

JANET WOLFF

Acknowledgements

This book evolved from my involvement with feminism, including campaign groups, study groups and consciousness raising groups.[1] There are several women who have been supportive of both my personal development and my writing whom I would like to thank, particularly, Myna Trustram and Lesley-Anne Sayers. Discussions with Valerie Briginshaw and Kay Lynn about feminist perspectives of dance have helped me to clarify my ideas and Valerie Briginshaw's continued encouragement and generous use of her house as my writing base has ensured that this book developed beyond the ideas stage. Word-processing has considerably changed writing practice and I am grateful to Anne Lloyd and Lesley-Anne Sayers for sharing their skills in this area with me. The dance work of women committed to feminism, especially Emilyn Claid, encouraged me to develop my ideas about feminist dance practice. I would like to thank the X6 Collective who took many risks and made public women's oppression within dance.

I am grateful to a number of people who have read one or more drafts of specific chapters and others who have read drafts of the complete book, made useful suggestions and been willing to discuss contentious issues with me; these include, Valerie Briginshaw, Ramsay Burt, Emilyn Claid, Linda Dawson, Maedée Duprès, Fergus Early, Rachel Harrison, Jackie Lansley, Kay Lynn, Julia Pascal, Mary Prestidge, Lesley-Anne Sayers, Maggie Semple, Joyce Sherlock, Jane Turner and Myna Trustram.

I was fortunate to be able to work in a number of libraries which often felt like treasure troves despite the limited resources for dance study in England. I am particularly grateful to archivist Jane Pritchard who gave me a wealth of information about tracing photographs.

A key aspect of feminism is collective action and an understanding that to achieve change, support rather than isolation is necessary. I am indebted to several people who understood this and gave me the necessary encouragement to enable me to complete my task. In particular I would like to thank Geoffrey Appleton, Geraldine Brennan and Tyra Till.

Finally, I would like to appreciate my mother, Joan Baker, who taught me how good mothering can combine with creating a career; my father, Jack Baker, who taught me the importance of trade unions and how generous men can be; my sister, for her warmth and loyalty; Robin, my journeyman, who has never hesitated to encourage my growth and has proved by his excellent full-time parenting that this job can indeed be achieved by both men and women; Bonnie, my daughter, who fills me with delight with her insightful perspectives on dance and who constantly demonstrates, through her drawings and models, the life of an artist; Tansy, my daughter, who shows me what good use of the body is like and who has an irrepressible joy in moving and dancing.

CHRISTY ADAIR

Introduction

My journey to writing this book has been a long and passionate one filled with experiences of many of the issues which I discuss. *Women and Dance: Sylphs and Sirens* is a personal and political statement drawn from my involvement in the dance world and my political perspectives, both of which began at an early age. My grandparents, following working-class traditions, were keen Old Time dancers, winning many competitions. Right from the start I was thrilled with the pleasure of learning new skills and dressing up but disliked the competitive atmosphere, and my love of dancing was severely curtailed by it. Nevertheless, I waltzed out ready to revolutionise the world through dance and education, teaching all ages from three year olds to adults in a variety of institutions. At the same time I became actively involved with anarchism and the politics of the Peace Movement. Emma Goldman (1869–1940)[1] was an inspiring but difficult model to follow! However, her writings and her lifestyle offered me a vision which countered the confined images and roles of women.

My background, which influences my perspective and writing, is that of a white, working-class woman who has been through the higher education system. The overt inclusion of my experiences when appropriate embraces the idea that 'the personal is political'. The emphasis on the political implications of personal life within feminism follows in the footsteps of Chinese and Cuban revolutionaries who insisted that there could be no division between personal life and pursuit of the politics of liberation. The activists of the American black Civil Rights Movement also took this stance. Through consciousness-raising groups in the 1960s and 1970s women made connections between our personal experiences and the patriarchal structures within which we live. However, these groups were primarily composed of white women so that the theory

1

and practice from these groups seldom took account of the differences between women of colour and white women (Case, 1988).[2]

Whilst I use the word 'our' rather than 'their' when discussing women's experiences which are also mine, I recognise that women are not an homogeneous group and that feminism today has become a social force which acknowledges women's differences. There are no easy solutions to the problem of creating viewpoints which are appropriate to women's experiences when the language which we use reflects a vision constructed from the point of view of men. There are many words which are generally assumed to represent both men's and women's experiences but closer investigation reveals that only a male viewpoint is represented (Barling, 1984/5). A change of pronoun does not create a new language but it does challenge the expectations of an 'objective' viewpoint and the ideology of sexism which

> generalises from the experience of one section of society, men, to create an explanation of the experience of both men and women, of the organisation of society as a whole, and of the power relations within it (Roberts, ed., 1981, p. 15).

Whilst individual men can and do challenge these power relations the dominant ideology reinforces a socially constructed male viewpoint. When I use the term 'male viewpoint', and similar terms it is this power-based constructed viewpoint and those who support it which I am challenging rather than individual men who may too be working against such patriarchal constructions.

Sexual politics provided many answers about my experiences within social hierarchies, particularly in dance and education.[3] However, the euphoric times of the late 1960s, when nothing short of complete social transformation was envisaged, have been succeeded by governmental onslaughts on resources which particularly affect women. In the 1980s and 1990s in Britain,[4] severe cuts in health and educational provisions have created serious setbacks to the 'collective socio-economic and political projects of women's liberation' (editorial, *Feminist Review*, 1989, p. 4). Nonetheless, 'black studies' and 'women's studies' which came into existence through their respective political movements have survived and are examples of a number of resistances to established practices which put sexism and racism clearly on the political agenda. So far, in the various feminist debates about cultural practices, dance has been frequently ignored. In this book my aim is to redress the balance and to open up some important areas for discussion. Whilst dance is evident in a variety of contexts in contemporary Western society, I am focussing on those forms of dance, usually regarded as art, which exist in a theatrical setting and are performed for an audience. This choice provides the opportunity to discuss the social context of dance training, the representation of women in dance and women's achievements as both dancers and choreographers.

The first half of this book is concerned with the complex interconnection of factors which contribute to the production and reception of dance, including attitudes to the body, dance training, funding policies, critical practices and the representation of women in dance. The second half of this book discusses and illustrates women's achievements in dance, in the context of the above factors, including those in ballet, modern dance, postmodern dance, black dance and new dance.

The Women's Movement has recognised the centrality of the arts in shaping our ideas about ourselves and our society. However, since women have rarely been the creators of art we usually see our images through male eyes. As de Beauvoir (1972) elaborates, 'humanness' has been defined solely in terms whereby man is 'subject' and woman is 'other'. As soon as we begin to discuss women's art, particularly if we are looking for feminist art, we come upon certain difficulties, such as the easy trap of essentialism; it is extremely difficult to say, if not impossible, what is 'truly female' or 'truly male'. Any difference established is historically-defined and transitory. For example, we should not assume that because women painted flowers and still lifes (whilst excluded from life drawing classes) that this then is part of our definition of women's art. Women's exclusion from certain areas of artistic practice and the hierarchies in which, for example, paintings are valued more than craft works, exist because of repressive conditions and prejudice (Eckler, 1986).

To consider aesthetics and art from a feminist perspective necessitates establishing gender issues, thereby contradicting the situation in which women have been presented with art as genderless, when in fact it is seen from a male perspective, and correcting the situation in which women's work has been labelled 'women's art' and marginalised accordingly. Many women recognise the invalidation attached to the label 'women's art'. They reject the label and struggle to transcend it, insisting that they are artists not 'women artists'. At the same time, of course, when women make work or analyse from our position as women, negative feedback from the status quo is frequent, because we present a challenge to the constructed gender-neutral facade. Another response to women's work is to ignore it. Women's dance work is usually small scale because women are infrequently appointed to positions of power in mainstream companies. As Mackrell (1982) points out, there is little critical discussion of the avant-garde and those reviews which do appear are frequently written by critics whose bias is for ballet and who frequently dismiss new work. Women's work, therefore, suffers from lack of recognition in critical writing.

Since the 1970s there has been a growing feminist analysis of art and culture. The most significant work has been within film, visual art and literature. Music and theatre have been discussed much less and dance hardly at all. The theories advanced within the former areas are useful reference points from which to consider a feminist analysis of dance.

The issues of defining women's art, such as what roles are available to women within a particular medium and how women are presented, are important areas for feminist analysis. We also need to understand fully the dilemmas confronting women in the arts, and here specific disciplines offer particular insights. There has been much discussion of the representation of women and of female sexuality both within film theory and the visual arts. The historical and sociological aspects of women's role within the arts have also been discussed particularly within the visual arts. There has been concern to show why women's work has been misrepresented and the effect on women artists of lack of access to resources (Greer, 1980; Lippard, 1976; Parker & Pollock, eds, 1987).

Music is an under-researched area with regard to women's roles and contribution within the medium. The little research that is available provides some interesting insights. Late nineteenth century music was analysed in terms of 'feminine' and 'masculine' and an influential music critic, George Upton, held that women could provide inspiration for male composers in the role of muse, they could interpret music especially as singers but they could not write music (Neuls-Bates, 1982).[5]

Women's work in theatre has been discussed by Wandor (1984, 1986) and Case (1988) who offer useful analyses of the influences of feminism on theatre: 'Feminist plays could stage a kind of utopian CR group, in which women could interact with a freedom of experience and expression not easily attained in their daily lives' (Case, 1988, p. 113). Within literature the portrayal of women has been analysed and challenged and the conditions within which women write have been questioned (Woolf, 1977; Smith, 1986).

Feminism in recent years has informed dance[6] through the reconsideration of the social structure and through the emphasis on the personal as political; taking seriously women's personal experience of the world and connecting this to wider issues.[7] These changes have taken place in a context of a reconsideration of women's contribution to, and role within, the arts. This is the context in which I discuss women's experiences in dance.

I have drawn upon a variety of resources for my research. In addition to written material, I have used information gained as a member of dance workshops led by a number of artists, as a member of the audience at performances, from videos, films, photographs and from interviews with dancers, choreographers, directors, dance company education officers and critics.[8] Whilst many of these resources are from all over Europe and the United States of America, I have in the main been limited to what has been available in England. It is quite possible, therefore, that I have missed some important examples of women's work.

Class and race are two key areas which affect any consideration of gender and dance. In many ways they are integral; however, it is important to recognise that these are two enormous areas which need research in their own right and are necessary future studies. There has been a growing number of texts speaking of black women's history, experiences and art. For example, *The Heart of the Race* (Bryan, Dadzie & Scafe, 1985) which also discusses dance and *Charting the Journey* (Grewal *et al.*, eds, 1988) which makes a case for a clear acknowledgement of the work of black women artists. As Brenda Edwards, a black ballet and contemporary dancer, makes clear, she was restricted from the start (Constanti, 1989). The majority of black dance which I discuss here is of women with an African-Caribbean heritage whose work uses Western techniques. However, some Asian dancers have begun to explore the links with Western techniques and Eastern techniques, for example, Shobhana Jeyasingh; in *Bharata Natyam* (1982) she describes some of the difficulties which she has encountered in practising her art.

Overall this book aims to be both a challenge to restrictive, hierarchical practices within dance and a celebration of the outstanding achievements of women's creativity.

1

Dancing hierarchies – dance in society

Women's position in dance is affected by a complex set of historical and cultural factors. The many aspects of dance production, which include dance training, the organisation of dance institutions, the funding policies and critics' responses to dance work, all influence women's role in dance. A brief historical account of dance, together with an analysis of the production of dance, will form a framework for the consideration of women's contributions to the art.

An historical perspective

Today in Western industrialised societies dance does not have a central place in the community as it does, for example, in some African societies. The European court ballets of the fifteenth and sixteenth centuries were derived from social dances of the time for the benefit of the ruling classes. The antagonism of the Christian church, particularly apparent at that time, ensured the decline of dance as a form of expression for working people. Western dance history, like many forms of history, tells the stories of the white aristocracy. Even in books concerned with so-called 'popular' dance, it is frequently difficult to discern whether the dance was open to all people or just a privileged section of the community.

Throughout the centuries, within Europe, dances which became popular in one country would be passed on to other countries. After the Renaissance, the movements which were presented for men and women, both in the codified theatrical dancing and social dancing, had particular differences. These were not considered arbitrary differences, but rather in line with moral laws, and upheld social conventions. Women learnt to weave lively, earthbound steps and to hold sensual poses while men were taught to use the air space, as well as the ground, with vigour (from Blasis, 1820, in Jackson, 1971).

Social class influences were evident in the typecasting which evolved in classical ballet in the seventeenth and eighteenth centuries. Dancers were either noble, demi-caractère (i.e. bourgeois) or folk-character, (i.e. peasant-plebian) (Jackson, 1971). It is to this latter category that most black dancers are assigned if they join a mainly white ballet company. The twentieth century saw a breaking away from the white aristocratic traditions. In the USA, for example, the effects of the economic structure, the diversity of its immigrants, the native peoples, together with changes in the morals and social class all influenced dance work. It was not until the 1920s that it was considered acceptable for middle and owning-class women to dance in public performances. On the other hand, the theatre was an avenue of opportunity for poor women performers who managed to attract wealthy lovers or husbands as was also the nineteenth century Romantic ballet in Europe.

Jazz music evolved among black people as part of the culture of an oppressed group. This music and black dance influenced both social dance and theatre dance. For example, the chorus lines in black productions influenced Broadway musicals (see Chapter 8). In the climate of change for women after the first world war, women challenged European ballet and created their own forms of modern dance, although some women had made important innovations before this time (for example, Isadora Duncan; see Chapter 6). The emphasis on creative independence, rather than following their predecessors, has ensured that each generation has rebelled against their ancestry and created their own forms of contemporary dance.[1]

The modern dance movement, like the postmodern and new dance movements which followed it, was an attempt to narrow the gap between dancer and audience and make dance relevant to contemporary society. There was a desire to overcome the specialisation which had developed with industrialisation and to re-unite performer and audience (Shipman, 1973).

The influence of Christian fundamentalists has been such in the USA (and parts of Europe) that there has been much criticism of what has been considered immoral behaviour in connection with dance. Even as late as 1932 one of the school boards in Florida tried to prohibit dancing and ruled that any teacher who danced in the school year would lose their job (Hanna, 1989). This example indicates the effects of social attitudes on dance practice. There were, of course, resistances to such attitudes evidenced by the popularity of performers such as Isadora Duncan and the wide participation in social dancing, particularly in the 1920s.

 Absence of a suitable place to dance does not stop the activity. So that for those who did/do not have access to theatre dance or dance halls the street has evolved into a cultural arena. For example, break dancing, predominantly the province of young, black, working-class men, was frequently performed in outdoor spaces. Many people have recognised the importance of dance and fought for its place within Western society. It can be an expression of communal activity with a constructive influence. As Boas says, 'The psychological implications of dance, and the methods of using it as a broadening educative medium on a par with the other arts must be widely understood and propagandized' (Boas, 1972, p. 2).

The production of dance

It is important to recognise how hierarchies and power relations work within those organisations which are involved in the production of cultural forms. Whilst it is common today to credit an individual artist for a piece of work this obscures the collective production of art. For example, dancers need training and access to dance spaces, and dance productions frequently rely on set designs, composed music, lighting designs and so on. The emphasis on individualism which developed with the rise of industrial capitalism is the context in which the idea of the artist as an asocial being with genius arose. As Janet Wolff (1982) points out, the artist in our society is more likely to be isolated and alienated from society than at any earlier time. The marginalisation of artists is exacerbated further within dance because of the low status of the art. Despite this marginalisation, the arts are potentially powerful.

Whilst dance is socially produced, it is not reducible to social and political factors. In certain conditions, dance as art can play a part in social change and the existence of state censorship is a recognition of the realisable power of the arts. As Janet Wolff (1982) argues, 'there is no contradiction between the view that art is socially and ideologically constructed, and the view that artistic and cultural intervention in politics is a possibility' (p. 75).

Dance gives both insight into itself and into aspects of the society in which it is made. The materials it draws on are the everyday movements and the special events (for example, celebrations and rituals) which then become transformed through the choreographers' and dancers' viewpoints according to the values and attitudes which they hold. This transformation is influenced also by the resources which the producers have access to and the audience's reception (see below and Chapter 4).

From the 1960s onward dance has enjoyed an increased popularity as attitudes to the body have changed. 'The body's real and symbolic power persists through a person's lifetime. This power is critical in understanding the potential of dance, for the body is the instrument of dance' (Hanna, 1983, p. 8).[2] It is important to recognise, however, the cultural specificity of nonverbal communication. It is not, as some performers/choreographers assume, a universally understood language. Each person will have different social experiences to some extent because of the attitudes, beliefs and the values of the group/s (i.e. gender, race, class, age) to which they belong and the society of which they are a part.

In order to understand the context of dance production it is necessary to consider the ways in which different styles, forms and genres have been ascribed particular values by specific groups in certain contexts. In addition, research reveals the different access which men and women have to dance production as a result of economic and ideological structures (see below and Chapter 4). These social structures affect everything we do since they frame our lives (Wolff, 1982). The general oppression which women experience in society is continued within dance; therefore, dance does not necessarily offer more opportunities to women than to men despite women's numerical majority in the art form. In the last twenty years much research and discussion has focussed on the reasons for women's lower social status.[3] Women do not have full equal rights with men anywhere in the world despite some governments' legislation for equal opportunities. Nor is it always the case that the relatively rich countries of the world provide better situations for women than the poorer countries (Seager & Olson, 1986).

Economics

The economic power of major industrialised nations and the multinational companies ensures control of the modern communications which convey art to a worldwide audience. So, for example, these nations produce 78% of book titles and 88% of records and audio tapes sold (Taylor, 1985c). This power results in money rather than creativity being the deciding factor in terms of the art available. The priorities and values of these nations and companies are discernible in the art product. This is particularly disconcerting when you consider that American films are available in many parts of the world and the USA dominates world television trade, accounting for approximately 60% of all exports (Taylor, 1985c). This, undoubtedly, means that people from many parts of the world are seeing and internalising images which are likely to be inappropriate to their lifestyles and cultures. It is vital that this is reversed because 'Those who can control image in fact control communication' (Mottram, 1977, p. 229). To remove people's ability to communicate is to deny them their power. This transmission of culture through the media has been termed 'cultural imperialism' which has (to some extent) replaced economic and political imperialism (Wolff, 1982, p. 73).

The preferences, ideas and values of those who influence the market affect the choreographer. To the extent that s/he makes 'acceptable' work, the form and content will be affected and may well be limited as may her/his creative potential (Vazquez in Wolff, 1982).

Women's economic situation is made very clear in The United Nations Report (1980). Despite working for nearly two-thirds of the world's work hours, women only collect one-tenth of the world's income, and only one-hundredth of world property is owned by women. Such working conditions and economic restraints are evident in the dance world. As with women who work in the media, women in dance are usually situated in the low-status, low-paid jobs. In an Arts Council Report, *The Glory of the Garden* (1984) it was found that dance was underfunded and salaries were low. Most companies operate on a shoestring budget allowing a severely restricted time scale for creating work.

Women are in the majority in dance, as dancers, but this does not work in their favour. Although in most companies there are equal numbers of women to men this apparent equality hides the fact that at auditions women compete for places. Whilst training, men are far more likely to receive individual recognition because, although they are in the minority, their power status within society is seen to legitimise the art. Therefore, teachers pay more attention to their male students in the hope that more men in dance will ease dance from its marginal position within the arts. Frequently, men start their training later than women and sometimes successfully compete for jobs against women with more training and experience (Perron & Woodward, 1976). It may well be the case that there are many women leading their own companies and choreographing on the fringe but that is not where the power lies. The funding is precarious and often heavy touring schedules make creating work difficult. The above factors make clear the fact that the choreographer and the performer are affected by the 'cultural context that shapes them and their dance' (Royce, 1977, p. 214).

Ideology

The term ideology has a number of meanings but here I am using it to mean a system of attitudes, opinions and values held by a particular group or class, which influences their actions, serves their interests and frames their view of 'reality'. The social class structures are reinforced by the dominant ideology. Usually it can be shown that, 'the economically and politically dominant sections of society are generally dominant ideologically too' (Wolff, 1982, p. 52). The value systems of the dominant ideology belonging to the ruling groups usually maintain the status quo. This is done through institutions of, for example, education, the legal system, the media and the funding bodies. This ideology is powerful and pervasive and frequently not recognised so that the dominant world view is assumed to be 'commonsense', apolitical and beyond challenge.

There are many facets of ideology which influence dance in a complex way. For example, gender, race, class and age will all contribute to the statements of meaning within the dance product. The dance may reinforce the status quo and, therefore, women's role within it, which is apparent in classical ballet, or may challenge it, as much postmodern and new dance work has done. The relationship of dance to society is 'relatively autonomous'[4] because whilst the economic base is a determining factor it is not the sole one (Barrett, 1984). So that at the time of writing in England, the government's minimal support for the arts and reinforcement of women's traditional role within the family has not prevented critical subversive works (for example, *Flag* (1988) – see Figure 27 – Anderson; *Germs* (1989), Snaith – see Chapter 10).

Statements of meaning in dance make reference to what exists outside of dance and in this way embody 'world views' of particular values. Unless such a 'world view' is recognised by the audience any interpretation of the work will be incomplete. It is important for viewers to understand and appreciate dance in relation to their own social context and experience, otherwise their power of understanding and the essential role they play in completing the meaning of a work will be undermined. So for women, understanding aspects of the production of dance which emphasise the display of women's bodies and the reasons for this will influence the way they receive dance as members of the audience.

In the cultural production of dance, forms of representations are ruled by conventions, genres and accepted methods of communication. However, these aspects alone do not explain what is represented (Barrett, 1984). For example, role reversal does not really work because of the power relations between men and women. The general use of women's bodies as a commodity has to be taken into account to understand why women models are used to persuade men to buy goods rather than the reverse. Not only have women's bodies become commodities but the link with consumerism is well established.[5]

For challenges to roles and stereotypes to be effective an understanding of the role of ideology and the creation of meanings is central. There is an integral connection between ideology and the relations of production. In addition to class, these relations include the divisions of gender and race, together with definitions of what work should be done and who should do it.

Dance training

Dance production and dance training are inevitably affected by negative attitudes towards the body inherited from the Judaeo-

Christian tradition which is a major factor contributing to the marginalisation of dance in Western society. These attitudes hold the body and sexuality to be indecent which in turn affects any expression through the body and hence dance. The primary focus on the verbal in Western cultures compounds a dismissal of dance as anything other than entertainment (Brinson, 1988).

There are different routes to dance training for ballet, contemporary, postmodern, African, African-Caribbean, Asian and other dance techniques. Ballet training usually begins at an early age with private dance classes after school. The majority of students come from white, middle class families who have the affluence and values to support such training. Prejudicial attitudes continue to ensure that girls' study of dance is viewed as beneficial but boys' study of dance is viewed with suspicion. The training then reinforces a race, class and gender bias which is further reinforced in the majority of performances which students see. For those students who show an aptitude for dance in these early classes there are vocational schools, some taking entrants from eight years of age. These schools are fee-paying and offer a wide range of dance subjects together with a traditional academic curriculum.[6]

Another route to dance training begins when some students become interested in dance through classes at state schools or dance clubs run after school. Whilst these classes may include mainly contemporary dance techniques some may not. The emphasis on improvisation and creating work is usually greater than in ballet classes where the emphasis is on learning the technique. Many contemporary dancers did not begin their dance training until in their late teens or early twenties. Their route into a three-year dance training course was often via evening classes at a school for contemporary dance.

Many of the postmodern dancers had a contemporary dance training and were experienced members of contemporary dance companies; some also had ballet training. However, in their rebellion against ballet and contemporary dance they questioned the value of technique and reassessed the type of training suitable for the work they were interested in. Techniques which were studied as a basis for dance work then widened considerably to include release techniques and martial arts.[7]

African, African-Caribbean, and Asian dance techniques are rarely taught as an integral part of dance training courses except, for example, in the dance establishments specialising in classical Indian dance forms. They are frequently found on community dance courses and viewed as an extra rather than rigorous training systems in their own right. The debt which the Western dance techniques and choreography of modern and postmodern dance owe to these forms is rarely acknowledged, nor is their influence on ballet.

Dance is assumed to be central in the life of most young dance students. An extreme example is that of the young dancers at the Russian Imperial Ballet school where, Nijinsky reported, parents gave up almost all rights when a child entered the school. He also mentioned that the organisation of the Russian imperial ballet was modelled on the military. In many US ballet schools, students' families are expected not to interfere. In addition, any academic study is not expected to impinge on rehearsals or performances. One student who chose to go through some graduation exercises at her school thereby missing an important rehearsal for an imminent performance, found herself dropped from the cast when she made a mistake at the following rehearsal (Forsyth & Kolenda, 1970).

Dance is a very time-consuming commitment and anyone who takes it up enters a particularly rarefied world within which traditional gender relationships are reinforced. The training through which body shape and physical skill are constructed contributes to this. In addition, the discipline which is crucial to a dancer's training is one of the means through which this construction is achieved. The self-discipline dancers acquire enables them to strive and reach the standards required which are initially imposed by the teacher's discipline in class. The hard work, repetition and structure of the daily class frequently results in 'unthinking' dancers, trained to accept unquestioningly the professional requirements. For women this structure mirrors women's expected role as passive rather than active in society.

Gender is a determining factor of the particular steps and movement qualities used within both classical and contemporary dance technique classes. The daily class illustrates the differences for women and men (Turner, ed., 1990). Whilst women are required to be more supple in their legs and backs men are expected to achieve spectacular jumps and turns. An adagio is a slow movement combination in which one leg is usually extended high, women are expected to attain these positions with ease whilst men are not expected to attain either the height or the ease to the same degree. Whereas the strength and control which the women require is hidden by the apparent ease in their performance the strength and control which men need for jumping is displayed (Laurie, 1989).

To begin training, particularly in ballet, one must have the required body shape. Daily, throughout training, the dancers are confronted with their body shapes in every class as they dance before walls of mirrors (see Figure 1). For women, who are socialised to pay a good deal of attention to their looks, this daily confrontation usually results in a dissatisfaction with themselves and a constant battle for perfection which frequently includes extreme dieting. As Natalia Makarova, a Russian ballerina, says, 'Mirrors are the big enemy. When you don't like your image, it's very depressing, but you try to work it out' (quoted in Shaw, 1989, p. 31). This regime is encouraged or exacted by the teachers. Gelsey Kirkland, a principal dancer with the New York City Ballet cites

1   Twentieth-century ballet class in England – Royal Ballet School – 'The Dancer's World'.

Balanchine, the company director, saying during a daily class, 'must see bones' as he banged her sternum and rib cage with his knuckles. 'He did not merely say "eat less". He said repeatedly, "eat nothing"' (1986, p. 56). Indeed, some companies make their dancers weigh in, and anorexia nervosa is an ever-present reality (Forsyth & Kolenda, 1970).

Undoubtedly, the dancer's training will be a fundamental aspect of the choreography s/he performs and/or makes. The notion of equality which was important for many postmodern and new dance choreographers was in opposition to the gender differentiation which they had internalised with their trainings and were attempting to free themselves from.

Dance institutions

The power relations within dance are quite clearly not in the hands of women, despite many women's remarkable achievements as pioneers and spectacular performers.[8] The British Theatre Directory of 1987–88 lists thirty-three ballet and opera companies, of which only six are directed by women. In London most of the major theatres are directed by men. A more detailed examination of four British ballet companies, London City Ballet, London Festival Ballet (now English National Ballet), Northern Ballet and Sadlers Wells Royal Ballet (now Birmingham Royal Ballet), reveals the dominance of men in the most powerful positions in dance. This is also the case for the Royal Ballet. All the directors are male, there are more ballet masters than mistresses and more male principal dancers. Of the administrators the majority are male. Men also dominate the electrical, lighting and music departments. Women work in the marketing, press, education and wardrobe departments at all levels and do all the secretarial work. From this information it can be seen that the structure of dance mirrors that of society, with men in the most powerful roles and women frequently doing 'back-up' work (Shaw, 1989). The above companies are larger than most contemporary companies and are hierarchically organised with dancers ranked as principals, soloists, coryphees and corps de ballet.[9]

Dancers' love of dance is exploited.[10] There are many dancers out of work so that dancers who do have a job are reluctant to demand more money (Hanna, 1988a). This is particularly relevant for women because the competition for jobs is greater for women as they are in the majority. Many company managements take any request for a raise as a personal attack and hold an attitude that the dancers should be grateful for the work which they have.

During a pay dispute with the New York City Ballet one dancer wrote:

> . . . how awful we feel, we only want enough money to pay the rent. Many of the younger kids simply cannot afford it. Mr B [Balanchine] takes it personally of course. We are his creation, his tools: without him we are nothing, and without us – well, he needs us, but he can always find dancers. The question seems rather basic: do we want to fight for our own pockets, or do we give a little for him? We . . . love him. We will show him that – and maybe scrimp a little more (Bentley, 1982, in Laurie, 1989, pp. 64–5).

The Royal Ballet Company in London, after years of putting up with unfair treatment, finally decided that they had had enough and voted to take industrial action to gain improved pay offers which they were eventually awarded (Benjamin, 1990; Whitfield, 1990). Most major dance companies are situated in the large cities which have notoriously high rents and more expensive living costs so that dancers are doubly disadvantaged. Dancers work a punishing schedule of classes and rehearsals, frequently having little time or energy just to do everyday tasks like shopping and washing.[11]

Dancers at the top of the ballet hierarchy might be able to decide to have children and earn enough to pay for childcare in order to continue their careers. However, for most dancers this is not an option. In recent studies in which women have discussed the issue of children and a dance career most of them viewed the combination as impossible not because of any physical difficulties but because of problems of organisation of childcare together with exhausting rehearsal schedules and gruelling touring programmes (Laurie, 1989; Shaw, 1989; Sherlock, 1988).

The more prestigious parts tend to go to those high up in the hierarchy if in a ballet company or to those with longest service in a contemporary company. Success for the dancers is measured by how many dances they are cast in and how much dancing they do. The daily classes also reinforce the company hierarchy, for example, with dancers taking set places at the barre or moving across the

floor according to their rank in the compar
Kolenda, 1970, p. 235). Although there is co
dancers this must not affect the overall co-c
dancers necessary for a successful performance. Ir
tion and monetary gain are secondary considerati
the company and audience satisfaction.

In order for the dancer to achieve high standar.. ..... contribute
to company cohesion the dance role must be the primary one in her/
his life. Other commitments are strongly discouraged by the
teachers and other company personnel. The shortage of work acts
as a controlling factor so that no matter how adverse the conditions
dancers do not withdraw easily from a company because there may
not be an alternative company with which to dance. There are few
opportunities for dancers to be involved in any interests outside of
the dance world. This inevitably affects their ability to question and
challenge the conditions of their work. In addition, the preoccupation with health, body and looks is time-consuming and self-
involving.

The standards of dance are harsh and frequently internalised so
that, for example, a leading dancer who omitted to fasten her
ribbons on her shoes in the correct way, which resulted in both of
them breaking during a performance, ostracised herself.

> She managed to keep the show going. That's vital. Nothing is to stop the
> show. She kept dancing. It was such a horrible thing to do that no one
> spoke about it. We avoided the topic. It was a horror. Next summer she
> had nothing whatsoever to do with dance (Forsyth & Kolenda, 1970, p.
> 233).

Dancers are pressurised by their own internal standards and the
standards of the company which are in turn affected by funding
policies.

Funding

Although the post 1979 Conservative government has tried to move
away from government funding of the arts, since 1945 that has been
the primary source of finance for the arts, administered by the Arts
Council and Regional Arts Boards. This is not without its problems.
England has a very strong class system and the values of this

..m, as mentioned above, are reinforced by the administering of
..nds from these councils. Robert Hutchinson (1982) in a study of
the politics of the Arts Council recognises that the Council
encourages and legitimises some forms of creativity whilst ignoring
others. Further, he points out that impartiality is unlikely when, as
for example in 1982, there were strong links between the director-
ship of the Royal Opera House and the Arts Council Chair.
Moreover, the Royal Opera House board members are also
dominated by men from public schools (Eton, also Oxford
University).

Women are usually bypassed for appointments to the Arts
Council or governing bodies of national companies and are,
therefore, under-represented. There were thirteen women among
the first sixty-six appointments at the Arts Council between 1945
and 1966 but only nine women among the next sixty-six between
1967 and 1980. Of the nineteen people who stayed at the Arts
Council for seven years or more only one was a woman. In addition,
black groups and other cultures are also very much under-
represented.

The values which are implicit in much of the Arts Council's work
equate the 'high' cultures of Western Europe with civilisation. This,
of course, ensures that working-class arts are neglected, and little
has been done to support black arts although that is changing
slowly. As Hutchinson (1982) says, 'Studying the Arts Council it is
easy to see what Marx and Engels meant when they denounced the
state as a committee for the management of the affairs of the
bourgeoisie' (p. 151). It is important to remember that the Arts
Council is not neutral but rather is a product of a class and has
loyalties to it. By the time they are appointed to the board the
members are likely to be affluent and unwilling to disturb the status
quo with radical reforms for women, blacks or any other oppressed
group.

Where the money comes from and how much is available are
crucial factors for any dance performer, company or new work. As
has been seen above, whether the work is organised within a major
company or by an independent artist, very much affects the funds
available. The funding policies of the particular country also affect
work. Recently, in England funding has been cut back drastically
with the resulting emphasis on making work which sells. This in
turn frequently means deeply reactionary work from both ballet and

contemporary dance companies, producing dance which entertains but does not challenge or offend. The demand from the government that artists seek business sponsorship is worrying because this is likely to lead to work which does not take risks (Peppiatt, 1984a; Murdin, 1990).

The new dance movement to date has resisted traditional values and offered alternatives, but without funding, these innovations will disappear. This is particularly precarious for women because it is mostly women who are working on the fringe and in situations without regular income. At the moment the arts are one form of unofficial opposition to the government, producing a critique of an ideology and practice which puts profits before people.

It is no accident, of course, that a government should attempt to suppress the arts because the arts have enormous subversive potential. By limiting and controlling education and the arts the government successfully confines the opportunities for people to think and act for themselves and resist oppressive policies.

The Arts Council's Report *Stepping Forward* (Devlin, 1989), makes clear the difficulties under which dance labours, with companies underfunded and overstretched. There is much discussion, disagreement and competition about who should be funded, which does not make for a healthy, co-operative art form. Four 'client companies', the Royal Ballet, Birmingham Royal Ballet, English National Ballet and Northern Ballet, use 76% of the Arts Council dance budget. This then leaves a mere 24% for all of the other ballet and contemporary dance companies and new dance initiatives. Unfortunately, and this is partly perhaps a reflection of increasingly conservative values in addition to inadequate funding, audiences have continued to support the ballet performances but the audiences for contemporary dance have decreased.

Dance companies are under enormous strain with taxing touring schedules and heavy educational commitments which are requirements of the Arts Council. Many of the contemporary dance companies have suffered because of such commitments and unrealistic funding. Black dance is finally receiving recognition and funding support is slightly more widely distributed. In the end, though, we should not limit ourselves to concern about who gets which bit of a pittance but why it is a pittance in the first place.

If, as appears clear from above, funding supports the status quo then women who want funding for producing choreographic work from their own perspective are not likely to have a particularly easy time. In order to obtain sponsorship a degree of forceful drive is necessary. This is a quality which is expected of males in our society but not of females. So to obtain backing for their work women have to go against the accepted social codes.

Critics

Dance critics play a part in the dance production process. The Arts Council takes notice of recent reviews when making decisions concerning companies' funding. It is interesting to note that a high proportion of critics writing for the national press have an Oxbridge background which endorses certain values; the Arts Council is then influenced by those values. It is significant, for example, that proportionally there has been a distinct emphasis on ballet in reviews which both reflects and perpetuates readership interest and preference (Davis, 1984).

This is what the critics are familiar with and feel safe writing about. As Royston Maldoom (1983) points out, it is much more disconcerting to be presented with as many techniques as performers/practitioners because then the critic, 'is faced with the problem of "seeing" dance rather than "comparing" it'. This is particularly problematic because women wanting to present new work will be working in ways which are unfamiliar to the critic. As Miranda Tufnell discovered when working with Dennis Greenwood, the critics had no categories for their work so for a long time they ignored it with the result that it remained invisible (Crickmay, 1982).

At a conference of the Association of Dance and Mime Artists (ADMA) in 1981 in London, many important issues were discussed including how artistic worth is defined. Such discussions need to be ongoing to ensure that values and attitudes are continually questioned and space made for groups which do not support the dominant ideology. Two other important issues, racism and sexism in dance, were discussed at the same ADMA Conference. Looking at the workshop reports now, the points made are still relevant and very much linked with funding. For example, one of the issues discussed at the 'sexism in dance group' was the need for better childcare facilities at dance classes and venues. The situation is only marginally better now than it was then. An issue discussed by the 'racism in dance group' was the need for a policy for combating racism in dance. Whilst the awareness of this issue has improved and recommendations have been made in the recent Arts Council Report (Devlin, 1989), there is still much to be done in terms of changing dance practice.

Conclusion

The power relations of the society within which dance is produced affect the work at the levels of economics and ideas. These relations affect women adversely because the social construction of gender places women in a less powerful position than men. For women who direct their own companies, choreograph their own work and attempt to retain some autonomy over their performances, finding ways of subverting these power structures is necessary for success. The Gay Liberation Movement and the Women's Movement have helped to change attitudes to dance partly by an acceptance of sensuality which is central to dance.

 . . . dance is about the body, the body as it moves in space and time, but nonetheless, the body. Our eyes are focused on the legs, arms, torso, neck and back as the dancer dips, turns, runs, leaps. No matter how sexually innocent the movement it still stirs a sensual response in its audience (Jacobs, 1976, p. 267).

 This body is not as is often argued 'natural' but 'socially constructed' and this construction will be the subject of the next chapter.

2

Cultured bodies – the social construction of the body

The body, which is central to dance, is socially constructed. This means that bodily behaviour is learnt rather than 'natural' and meanings which may be attributed to the body change over time and according to social circumstances. Whilst social context is significant it is also important to recognise the subversive potential of the body. Such a stance offers a challenge to the traditional interpretations of the body and so it is of particular advantage to women and to the status of dance. In this chapter I discuss how the body is socially constructed through concepts such as dualism, 'the natural', 'the essential self' and 'the feminine' which are evident in institutional practices such as the family, education and the arts. The subversive potential of the body is diminished through such constructions and women in dance, in order to have their work taken seriously, have to confront negative attitudes which arise from these constructions. In Western society we are surrounded with paradoxical messages about the body. On the one hand we are urged to keep fit, be healthy and enjoy physicality, on the other hand physical education and dance are generally perceived to be of less value than 'academic' subjects and manual work is often viewed as less significant than 'intellectual' work.

Dualism

These messages are examples of dualism which is concerned with two independent principles of, for example, good and evil and separates mind from body. Dualism is an obstacle to reclaiming women's power in Western society because women are traditionally denigrated through their perceived association with evil, the body and nature. At the same time, men are traditionally elevated by their perceived association with good, the mind and culture. Without the dualism which permeates our language, it would not be possible to write of 'the body' or of 'the mind'. The terms would be meaningless. However, the references in this book to 'the body' refer to the 'lived body' which assumes a body/mind position as far as possible, rather than in opposition to 'the mind' (Fraleigh, 1987).

References in dance classes and dance literature to the 'body as an instrument' and the need to be 'present with both mind and body' reinforce a notion of separation so that it is more 'mind over matter' than a 'lived body' or a 'thinking body' (Fraleigh, 1987, p. 9). Such references in the teaching and learning of dance encourage dancers to view dance training as purely physical. This results in a perception of the body as a machine, an object to be worked into shape. It is this approach which can lead to damage through injury when dancers push themselves too hard. In addition, dance training which endorses this approach limits the potency of the body through harsh control. But dance also offers the potential for an anti-dualist stance with the recognition that the 'body is not something I possess to dance with. . . . I do not order my body to bend here and whirl there. I do not think "move", and then move. . . . My dance is my body as my body is myself' (Fraleigh, 1987, p. 32). However, if dance is marginalised within society this liberating potential is hidden and reduced (Dempster, 1988). These values associated with a dualist position, which evolved during the Enlightenment when men were identified as more rational than women, restrict both women's and men's potential (Caplan, ed., 1987).

The early modern dancers in the USA in the 1920s and 1930s countered many of the negative connotations associated with the body. The dancers were one of the main symbols of the New Woman who emerged after decades of women trying to free their bodies through art, exercise and dress reform (Kendall, 1979). Doris Humphrey, an American modern dance choreographer in this period, began her lectures by describing modern dance as a theatre art 'of our time' saying that,

Dancers found that they were people first with new attitudes and feelings about life in a world of vast sociological, psychological and historical change . . . The old forms would not do, the resources of the human body had to be enlarged (renewed), revitalized to contain the new dance (Cohen, 1972, p. 118).

The women dancers of this time created movement from themselves as 'thinking bodies', recognising the futility of a practice which attempted to separate physical and thought processes. The path of modern dance parallels women's growing awareness that we have a right to instigate change and be involved in the social, political and economic areas of society.

The portrayal of women as either good or bad, virgin or whore, mother or mistress is another manifestation of dualism which confines women. Isadora Duncan, a pioneer of modern dance at the beginning of the twentieth century, attempted to solve this polarisation by thinking of her body as a temple which was exulted by the intellect and spirit which it encased. To her the idea that lust could be evoked in the audience by her body was unthinkable (Jowitt, 1988). Whilst this solution did not avoid dualism it can be seen as a positive view rejecting women's denigration. However, women in dance have to combat the frequently made connection between sexuality and dance if they wish to convey their own message. Sexual display and meanings are evident both in ballet and contemporary dance when for example, women are presented as desirable. Such meanings fit in very well with society's demand for a perfect body. Dance also provides images of 'the superhuman body in motion' (Copeland, 1986b, p. 12) and is sometimes viewed as a threat to moral standards (see Chapter 1).

It is commonly assumed that women are to be identified more with the body than men because of our bodily cycles and reproductive abilities. 'This closeness to the body is a potential source of danger in a rational technically orientated culture, in that this "nature" can erupt into the culture in the form of erratic or irrational behaviour' (Thomas, 1982b, p. 6). This potential subversiveness of the body offers a rich resource for women for social change. However, the fear of the eruption of 'nature' into culture results in a wide variety of social controls. Yolande Snaith uses some of these controls as an inspiration for her dance *Germs* (1989, a development of *Lessons in Social Skills*, 1988):

Extracts from *The Young Ladies Journal* 1866 provide the ingredients for a concoction of surrealist recipes, absurd demonstrations and moral sermons on matters such as vice and virtue, domestic education, etiquette and acceptable social behaviour (programme note).

The 'natural'

What is 'natural'? When comparing different societies it becomes apparent that a 'natural' way of doing things is culturally specific and not 'natural' at all. Margaret Mead's (1970) studies were influential for women's understanding of our roles and for the details they provided of the varied manifestations of gender in different societies. In particular her evidence made clear that that which is associated with men has status and power and that which is associated with women does not.

Until about 1860, sexual roles, marriage and the family were assumed to be 'natural'. However, for the next thirty years anthropologists showed that the Victorian middle class ideal family was not part of nature but the result of a resistance to nature. Such discoveries did not benefit women, because the male anthropologists used this information to justify women's confined roles within English culture (Caplan, ed., 1987). Victorian England was shown to be elevated from a 'savage state'. 'Savages' were equated with nature and sexuality connected with animality. Many anthropologists argued that the control of sexuality was crucial to the continuation of civilisation.

These Victorian values have continued to influence current attitudes. Some major dance studies have been criticised for ethnocentric approaches. For example, Sachs, in his much quoted study, *World History of the Dance* (1963) treats his own culture as complex and dispersed and other so called 'primitive' cultures as simple and static. In much dance history 'primitive' dance is cited and then Western dance is discussed more fully. The lack of detail applied to the former is, as Youngerman (1974) argues, to imply its inferiority. Rust (1969), Lomax (1978) and Langer (1973) all fall into the trap of assuming that because dance is important in some small-scale societies it is important in all of them (Thomas, 1986). Nonetheless, it is important to consider these studies as they illustrate some of the values which underpin the study of dance.

In Western societies dance as social activity and dance as art have become separate areas with art holding an elevated position. This has particular repercussions for women who have 'object-status' as performers.

Some artists, for example, Susan Hiller and Mary Kelly are concerned to deconstruct the 'natural' in their work. Marianne Wex (1979) is also concerned with this task in her photographic study of female and male postures and gestures. Her book makes clear the fact that women learn acceptable bodily posture and behaviour which is different from that of men. One example of this is a page of photographs of men's and women's standing postures. The line of male photographs are at the top of the page with the line of female photographs at the bottom. She organises them in this way, because this order reflects the patriarchal hierarchy. The men are all standing with their legs apart and hands clasped behind their back. The women are standing with their legs together and their arms crossed in front of them. The differing attitudes to their bodies and the amount of space used is very illuminating. Men clearly feel more at ease in presenting themselves and taking up a good deal of space whereas women shrink from the space and try to enclose themselves.

Another example from Wex's book is one of sitting postures. In these photographs the men sit legs apart sprawled out into space whereas the women sit with legs closed, again with arms crossed over themselves, as if for protection. Wex says that she takes for granted that women and men learn to move differently from an early age. She argues that this female and male body language is related to other female and male tasks.

'The essential self'

Theories of 'the natural body' and 'the essential self' have an appeal which has attracted some feminists. But does an 'essential self' exist? It is tempting when faced with a restrictive, oppressive set of social structures and practices to seek for a core untainted by such social confinement. However, whilst attempts to reclaim our identities and creations of utopian visions may empower us and enable us to envisage alternatives, they cannot be a substitute for a clear perception of the factors which contribute to a socially constructed body (see Brown & Adams, 1979).

A reconsideration of the body from a feminist perspective entails a re-evaluation of the meaning of biology and its relation to psychological, social and cultural factors. Analysis of the body which resists binary oppositions offers a challenge to traditional perceptions and possibilities of new identities. Some French feminists, particularly, Luce Irigaray and Hélène Cixous, have focussed on a deconstruction of binary oppositions influenced by the philosophy of Jacques Derrida. Their analyses of sexual difference reject the belief of fixed gender identities and a polarised opposition between male and female and offer instead a more fluid interchange of diverse elements. However, whilst the above can be a useful concept there is a danger of essentialism in their theses despite attempts to circumvent this. There is also the objection that their positions tend to discuss women universally without taking sufficient account of women's differences. Whilst Cixous' stance on the one hand usefully attempts to move away from a focus on the sex of the artist to a discussion of the place of sexuality and desire within the text (i.e. dance), Moi (1985) suggests that in other ways Cixous may actually not be undermining patriarchal ideology for example 'in her eagerness to appropriate imagination and the pleasure principle for women' (p. 123).

Cixous says, 'by writing herself woman will return to the body which has been more than confiscated from her, which has been turned into the uncanny stranger on display . . . Write yourself. Your body must be heard. Only then will the immense resources of the unconscious spring forth' (in Marks & Courtivron, eds, 1985). The idea of the body being a means to discovery of the unconscious, 'the real self' is evident in some new dance practice (see Chapter 9). An underlying theme in many new dance workshops is the desire to free oneself of social constructions (Adair *et al.*, 1988). The value of such an approach is that it can offer a vision, as Cixous does, of women's creativity. Such a vision was Isadora Duncan's concern as she saw herself 'dancing the freedom of women' (see Chapter 6). However, the focus on expressing 'the essential self' and on the issue of whether women dance differently simply because they belong to the category 'woman' leads back to biological essentialism. These arguments result in a determined position, with no room for social change. The important point is that 'women do not [dance] differently by virtue of being born with wombs but because they [have] learnt to become women' (Gunew, 1988).

Perceptions of the body do not remain constant. As Coward (1989) points out, the

> body is no longer viewed as degenerate, subject to natural impulses, especially sexual impulses, which dragged man down among the animals . . . Nor, indeed, is it the sexually free body of the 1960s, where sexual connection was essentially the most important self-expression of the body. Instead, we have an essentially innocent body, born with wholesome impulses but gradually worn down by the hostile world (pp. 50–1).

The 'feminine'

In the theatrical tradition of Western culture, the dancing body is often discussed in terms of the 'feminine', as for example Balanchine's statement that ballet is a 'woman, a garden of beautiful flowers' (quoted in Dempster, 1988, p. 38). As Dempster points out, 'it follows within the logic of patriarchal social order that its power [the 'feminine'] and the power of the body must be controlled, constrained, disguised or denied' (1988, p. 38). Aspects of this control are evident in traditional dance training.

Part of this control is woman's social role in which she learns to defer to others rather than to be the main actor in her own life. Given this framework, it is not surprising that female dancers accept male choreography which reinforces this view. This deference results in women undervaluing and feeling insecure about ourselves and our opinions. We also learn that part of our social role is to be connected to others and to shape our lives according to a man.

> The social taboo against being an autonomous woman is internalised. Self-containment and separateness feel selfish, self-centred, and even aggressive for a woman . . . Since connection to others must be maintained, a woman must make herself into a person others will find pleasing; in making herself in their image she may end up not knowing who she is (Eichenbaum & Orbach, 1982, p. 28).

Here then is part of the dilemma for female dancers. They are socialised as women to please others, their training encourages them to be performers rather than creators. The image of the ballerina is a popular one with young girls and idealises 'feminine' aspects of woman. The reason more women do not challenge such an image, either as dancers or as audience, can be understood when one recognises how much woman's socialisation complements the female dancer's role and how much most dance images epitomise the 'feminine' (Furse & Lansley, 1977).

However, as McRobbie (1984) points out, there are contradictory aspects to women's role within dance. On the one hand there are social expectations that girls learn dance because it is a suitable 'feminine' leisure activity or career. The control of the body and presentation of girls and women for admiration are part of these expectations. On the other hand there are aspects of dance which can provide a space for resistance. Within fantasy, dance plays a role in an area which 'cannot be totally colonised' (p. 134). Also the popular ballet stories in girls' comics and books offer an alternative to the roles of domesticity which are the usual social realms for women.

Another role women learn is to nurture. The expectation is that women will care for others and assist them to express what they need. So if we look at the female dancer's role and male choreographer's role from knowledge of these socialising methods, it can be seen that they match exactly. The male choreographer has been taught that he has a right to consider the world his, that he is a human being rather than just a man and that women are there to meet his emotional needs. The female dancer has been taught that her role is to defer to others and to help them express their needs. The two are an ideal fit. The roles mirror those of society and it is hardly surprising that choreography is predominantly a male occupation.

Bodily expression

Women's physical expression is a key question in relation to dance. However, there has been an understandable ambivalence towards the body in feminist theory. The body has been cited as a source of women's oppression and there has been a good deal of focus on control of the body in terms of reproduction rights and fighting sexual harassment. It is not surprising that some feminists have taken on the mind over body stance of dualism, ignoring the 'lived-body'. Nevertheless, a significant feminist theme has been the transformation of biological sexual differences into culturally gendered identities. Discussion of women's bodily oppression and the cultural meanings associated with our bodies has come from women's lived experiences and feminist research. So from the oppressive effects of rape, pornography and domestic violence to the potential of sexuality, reproduction, sport and fitness, dress reform and paid work, new theories of the body are being formed (Allen & Grosz, 1987). Women's performance work has particularly challenged cultural norms and forged new perceptions as evidenced, for example, in M. Roth's book *The Amazing Decade* (1983).

So is bodily expression 'natural' or socially constructed? There have been two major traditions of study. The first is the evolutionary tradition, following Darwin. The universalists hold the view that bodily expression is either innate or inherited and cross-culturally universal. They, therefore, assume that similar behaviour patterns can be understood by people from different cultures without reference to the social context in which they take place. This view reinforces the 'natural' and does not offer the potential of social change for women. In contrast, the interpretative symbolic tradition following Durkheim presents the view that movement is learnt and culturally variable. This view offers women the potential for change because learnt behaviour can clearly be modified.

Mauss (1973) considers different bodily techniques in a variety of cultures. He takes into account the biological and psychological aspects and concludes that these techniques are governed by what we learn in society.

> Dance as a symbolic art form consciously attends to its bodily technique through its encoded system. What Mauss seeks to show is that natural everyday movement is also a symbolic form with an encoded system, but that its form is treated by societal members as natural (non-social) behaviour (Thomas, 1982a, p. 5).

Douglas develops Mauss' work further and maintains that there is a reciprocal relationship between society and the body, with each symbolising the other. In *Purity and Danger* (1970) she considers the body's boundaries and maintenance of these, illustrating the information about a society which these offer. In *Natural Symbols* (1973) she concludes from the fact that all societies have a form of bodily symbolism that there is a natural tendency for the body to express society, although this needs to be considered within a particular system. She says that the 'social body constrains the way the physical body is perceived. The physical experience of the body, always modified by the social categories through which it is known, sustains a particular view of society' (1973, p. 93). So in viewing the body in dance, we will also be viewing aspects of society.

One aspect of which is, as Thomas (1982b) points out, how bodily expression is discussed in different categories of literature. The popular journalism approach aims to teach people how to understand gestures and postures. A typical focus of such books is advice for men on how to interpret women's body language so that sexual advances may be made more easily (for example, see J. Fast, 1971). There are also psychological studies which stress the positive aspects of communicating non-verbally (Montagu, 1978).

Nancy Henley (1977) in her book *Body Politics* attempts to show that differences in non-verbal behaviour in terms of sex, race and class can be shown to be power differences which are learnt to keep the status quo. Henley recognises that although the body can be studied in isolation the main concern is to understand bodily behaviour in its social context. People are concerned about this form of communication because there is an assumption that it can reveal our 'true selves' in ways that speech cannot. 'We view body movement as pre-linguistic, and expressive of some inner emotional state' (Thomas, 1982b, p. 4). This is also an existing notion in dance theory and dance anthropology. However, the study of non-verbal behaviour can only tell us about particular socially learnt traits which we display bodily. It can be an important aspect of change to alter physical behaviour patterns, for example, so that women take up more space and men stop invading women's space; women stop smiling inappropriately and men begin displaying emotion. However, such action is not a substitute for changing the social order, rather a step towards it.

The American tradition of study of the body as a medium of expression has been developed by ethnographers and anthropologists. Birdwhistell (1972) and Hall (1969) have studied everyday movement and interpersonal spatial relations using communication and linguistic models. They have developed theories concerned with the way the conceptual sense of the physical body is socially constructed. Goffman's (1972) tradition is concerned with uncovering the social rules governing people's spatial behaviour and territoriality. This work can inform us of the ways in which dance technique, choreography and performance convey meanings which we understand and interpret in the social setting and also the ways in which social values inform our viewing, production and performance of dance. It is interesting to note, however, that, despite the power of bodily communication which these studies make clear, when dancers want to make their work more accessible or political they frequently include verbal language. Hence many women's choreographies with a political bias have used words, for example, Lansley *Frank* (1986), Sergy *Gold* (1988), Claid *Grace and Glitter* (1987), Snaith *Lessons in Social Skills* (1988).

A reviewer writing about *Real Life Adventures* (1985), (see Figure 26) choreographed and performed by Mary Fulkerson, lamented the fact that the dancers needed speech training but enjoyed the way they could not hide behind their technique and were forced to contact the audience. She concluded, 'Perhaps there was something unnatural about those silent bodies and it's simply a relief to know that they can speak' (Mackrell, 1985, p. 35). This comment demonstrates our uneasiness with physical communication without the much safer, known world of language. For women, however, because bodily communication is largely unrecognised and unvalued, the female performer can be viewed as an object. When women use voice in performance they challenge this view, they become speaking human beings to be taken seriously rather than objects to be dismissed.

Institutional practices

Clearly, attitudes towards the body have not remained static in the course of history. Such changes are apparent in the institutions and practices of, for example, religion, education, medicine, the family and art. These changes are also revealed in dance styles. The formal placement of the ballet dancer which evolved from the aristocracy of Western Europe, was challenged by modern dancers whose expressionist style was determined by their specific creative needs. Each choreographer shaped the body in their own particular way. The postmodern dancers jettisoned 'trained bodies' for 'any old bodies of our any old lives' (Johnstone, 1971, p. 137). It is evident that, whilst it has not necessarily been the case in the past, there is the possibility for these changing attitudes and assumptions towards the body to benefit women.

In *Discipline and Punish* (1977) Foucault argues that the economic changes of the eighteenth century which elicited popular dissent led to a requirement for more systematic control over individuals. The invention of prisons and legal hierarchies were for the purpose of social control with an emphasis on 'reform' rather than punishment. This resulted in training individuals to be docile and useful and similar forces were apparent in the army, education and the work place. Foucault's description of training docile but useful bodies can be applied to dance training. From 'an inept body, the machine required can be constructed; a calculated constraint runs slowly through each part of the body, mastering it, making it pliable, ready at all times, turning silently into the automatism of habit' (p. 135). Traditional dance classes emphasise control of the body, working for stamina, flexibility and strength at the same time as creating automatic responses. The power employed in such training is not only repressive but also productive. The role of the body is significant here because it is trained to be active and useful. 'The power of the body corresponds to the exercise of power over it. Hence the possibility of a reversal of that power' (Sheridan, 1980, p. 219).

The discipline of the above institutions is in addition to learnt behaviour within the family. It is within the family that we learn what is socially acceptable and what is not, including bodily control. The role of the family changed in the twentieth century. Earlier the family, as part of the capitalist structure, distributed property. Today one of its main roles is that of consumer. The myth of the idealised family and the particular organisation and ideology which goes with it is central to women's oppression. Part of this oppression is the way sexual desire is restrained and used by the dominant power (Foucault, 1981).

The potential power of the body is limited by the commercialisation and commodification of sex. We receive the message that sex and bodies exist to be consumed. Consumerism works by creating everlasting desire in the consumer and much of this is focussed on the body. Foucault suggests that the revolt of the body is no longer controlled by repression but rather by stimulation. So now we are told to display as much of our bodies as we can, provided they are attractive and slender (Foucault, Gordon, ed., 1980). However, Outram (1989) suggests that a Foucaultian analysis is less than adequate in terms of women and men. There is no place for the question 'Whose body?', which is clearly of central importance to women as it is our bodily experience which is so often confined.

Changes in attitudes and social conditions

Dance roles are very much influenced by the prevailing views of societies which change over periods of time as do attitudes to the body. A hierarchical model of the body has existed from ancient times to the eighteenth century. This model established woman's body as inferior and an inverted version of the male body. In this view, woman's reproductive organs were considered as underdeveloped equivalents of male organs (Gallagher & Lacqueur, eds, 1987).

In Victorian society the body was central to social communication. There was an obsession with sanitation and with excluding body contact where possible (Gallagher & Lacqueur, eds, 1987). Class and gender differences were consolidated through notions of correct behaviour which were partly realised through the body so that by their external behaviour, 'ladies and gentlemen' were clearly distinguishable from each other and from other classes (Stone, 1977, p. 257; also Davidoff, 1983).

The dominant views about women have permeated all forms of knowledge so that scientists generally reinforce the idea that nature is a basis for social inequality. In the study of anatomy, in the early nineteenth century, the 'ideal' woman's skeleton was thought to be a wide pelvis, narrow neck, small rib cage and relatively tiny skull. The smallness of skulls and special adaptation of pelvises in female skeletons led scientists to assume that women were 'in the depth of their bones . . . unsuitable for intellectual labour' (Gallagher & Lacqueur, eds, 1987, p. ix). There is a paradox central to modern science with regard to women. Women were denied equality (and access to science) in the eighteenth century so that when scientific investigations into the nature of women were undertaken, women were excluded from the body of researchers. Yet it is frequently scientific results which are used to justify our exclusion. It was argued that woman's ability to produce children, even if she did not do so, dictated her health and she was, therefore, defined by her reproductive ability (Gallagher & Lacqueur, eds, 1987). Women's viewpoints were totally disregarded. Only scientific language was listened to by the medical profession and as women had been excluded they inevitably spoke a different language.

The female body was, then, a silenced body and a space in which meanings could proliferate. 'What medical men identified as women's sexuality was obviously as thoroughly what they did not want to see in themselves as it was what real women felt' (Poovey, 1987, p. 155). The female dancing body too is usually silent and attracts many meanings. However, silent images can be powerful and women in new dance recognised both the potential and the need to connect their dancing with the wider social context. They were concerned not to create just another new 'look' which could easily be appropriated, but to express their own viewpoints (Furse and Lansley, 1977; see Chapter 9).

Breaking the bounds of silence

The colonisation of women's bodies within the media and art practices has been so pervasive that we may be forgiven for assuming that this must always have been the case. However, whilst in the visual arts, in the past two hundred years, it is the female nude which has so obsessed artists, for nearly two thousand years previously, it was the male nude which was central to visual arts (Walters, 1978). The Boy David

In the two formative periods of Western art, the Classical Greek and the early Italian Renaissance, the male body was of crucial importance. At both of these times there was a curiosity about the make-up of the human body and the belief of man as god and central to the world. Hence the figures which artists created reflected these beliefs and they produced idealised images of the human body. The study of the nude has been central to artistic training from the fifteenth century to the present day. However, gender stereotypes abound, with the posture and movements of the male nude suggesting potency and those of the female suggesting passivity. Giorgione's Venus, whose eyes are closed, 'is at once receptive and mysterious, endlessly desirable because any desire can be projected on to her' (Walters, 1978, p. 8; this point is developed in relation to dance in Chapter 4).

Feminism is concerned with intervening in cultural practices and making new readings. The issues of sexual difference, power, sexuality and gender are now seen as relevant to art work. Radical social change is the aim of the Women's Movement, which in turn threatens male domination of politics and ideology, often resulting in hostility. Many feminist art practices focus on women's bodies, for example, those of Sonia Boyce, Judy Chicago, Cate Elwes, Suzanne Santoro and Susan Hiller. Some of these attempt to celebrate women's bodies, and bodily processes. Whilst these works fulfill an important function of removing the mystery, secrecy and disgust frequently associated with women's bodies, they are limited by the social context in which they are read. Unfortunately, attempts to decolonise women's bodies in art can frequently be reappropriated (Pollock, 1977). In addition, there is a contradiction in trying to form a women's culture based on our bodies and ideas of the feminine when we are also saying that these are distorted by patriarchal structures. Instead we need an understanding 'of *culture* as a collection of (ideological) representational practices and a concept of *women* produced as a category within the social totality' (Tickner, 1984, p. 16).

Conclusion

The above discussion indicates the changing attitudes and meanings attributed to the body which do not remain static. Rather the historical and class contexts affect attitudes and meanings towards the body and towards gender. Whilst it is clear that there are physiological differences between the sexes, what is important is how these differences are given meaning. The early training we receive in the family, through the education system and the messages we receive from the dominant culture, all contribute to the social construction of the body. The cultural practices of any particular group define and reflect ideas about the world and the behaviour which is expected of people within it. From this view-point it is possible to see that behaviour and attitudes are not fixed but are affected by cultural practices and social contexts. Therefore, challenges to the social structure and dominant culture can affect women's experiences of our bodies and contribute towards ending our oppression. In the next chapter, *Colonised Bodies* I discuss the specific connections between women's oppression and our bodily experiences.

3

Colonised bodies – the oppression of women

Women's bodies are colonised when treated as commodities. The social constructions, discussed in the last chapter, also contribute to this colonisation, forming part of the complex relationship between cultural practices and bodily experiences which both inform and influence each other. The physical expression of Martha Graham, a founder of modern dance (see Chapter 6), or Yvonne Rainer, a founder member of the Judson Church Collective (see Chapter 7), who formed their own dance practices, is clearly established in the radical changes they instituted in body stance and movement. Women's numerical majority in dance has led to assertions that women dominate dance and do not suffer oppression within the art form. But women performers and choreographers live and work within a social framework and will, therefore, be affected by social factors, of which women's oppression is a significant example.

Gendered movement

Whilst it is undoubtedly difficult for women to feel physically at ease because of the objectification of women's bodies, those dancers and women who have recognised the potential for rejecting restrictions and finding self-determined expression, are proving that the body can be a means to assert one's power. This, of course, relies on the extent to which one can free oneself of learnt physical behaviour.

Males and females often learn different movements; for example, boys learn to punch whereas girls rarely learn this movement except when learning a martial art. As Bray (1987) points out, movement is gendered but research into how girls and women learn to move has been overlooked. She uses four categories as a first step to understanding women's physical or motor learning: passivity, received knowledge, playfulness and skill. Passivity is a common characteristic of women's physical experience; the still groups in the playground, restricted movement of women on the street wearing tight clothes and the almost stationary positions on the factory floor. Received knowledge is the internalisation of other voices rather than women's own, resulting in 'ladylike' behaviour, bearing weight hesitantly, shortening strides and generally limiting physicality. Playfulness is often abandoned by adults who are not so ready to create new movement and new games. Skill is an important aspect of physicality but many women's skills are overlooked, as for example, in childcare. Dance provides a very important means to challenge the above social expectations of women's physicality. Dance technique provides a means to skill, expansive movement and a range of physicality. Dance improvisation and choreography offer the opportunity for creating new movement and creating new cultural practices.

Intruding into culture

Women are frequently defined as nearer to nature because of reproductive capabilities and men are defined as nearer to culture because of production activities. 'A woman who is visibly pregnant or is known to be breastfeeding is at her most explicitly female' (Rodgers in Ardener ed., 1981, p. 60). In describing some of the attitudes to women in English society, Rodgers (1981) uses the example of the House of Commons which, she says, 'turns women into fictive men' (p. 20). As women's primary social role is that of mother and homeworker, when she is outside working, by definition she is encroaching on the male domain. When women require different hours or childcare facilities, the threat to the male role is highlighted. In situations where other women's femaleness is inevitably apparent, such as when breastfeeding, other women may be hostile because 'women whose success has been geared to the male construct have discarded the symbols by which they would be anchored into the traditionally female domain of domesticity and nature' (p. 60). To be acceptable in the male world they cannot afford to appear different or to support those who do.

Whilst Rodger's example is specific to the House of Commons, much of what she says can be applied to many other situations. The female activities of menstruation, pregnancy and lactation are to be kept in the private domain of 'nature' rather than intrude into the public domain of 'culture'[1] (Rodgers, 1981, p. 61). These issues obviously affect women dancers and some women have refused to 'be kept private' and have rudely interrupted 'culture' by foregrounding menstruation and pregnancy in their performance work (see Chapter 9).

Rendering women's physical processes invisible is a means to control women in a context where 'patriarchal authority is based on male control over the woman's productive capacity and over her person' (Rowbotham, 1973, p. 117). Paradoxically, this control is shown through the body, as patriarchal culture encourages women to use our bodies to get male approval and rewards us for being 'sexy'. Some female dancers in the nineteenth century were known more for their sexual adventures than for their artistry, fitting in very well with their socialised role (Sorell, 1981).[2]

Nature/culture

Consideration of women's place and role in society has led to much discussion about the 'nature' of women. Within the realm of psychology, the Freudian school has been criticised for a theory which equates 'anatomy with destiny'. However, Melanie Klein suggests that 'feminine characteristics are almost completely relative to the society, history, culture and very little can be said to be "innately masculine or feminine"' (Millum, 1975, p. 71).

Elizabeth Spelman (1982) has demonstrated that although Plato appeared to value the equality of the sexes, particularly in *The Republic*, he thought that women illustrated the inability to value the soul above the body. But it is not only philosophers who would have women transcend our bodies. Some feminists too have argued from this position. Simone de Beauvoir, whose ideas inspired many, implies that women's emancipation will come when women, like men, are freed from association with the body. Betty Friedan's view of women's liberation could only have been for middle-class women, as it requires women to pursue 'higher' intellectual pursuits and allow others (i.e. working-class women) to do the 'menial' tasks. Whilst Friedan was not noted for the radicalness of her views and such a stance may not be so surprising, Shulamith Firestone was considered radical. However, her attitudes towards the body have much in common with Friedan. It is not only the institutional structures surrounding pregnancy and childbirth which Firestone finds oppressive but the experiences themselves. She describes pregnancy as a 'deformation' of the body (Spelman, 1982, p. 123). She suggests that woman's 'essential self' is her mind not her body (see discussion of this point in Chapter 2). These feminists are arguing that women's liberation 'ultimately means liberation from our bodies' (Spelman, 1982, p. 124). I am arguing the reverse, that whilst undoubtedly our oppression has been sited in our bodies, our liberation will be achieved through a non-dualist stance, changing personal and political practice, together with a change in institutional structures.

In a paper entitled 'Is Female to Male as Nature is to Culture?', Sherry Ortner (1974) seeks an explanation for the secondary status of women. However, she overlooks the fact that women's power and contributions vary greatly from culture to culture and within any given culture at different points in history. Her finding that the equation of women with nature is the reason for our secondary status is limited. Within feminist theory some feminists challenge 'the natural' as socially constructed, whilst others try to celebrate 'the natural' in opposition to a male-defined society. But as Coward (1989) argues, revering women's bodies misses the point that women are interpreted as symbols. This symbolic status ensures that women are then defined from outside and endure that identity. We have minority status, regardless of number, and the fantasies and projections of others have more influence than our own statements about ourselves. Our individual differences are submerged by the group identity of 'woman'. However, women should avoid seeing ourselves as innocent or passive beings as we then overlook the effect of our own actions, and the areas in which we have and exert power (Flax, 1987).

For women, control of our bodies, particularly in relation to our reproductive systems, is frequently denied us. We become a colonised space. We are denied access to abortion or forced to undergo sterilisation depending on the particular race and society to which we belong, because fertility and politics are connected. For heterosexual women, the patriarchal structures often mean worrying about being pregnant or lactating or worrying about not being pregnant or lactating because contraception is still far from adequate and there are numerous pressures connected with breast-feeding. Because of her reproductive functions woman *appears* closer to nature but in reality is no closer or further from nature than man. This issue is so important that, as Barrett (1984) suggests, 'the possibility of women's liberation lies crucially in a re-allocation of childcare, and this is why the erosion of gender division in the sphere of wage labour will not bring an end to women's oppression' (p. 226).

Women's oppression

Women are subjected to systematic mistreatment and social injustice because of our sex. This statement, the acceptance of which is the essence of feminism, defines women's oppression (Radcliffe Richards, 1982).[3] However, there are many variations of feminism, all with a specific view of the role of woman's body in her oppression. Both the revulsion of anti-feminists and the reverence of radical feminists towards women's bodies place too much emphasis on biology. But denying our biology as liberal feminists do is no answer either. Despite classical Marxism's limitations, it does offer a theory which recognises that 'biology does have a direct influence on women's lives and . . . that, despite their shared biology, women of different classes nevertheless have different, and sometimes conflicting, interests even in regard to their shared biology' (Sayers, 1982, p. 200).

In searching for reasons for women's subordinate position, the family structure and women's domestic responsibilities are clearly implicated; for example, 'the construction of a family form in which the male head of household is supposedly responsible for the financial support of a dependent wife and children has militated against demands for equal pay and an equal "right to work" for women' (Barrett, 1984, p. 157). In addition, the work which women tend to do is service work, work in the 'caring professions' and domestic work which mirrors women's roles in the family. Such division of labour results in women's dependence on men and inequality in relation to men. Although some women benefit from the class system there are certain aspects which cut across class boundaries. The notion of dependence, which is a central feature of family-household structures is an example (Barrett, 1984).[4]

An important move towards women and men participating equally in creative, cultural tasks would be to eradicate the internalisation of women's oppression which goes alongside the oppression which is rooted in the economic system. However, the construction of gender identity within the family and education system has resulted in our internalisation of that oppression. This internalisation is one of the divisions which exist between women. The role of feminist consciousness-raising groups was to share and recognise the many levels on which our oppression operates.[5]

Another aspect of women's oppression is rooted in the socialisation processes, through which young people learn what is expected of them and the values and attitudes they are to adhere to. The family is one of the main units where this learning takes place. Our understandings of gender and sexuality are formed through notions of romantic love, feminine nurturing, self-sacrifice and masculine support and protection which characterise the ideology of the family. The pressure to conform for individuals is often felt in terms of fear of disapproval from the family.

The family-household constitutes both the ideological ground on which gender difference and women's oppression are constructed, and the material relations in which men and women are differentially engaged in wage labour and the class structure (Barrett, 1984, p. 211).

Both ideologically and economically women's dependence on men is perpetuated. An important aspect of the family unit is that it tends to encourage conservatism and restrict challenges. The close connection between economics and personal relationships is an important aspect in this.

The family is promoted as a moral unit with particular roles. The husband and father provide financial security, the mother provides domesticity, and obedience is expected from the children. These role models are held up as the ideal for all and presented as inevitable and 'natural'. Challenges to the family in terms of laws on divorce, abortion and homosexuality are fiercely contested by the supporters of the 'traditional' family.

Gender identity

In Western society, boys and girls learn specific gender identities with the ideology of family life so that girls are expected to be dependent, helpful and caring whereas boys are encouraged to be independent, active and protective. All men benefit from the privileges of masculinity and yet the rigid definition of this constructed gender identity is also oppressive to men, as members of men's groups and the male gay movement have documented (Hearn, 1987). Maria Black and Rosalind Coward (1981) point out that there

> is a discourse available to men which allows them to represent themselves as people, humanity, mankind. This discourse, by its very existence, excludes and marginalises women . . . [It is, therefore, necessary] not just to validate the new meanings of women but to confront men with their maleness (pp. 70–85).

The tendency for women to be involved with feelings, people and things rather than abstract notions is evident in some dance work. For example, Gaby Agis in *Undine and the Still* (1985) with an all women group, uses a style which works *with* the body rather than attempting to transform it. There are images of women helping each other and rediscovering their bodies. Agis emphasises the feeling of sensuality which women share but whilst this is an important statement it does border on reinforcing an 'essentialist' position (Savage-King, 1985a; see discussion of Agis' work in Chapter 9 and 10).

As Chodorow (1978)[6] argues, however, women's tendencies to be involved with people and feelings are not to be seen as innate. They are part of family structures in which women are mainly responsible for childcare and socialisation of females if not of males. In addition, 'the structural situation of child rearing, reinforced by female and male role training, produces these differences' (p. 44). She develops her argument by saying that boys and girls personally identify with the mother who is usually the early socialiser.

For women, as we come to recognise our sameness with this body, we struggle to find ways in which to avoid the oppression which we connected with this identity. For men, one way of suppressing these early feelings is to control woman's body which had so much power over them. 'Woman though she inhabits her own body, does not possess it' (Morgan, 1983, p. 42). Within patriarchal relations man possesses it. We are then surrounded by images of woman's body used for male gratification. Indeed, as Joan Smith (1989) points out, antipathy to women and male fear of our power and sexuality is evident in most of our culture (including dance).[7]

Women are made 'other' by being identified by our bodies (which are unlike male bodies) and yet women are often ill at ease with our bodies. Eichenbaum and Orbach (1984) suggest this sense of other 'has found a cultural translation in patriarchy in the exclusion of women from political, economic and social, sexual or legal equity, so that it is the woman who becomes and carries the emotional burden of being the outsider, "the other"' (1984, p. 124).

Sexuality – female cycles

Women's sexuality is clearly evident during menstruation, childbirth and when breastfeeding and is subjected to severe controls within patriarchal structures. As women dancers use their bodies as the medium of their expression these controls will inevitably limit that expression although, of course, women also consistently resist such controls. Female dancers are usually, not surprisingly, extremely aware of their bodily cycles. However, how at ease they are with their body image and changes of energy during menstruation and how they view the possibility of having children will depend upon their individual background, circumstances and working situation.

Culturally, the red fluid of menstruation has negative associations, such as being in pain. It is tabooed, despised and neglected and in this context it often hurts. The other fluid women produce is white or clear, indicating ovulation and in contrast to menstruation, is an indication of the possible production of new life. Research into childbirth has shown that without fear giving birth can often be without trauma.[8] Shuttle and Redgrove (1978) suggest that this too could apply to menstruation. They discuss the powerful nature of the cycle and the radical implications of reclaiming it, suggesting that the suffering connected with it is a learned response to oppression. To question the changes women go through or to consider the context in which these happen, would be to question the structure of society itself. It is not surprising, therefore, that many women believe that men are in a better position because of their biology, i.e. they do not menstruate, are free from cramps and extra encroachments on their time and money and, therefore, accept the menstrual taboo and its misconceptions. Shuttle and Redgrove point to the importance of redefining this area of experience from a female point of view because it is part of our identity. This information is relevant for female dancers, particularly as the combination of intense exercise and restricted diets frequently results in irregular menstrual cycles or cessation of menstruation (Druss & Silverman, 1979).

The other cycles in women's lives which may affect women's dancing are those of pregnancy, childbirth and lactation. During pregnancy women can learn much about our bodies which can be beneficial for the dancer.[9] One dancer found that for the first time in her career 'she really located her center of gravity' (Pierpont, 1981, p. 86). Dancers have performed into the sixth month of pregnancy and Ninette de Valois (1957) mentions a Madame Zanfretta dancing seven months pregnant at Covent Garden. Such dancers, however, tend to be the exception partly because of the physical strain and also because dancers who are noticeably pregnant offer a challenge to the traditional dance image of the 'ideal' woman. Whilst a dancer who is pregnant may not be able to dance the classics in ballet because of the strain on the heart and breathing, it could well be possible, using ballet and contemporary technique, to dance an alternative choreography.[10] However, whilst most choreographers are men and the image required is that of the 'ideal' woman this possibility is unlikely to become anything more than an occasional exception. Some dancers in new dance have, however, incorporated the experience of pregnancy into their careers, demystifying misconceptions about pregnant women being ungainly, fragile or limited in movement (see Chapter 9).[11]

The act of childbirth itself has changed considerably in women's history (Reed, 1975). At one time only females were involved with childbirth and women were segregated, as they were during menstruation because of fear. The idea that childbirth is inherently dangerous, painful and terrifying is from Christianity, absorbed from the Hebrew view of Eve's transgression. This was explained as the cause of women's travails in childbirth, 'thus setting the foundation for the negative attitudes towards women's sexuality and child-bearing which have continued in Western civilization for nearly 2000 years' (Arms in Ardener, ed., 1978 p. 14). An important shift in reproduction care in the past century has been care from experienced, untrained women to a profession of formally trained men (Ardener, ed., 1978). The changes in attitudes which have accompanied this shift have increasingly placed the pregnant woman as patient. The risks of pregnancy have been emphasised by doctors who see their role as one of controlling the birth process and the new technology greatly reinforces these attitudes. Male fear of women's bodies can be read from such practices and it seems highly likely to be combined with a desire to cleanse and control women's bodily functions. 'After all, to give birth lying down is the worst and most painful position for women but it is altogether less threatening and more convenient for the male doctor' (Coward, 1989, p. 157).

My own experiences of pregnancy and childbirth brought me into contact with both the medical establishment and the organisations which women have established in attempts to avoid male control of an extremely powerful female event. Despite the changes in attitudes which have filtered into hospitals as a result of the writings and practices of, for example, Grantly Dick-Read (1957), Sheila Kitzinger (1981), Frederick Leboyer (1982), Michel Odent (1984) and the Radical Midwives Association, I was struck by the inappropriateness of hospital as a place for most births. To enter a hospital is to be reminded of illness, pain and to lose power in the role of patient. This is the antithesis of an ideal setting for birth. In the birth event it is the mother who needs to be central with the attendants playing a minimum role just giving her the support and encouragement she needs to allow and assist the process of the baby's birth (with the aid of technology if necessary). However, reproductive technology has become increasingly complex making issues of women's control of our bodies even more urgent (Kroker & Kroker, 1988).

The control in dance companies frequently intrudes on a dancer's decision to have a child. So for example, women in the New York City Ballet Company who decided to have a child risked their career as the management disapproved (Abra, 1987/88). Motherhood does not combine with a dancer's life (or many other jobs) particularly easily. Many dancers view the choice to have a child as the end of their career (Laurie, 1989). The main reasons for this are practical.

Those dancers who do have children and continue dancing almost certainly need to have full-time help at home and for those dancers on a low salary this can make the dual roles impossible. Touring also makes childcare arrangements extremely difficult particularly when provision for the under-fives is poor as it is in this country. Creche facilities would help but these are unlikely to be available in the near future not least because of the precarious economic position of most companies. Art does not have the status of industry, therefore, it has fewer resources.

Sexual orientation and autonomy

In Western society today, sexual orientation is an important part of identity, and sexuality is frequently assumed to be the 'core of the self' (Caplan, 1987, p. 2). However, as Caplan (1987) points out, 'what is sexual in one context may not be so in another: an experience becomes sexual by application of socially learned meanings' (p. 2). Heterosexual relationships are viewed as the norm in our society and homosexuality is viewed with censure, not least because homosexual relationships threaten the view that sex is 'natural'.

In dance the meanings conveyed will frequently be informed by sexual values because it is very difficult to separate bodies and their movements from sexuality. In the patriarchal relations of a society these values are inevitably interpreted as male. So that the ways in which women's bodies are displayed before an audience and the dance roles they have to interpret can be oppressive to women, both as dancers and as audience. The majority of dance choreography frequently incorporates male/female sexual relationships, usually from a male perspective. The romantic ballets are one example but such a perspective is also evident in the work of contemporary dance choreographers such as Paul Taylor. The early work of Martha Graham was a significant counter to such work, conveying a female perspective. However, even when the intention is not to convey sexuality the audience may perceive it.

Women's autonomy poses a threat to male dominance as it refuses a female subservient role. Women's dance in this century has, in many cases, foregrounded this autonomy, as in the work of

Isadora Duncan, Martha Graham and Yvonne Rainer (see also Chapter 10). There is still much greater social acceptance for women to express their sensuality than for men and this has been of benefit to women in dance. Women are allowed more physical touch between friends than men are before homophobia becomes an issue, and in many women's lives day to day caring for children can have sensuous, pleasurable moments.

It is not surprising in a context in which women's bodies are displayed as sexual objects for male desire, that women's sexuality is a site of confusion, oppression and a focus for campaigns for change. The Women's Movement has made clear that rape is not the result of individual men's sexual desires but the result of a social structure in which male violence is condoned. Within a patriarchal structure power and control are central and are evident in sexual behaviour. This behaviour is legally controlled by the state as are, to some extent, ideological and cultural representations of sexuality.[12] However, the state reinforces assumptions based on the division of gender. For example, by judging sexual behaviour in girls to mean they are in need of 'care and control' when similar behaviour in boys would be overlooked (Heidensohn, 1985).

Ballet is deeply imbued with sexuality as Agnes de Mille (1951), who was herself a classical ballet dancer, points out. The woman's body becomes the symbol of beauty and power. However, de Mille is suggesting that the ballerina is powerful in her role, overlooking the fact that she is interpreting a male viewpoint. She suggests that the female dancer pays for the success of her career because by 'dedicating her life to her own body, she sacrifices the reality of her children's bodies and in effect that of her husband . . . literally and profoundly they wed their work' (p. 59).

Women are encouraged to believe that we will achieve our desires by presenting ourselves as an attractive image so that 'Mr Right' will solve all our problems. It is little wonder that many women spend hours trying to perfect 'the package'. This packaging is evident within dance in the display of women's bodies. The power of the experience for the dancer and the subversive potential of being totally ourselves in the present in movement, is flattened to fit the proscenium arch and the glossy magazine. Jeffrey Weeks (1981) suggests that there is a dichotomy between the objectification of women in modern society through visual representation and the relatively recent choices we have about our lives because of the easier access to birth control and abortion (although as with all advances not all women benefit to the same extent). The eroticisation of modern culture, with the advent of the pill, was able to focus on the female body without the consequences of earlier times (i.e. pregnancy).

It has not, until recently, been deemed necessary to control our sexual activity because of women's lack of status and power in Western society. In the nineteenth century, women's individual sexual identity did not exist publically outside of heterosexual relationships although, of course, some women resisted this (Cooper, 1986, p. xvi). Male superiority was so entrenched that the sexual independence of lesbianism was not generally recognised before this century. Both in Western society as a whole and in dance in particular, lesbianism has mainly remained hidden. Unlike male homosexuality, lesbianism was not a crime and, therefore, did not generate political activity in protest. However, because it challenges the 'norm', the stigmas attached to it ensure that lesbians in dance are often unknown. Given Loie Fuller's undoubted talent in staging, lighting, costume and influence in terms of Art Nouveau (see Figure 16) it is curious that she is not more well known. Perron suggests that Fuller's role as a founder of American modern dance would have been given more acknowledgement if she had not been lesbian (in Hanna, 1987a). The Gay Movement and the Women's Movement both ensured that lesbianism became a political issue.

Feminist studies of art have created a new awareness of how art embodies values and attitudes of the society in which it has been created, though few mention lesbianism. In 1969 Kate Millett stated that 'Lesbianism would appear to be so little a threat at the moment that it is hardly ever mentioned' (Cooper, 1986, p. 238). Lesbian artists can deal with their identity in terms of their art in one of three ways (Cooper, 1986). Firstly, they can present themselves as artists, whilst ignoring their sexuality. Secondly, they can identify as feminists with lesbianism as part of the wider Women's Movement and participate in the debates with regard to women-only spaces, and challenge conventional aesthetics. Thirdly, they can make lesbianism an issue in their work and take account of this experience as a major influence in their artistic practice (see Chapter 10). In dance the second two options are still rare.

The sex industry

The sex industry is another area in which women are viewed as under male control. Women lack resources and money but at the same time we have the important task of caring for children. One survival technique open to women is the sex industry (mostly employing working-class women). This industry is one end of a continuum in which men are serviced by women. Often women who do this work are considered immoral and yet, as one of them says it is 'immoral that men want to use women's bodies without relating to us as human beings, without considering our feelings' (Roberts, 1986, p. 236). She is referring to society generally and not just to the sex industry. Worldwide, men hold the power and, unsurprisingly, it is their definition of what is important with regard to money, sex and power, that is upheld.

Patriarchal culture encourages women to use our bodies to get male approval and the internalisation of these values and poverty ensures the sex industry continues. Black women are doubly oppressed and exploited within this industry, including being represented and signified as animals in pornography which reinforces the messages and myths of male superiority and white supremacy. The pornography industry reveals the mystery of the female body as nothing more than flesh, under culture's control. Many of the images show that women exist for male pleasure, making clear that pornography is essentially to do with power (Griffen, 1981). It is not only in pornography that these images surface. The conventions of pornography are used, with modification, in mainstream media, including popular magazines (see Coward, 1984, p. 60).

The women in the sex industry support each other. They know they are doing their best to survive. It is work, a way of getting access to money which is usually denied to women, it is men's fantasy that it is anything but work for them. The women in this industry are vulnerable but cover this with harshness. When describing her life as a stripper, Nickie Roberts (1986) talks about the stripper's need for some psychological defence against the 'punters' in her vulnerable, unprotectedness when naked on stage. For women entering this industry the first strip is like an initiation and after the fear, the familiarity turns to anger at the need to do such work to get money. The experiences in Nickie Robert's book were used as an inspiration for a scene in Claid and Semple's production of *Grace and Glitter* (1986; see Chapter 10 and Figure 28). The vulnerability of the stripper is portrayed, but also her anger. The performer enters the stage wearing a tutu ready to begin her ballet solo but sleazy music is playing. As her fear turns to anger the objectification of women, whether stripper or ballet dancer, is emphasised. The performance makes clear that the issue is power rather than sexuality.

The body as a commodity

Women's bodies are distorted by being reduced to commodities to be improved by physical exercise, diets and general management. There is a great deal of competition attached to this management, for to have an ideal body and to work hard at achieving that ideal is to improve performance at work, at sex and increase life, or so the myth would have us believe. As Turner points out 'successful images require successful bodies, which have been trained, disciplined and orchestrated to enhance our personal value' (1984, p. 111; see also Foucault, 1981).

Today the healthy body is a necessary possession. However, the healthy body has not always had the current, positive associations. For example, in Nazi Germany the healthy ideal had strong racist and anti-semitic connotations. Rosalind Coward (1989) argues that contemporary views of the healthy body in Western society, as evident in alternative therapies for example, are basically conservative. The emphasis on transformation by human willpower enhances a world view in which the talented are rewarded and hardship is the result of weakness. These views underlie much dance practice, with the emphasis in technique classes on the achievements of the 'talented' and the exhortation of the 'weaker' students to work harder.

The emphasis in the health movement is change through individual personal control. 'This new concern with the body is a place where people can express dissatisfaction with contemporary society *and* feel they are doing something personally to resist the encroachments of that society' (Coward, 1989, p. 197). But the problem is that such individual solutions are within the existing social structures. They do not challenge them.

Within the fitness industry we are offered the model of the body as a machine, underlined by the language of servicing and maintaining the body. There is a different message for women than for men here. Women have always been required to change ourselves to fit the ideals of femininity and the emphasis on fitness and keeping healthy is just another aspect of this. There is tremendous emphasis in the fitness literature on achieving freedom and a sense of self through mastering and controlling the body. However, as Hilary Bichovsky-Little (1987) comments, beneath these exhortations to be in control is an underlying sense of powerlessness. It is clear we are not in total control of our bodies. Indeed the certain facts of our lives to date are that we are born, we age and we die and no-one so far has controlled the ageing or the dying process. Another important aspect to consider about exercise and getting fit is that that is a risk in itself. It is quite possible, particularly for the unwary, to injure themselves whilst going through some of the 'health-giving' motions. It is, of course, not only our individual actions that affect our health; the environment in which we live also plays a big part and there is much evidence that the interventions of industry and nuclear energy are doing much to make a beautiful world a dangerous place in which to live.

Recently, weight-training and body building for women have become more popular. Anna Wilson (1987) points out some of the contradictions behind these activities. She suggests that these are presented as liberating activities which offer the muscular woman as a pure ideal, different from previous ideals because she is supposedly free from social pressures. (Wilson, 1987; also Greig, 1986; and Kuhn, 1988). The ideology behind the activities is that everyone can have a perfect body and have only themselves to blame if they don't succeed.

In searching for the origins of the fitness movement Bichovsky-Little suggests that the military's need for fit recruits is a source. In the 1950s the USA army discovered that a large number of recruits who were called in were unfit. So health education and fitness campaigns began. In the late 1960s Britain too was referring to the number of unfit recruits to the forces. It seems more than a little ironic that our health and fitness is associated with the same war machine that threatens our existence.

The significance of the Health 'n' Fitness cult is not that it attempts to replace political action as a means of changing an individual's world but that – in the short term – it succeeds in so doing (Bichovsky-Little, 1987, p. 23).

Along with the emphasis on individual responsibility for our health goes the marketing of products for achieving this. We are urged to combat any signs of ageing, and the look which we are surrounded with and urged to achieve is that of the 'body beautiful', which is young, sexual and takes money and hard work to achieve and maintain. The message is that if we do not achieve this, it is our own weakness.

The body and body maintenance provide a growing market for the sale of goods. Not only does advertising appeal to our current needs but business leaders and advertisers do their best to create new needs. The concentration on the body market has left us with a heightened awareness of our 'imperfections', to which we frequently respond by buying a product. We have been sold the image of luxury and ease which was once enjoyed by only a few but is now supposedly within everyone's reach; freedom is associated with the freedom to consume. However, poverty and unemployment amidst affluence illustrate the other side of consumer culture. The only consumption the poor are left with is that of images (Featherstone, 1982).

The display of the human body is very much part of this consumer culture and we are encouraged to view the body as a vehicle of pleasure. The images and messages which surround us persuade us to believe that the body is infinitely malleable and changeable and with the right product and correct work, perfection is well within our grasp. The responsibility for organising the purchase and consumption of products, together with the symbolic use of our bodies in advertisements, traps women in a narcissistic world of images (Winship, 1980; Pollock, 1977). It is considered quite acceptable to spend one's leisure time on body maintenance and this appears almost necessary as the slim body becomes the required form. With rich food and declining amounts of exertion in daily life it is no easy achievement to present a slender shape. Also,

> with appearance being taken as a reflex of the self the penalties of bodily neglect are a lowering of one's acceptability as a person, as well as an indication of laziness, low self esteem and even moral failure . . . it is hardly surprising that ageing and death are viewed negatively (Featherstone, 1982, p. 26).

When Martha Graham, a major modern dance innovator and choreographer, continued to dance as she aged there was much controversy about the wisdom of her action. But as one critic pointed out, she contributed a vital presence. However, the critic also revealed frequently held prejudices about older women when she suggested that Graham should not perform in costumes which were sleeveless and low necked (i.e. her ageing body should be hidden) (Clarke, 1967, pp. 460–1). The emphasis on youth sometimes means that the tremendously valuable experience of ballerinas who perform in their forties and fifties can be underappreciated (Tobias, 1982).

The body maintenance which ballet dancers undergo entails daily discipline and pain. Makarova, describing her working life, says 'Even with arthritis, which I have in several places, muscles eventually respond. I'm used to pain. We all are. Some days when you don't have pain it's strange' (Coleman, 1989). Although exercising and keeping fit is generally associated with health, the extremes which dancers go to in order to achieve high standards of technique and adhere to a required 'look' frequently result in bodily stress and strain. Many dancers smoke, often in an effort to cope with the daily stress and to keep weight down (Mackrell, 1989). There are a number of occupational hazards including injury, which is often a result of being over-tired and over-worked. Frequently, dancers work in poor conditions with unsprung floors and in cold rooms. In addition, the pressure to keep thin and achieve ever more demanding standards takes its toll with dancers often surviving on poor diets (Abra, 1987/88; Mackrell,1989)[13]

An alternative approach is that of the American postmodern choreographer Anna Halprin who has worked a great deal on discovering the dance from the person's own life and experiences rather than attempt to impose or create a particular 'look' (see Chapter 7). This seems to me to be a very powerful way of working and is an opportunity for women to work from their own viewpoints and experiences. This form of dance is the antithesis of bodily colonisation through emphasis on the 'look'.

Body management reinforces the emphasis on the 'look' in dance. This is not without implications for the different classes within a class society, as it is the middle classes and owning classes who have access to the resources required to create the acceptable images. However, it is important to remember that the 'pleasures of the body are never wholly incorporated by consumerism and may become features of individualistic protest and opposition' (Turner, 1984, p. 251).

In *A Dream I Wished* (circa 1981) Ulla Koivisto's performance subverts our expectations as she presents a heroic, whirling, female presence which contradicts the light, delicate image women dancers often have. She is clearly a woman in control, enjoying dancing her own dance. The importance of such work is that it widens narrow perceptions and allows new possibilities. I remember being awe-struck that a woman would dare to dance so forcefully and confidently particularly when she so clearly did not fit the image of a woman dancer. I was also immensely elated.

Body image

Women's awareness of body image is even more apparent with female dancers. An image is complex, conjuring up many associations, feelings and meanings for the spectator. Initially, when watching a dance we gain an overall impression connected with, for example, age, gender, race and then begin to consider the relationship of one dancer to another. In considering the dancers' appearances further, we may then consider the body images we are confronted with.

Most of the studies of body image are from the disciplines of psychology and psychiatry. These rarely differentiate between male and female experience despite the vast differences resulting from social inequality. Fisher (1973), who has completed a number of studies in this area, is unquestioning of the designated roles between men and women and proceeds to explain them in psychological terms, with little regard to the social context in which these roles exist. He doesn't question his evidence that most women want to be small and most men want to be large and yet this seems to be crucial information when we consider male/female roles. Men are conditioned to act powerfully in a dominant role, therefore, the larger they are the more visual affirmation there will be of their prescribed social role and vice-versa for women.

Dance and sports literature often stress enhanced body image as one of the benefits of these activities. However, in two studies which Susan Puretz (1982) carried out with students in the USA she found that this was not necessarily the case. Her data was gained through a variety of tests on students studying ballet, folk dance and contemporary dance. Whereas in ballet and folk dance the movements are structured and allow little space for individual additions, contemporary dance frequently has an improvisation section giving the opportunity for individuals to explore creatively. Puretz, therefore, expected in contemporary dance an enhanced body image because of the involvement of the individual's own ideas and self. In fact the data showed that not only was there no improvement of body image of those students who studied contemporary dance but rather the students' body images became poorer the more contemporary dance they studied. In contrast to this the students who took physical conditioning classes did have an enhanced body image.

Puretz suggests that an explanation for this, which I would endorse, is that the physical conditioning group registered any improvement in flexibility and strength as success and feeling good about oneself and one's body, as they had no external standards to judge by. The contemporary dance students on the other hand were continually monitoring their achievements against expected standards. The more they learnt the more aware they became of any faults and the striving for perfect technique would mean constant criticism of oneself in relation to the 'dance ideal image' (1982).

Psychoanalysis offers a useful way of making sense of our experiences and many feminists have used this approach to provide a theoretical framework to explain women's roles.[14] In Parveen Adams' *Versions of the Body* (1986), she points out that we gain knowledge of our own bodies through body image, which is socially constructed and of key importance. Women 'search and search for the perfect image' (Parker, 1987, p. 26). We are surrounded by ideal images and consequently frequently feel that we are not making the grade, that we are not perfect, that we take up too much space. Dr Marcia Hutchinson endorses this point in her book, *Transforming Body Image*. She states that women are only allowed to take up a certain amount of space in a patriarchal society (in Parker, 1987).

Parker attempts to locate more positive images for women who do not fulfill the very thin ideal we are surrounded with in the media. To do this she goes back to a time of Goddess worship; she says the image embodied 'the curving, fertile power of the female body and soul' (p. 26). She also cites artists who celebrate feminine beauty and power through archetypal images, such as Rubens, Ingres and Renoir. Power and prosperity were indicated by a large woman then. This is still so in some parts of the world. She argues, however, that these images were suppressed as Judaism and Christianity took hold with their patriarchal messages. Now women with large bodies are cruelly stereotyped as lacking will power, gluttonous, pathetic. Today, in the West, the ideal image for women is that of the adolescent boy with female curves barely formed, hidden or dieted out of existence. Consequently many women spend precious energy fighting ourselves, our bodies, in order to fit this impossible ideal and consequently not recognising or experiencing our power (see Chernin, 1983; and Farnham, 1983).

Eating disorders, which are common in the dance world, illustrate the pressures on women to conform to an ideal, relinquish our power and turn our anger on ourselves. In a study of ballerinas it was found that they tended to feel overweight in spite of being thin, and in order to become even thinner dieted or used other means. Eating, a basic bodily pleasure, was kept strictly controlled (Druss and Silverman, 1979). Vincent (1979) condemns the risks which dancers take (he discusses women because whilst men have to keep to an ideal it is not as narrow or restrictive as for women) to attain the 'unhealthy ideal body form' (Naess, 1981, p. 53). Vincent suggests that dancers need to listen to their bodies rather than to fight them. The body image we have is defined by two kinds of experiences.

> The first is our experience of body sensations (inner organs, muscle and sensory receptors); inner thoughts and feelings. The second kind of experience is of outer events and expectations which influence our behaviour and attitudes towards ourselves. The mirror is the interface, the literal mirror on the wall or the reflections where each person judges the bit between inner, personal psychological realities and outer expectations (1979, p. 54).

Vincent gives examples of dancers' sufferings because of these judgements and the difficulties of maintaining the ideal image which is a necessary part of aesthetic or personal excellence in their work. Female dancers are in a constant dilemma whilst training and performing. There is a deep conflict, 'between their art and their needs as human beings' (p. 54). Vincent makes clear that all dancers are thinner or perceive the need to be thinner than the 'average' person and the classical dancer is the thinnest of all the types of dancers. Also clear is the discrepancy between artistic and health considerations. A choreographer need only be concerned with a dancer to fulfill her/his artistic vision. Therefore, if a particular body shape is required for a dance, then the dancer has the choice of shaping up or being expendable.

Whilst Vincent gives an excellent account, with many examples, why this striving after an ideal image is dangerous to health, he does not address the issue of why this happens and why it is particularly women who are affected. For answers to these questions one needs to look at women's experiences and our position in society as I have outlined above.[15]

Conclusion

Much of this discussion is a direct result of the Women's Movement. There was a questioning of conditioning processes and all aspects of women's experiences. The theory came from women's own personal experiences, much of which was shared in consciousness-raising groups.[16] These discussions made clear that it was not individuals' personal inadequacies that were the problem, but that there was a common experience of difficulties encountered in a structure which did not take account of women's lives. This situation, once named, began to be challenged. Much of the information and experience of the Women's Movement, detailed in this chapter, informed new dance which will be discussed in Chapter 9. Many women involved with this dance practice were aware of and/or involved with feminist theory and practice and this was evident in their work.

Physical movement is one way of resisting rigidity and many women in dance have challenged restricted bodily expression. Through redefinitions of 'the feminine', women have presented our own viewpoints. However, the oppression of women in all its manifestations from the socialisation processes, the control of women's bodies and the commodification of women's bodies has serious repercussions on women's lives and on women's dance opportunities and experiences. The emphasis in dance on the objectification of women's bodies and the display of the dancer limits female dancers' potential power. This will be the topic of the next chapter.

4

Viewing women – the production and reception of dance

An understanding of the production and reception of dance is central to an assessment of the representation of women in dance. Dance production and reception are inextricably linked. Both involve the display of women's bodies, 'the gaze' of the audience, the desire and pleasure of both the female performer and of the audience. This chapter explores the role these aspects play in the representation of women in order to locate meanings in dance.

Meaning cannot be ascertained without a context because the same movement has different meanings in different situations (Best, 1979). How the work is produced and the interaction between the performer and the audience contribute to the creation of meaning in dance. When someone from a dance audience asks, 'But what did it mean?' there is frequently an assumption that the dance had one meaning which the speaker missed. However, dances are multi-layered and can be read in a number of ways. Educated viewers, that is those who have had the opportunity to see a good deal of dance, to listen to pre-performance talks, to participate in after-show debates, to read about dance and perhaps participate in technique classes and choreographic workshops, are more likely to be able to absorb more of the layerings than those who have seen or know very little of dance. This is not to say, of course, that one has to be dance-educated in order to appreciate dance. The power of dance is that it communicates through the kineasthetic sense which we all have. Watching physical movement can be a liberating experience. Although there is no one meaning or interpretation of a dance, some interpretations can be more easily substantiated than others. This is because of the shared visual symbols of everyday life, which are also used in dance, which we understand to have specific meanings in particular contexts.

There are several factors which combine to make meaning in a dance. The primary factor is the body. It is the movement of the body, the technique used, and the look of the body which is central to any dance work. However, the dancers' movements, their visual appearance and the relationships between dancers frequently present a stereotypical view of women. This is particularly evident in many male/female pas de deux.

Nevertheless, much dance criticism elevates the dance work and discusses the text (dance) independently from the conditions of production and reception of the work. The socio-historical context is thus ignored with no consideration of issues of gender, class and race. Analysis of the context and production of the work counters the idealist view that dance can transcend its conditions of production. Eagleton (1990) argues (in a discussion of literary text but I would suggest it is also relevant for dance) that these conditions are internalised in the work.

Conditions of production and reception

The conditions of production for men and women are materially different. Virginia Woolf's (1977) analysis of women's access to literary production is still relevant today and it is relevant to a discussion of women and dance. She argues that the material conditions, money, housing, health and so on affect writing. These conditions affect the artist's perceptions and indeed the form chosen.

Access to the material means of producing dance has been and is available to women. If the aspiring dancer can pay for dance classes, it is comparatively easy to gain access to dance training. However, whilst it is socially acceptable for women to undertake dance training because it reinforces 'the feminine' it is not so acceptable for them to portray their own perspectives through choreography (see Chapter 3). It is not surprising that women are judged as not achieving the standards of male artists. There are two main explanations usually given for this. The first is that women have been constrained by the conditions in which their work was produced. The second is that women have achieved work of equal aesthetic value to men but because of prejudice in a male-dominated society this is not recognised as such. However, as Barrett (1984) points out, to take up either of these explanations is unhelpful, as they continue to reinforce the notion that aesthetic judgements can be made outside of a historical and social context. It is therefore important not to forget the fact that there is no consensus by which products can be judged aesthetically across classes or cultures.

It is not only the production of dance which is important, but also its reception. It is clear that the cultural specificity of the production of a dance work needs to be taken into account by the audience. How a dance work is read will contribute to its meaning, since we cannot assume that a specific meaning is intrinsic to the text. Also, the imagery of gender affects both men and women deeply although these effects may be different.

There are several processes through which ideology concerned with gender is reproduced. Barrett identifies these processes as stereotypes, compensation, collusion and recuperation which operate in a number of cultural practices (that is, the various forms of artistic expression). Stereotypes are significant because they are an imitation and are used repetitively by the media as the main symbol so that people associate and accept the imitation for the real (see Dyer, ed., 1977 and Davis *et al.*, eds, 1987). Through repetition, images begin to be internalised or accepted. In dance the romantic myth of a man being central in a woman's life and supporting her is a familiar image. In both ballet and contemporary dance women are frequently portrayed as decorative and dependent as, say, Odette in Swan Lake (see Chapter 5).

The notion of compensation elevates women's prescribed roles, such as mother and housewife, so that they are represented as having moral worth. This romanticises women's roles. An example of this is evident in *La Fille Mal Gardée* (Ashton, 1960 after Dauberval, 1789). In Act II there is a mime scene in which the central character, Lise, a young woman, is left locked in the house on her own. She begins to daydream of marrying Colas, the man she loves and we see her imagining the progression of her future. She dreams of her 'happy ever after' life as a bride and then a mother. This idealisation and romanticisation of women's roles is typical of many female roles within ballet (see Chapter 5).

Feminists have turned to psychoanalysis for explanations for women's 'collusion' with objectification. Collusion is evident for example, when women wear tight-fitting shoes and clothes which are difficult to move in, thus increasing their 'passivity'. Women in dance companies who keep their weight very low in order to conform to the company image offer another example of collusion. Whilst it is important to take into account the material aspects of women's oppression, how we internalise our oppression is equally important. This was a major understanding formed in women's consciousness raising groups and developed in feminist counselling and therapy (for examples see Ernst & Goodison, 1981; and Krzowski & Land, eds, 1988).

Recuperation describes a process which we are increasingly seeing in which women are initially portrayed as autonomous and powerful, only to have that independence eroded. For example, an advertisement for Reed employment agencies portrayed a woman climbing a mountain which supposedly emphasised her independence. But this message was limited by the display of her body in a bright, tight fitting, shiny lycra outfit. Her 'look' was what counted, not her activity. Dance images are frequently used in advertisements. For example, those for menstrual products often portray dancers as independent and active with the message that women's menstrual cycles need not restrict our movements. However, the sense of shame at something which needs to be hidden and ignored is communicated at the same time.[1]

By taking the viewpoint that gender is not just difference but oppression, changes are possible in the making and viewing of dance. The recognition that dance cannot be separated from the material conditions of a particular time and that choreographers cannot totally control the reception of their work have implications for feminist producers of dance. The effectiveness of their work may often be limited by the means available to produce it. In addition, despite very clear intentions on the choreographer's part to present the female performer in a way which does not objectify her body, some members of the audience may still read the performance in an objectifying way. Nonetheless, it is crucial, and possible, to challenge assumptions concerned with gender.

Issues of class and race also need to be addressed, otherwise gender issues tend to be limited to those from a ruling, white, middle-class perspective. The focus on gender issues of the last twenty years has meant that class issues have been somewhat neglected, particularly in decoding images (Eagleton, 1990). How-

ever, there are significant differences between the roles and representations of women from different classes. For example, the world
view of Victorian society created by those who had the power was
illustrated in visual images. These images emphasised the powerlessness of working-class people and their potential threat to those
who exploited or employed them. Middle-class woman's role was to
keep a well-ordered home and to be decorative, whilst working class
women did extremely heavy, dirty, manual work (Davidoff, 1983).
The romanticisation of women's domestic labour (as in the example
of *La Fille Mal Gardée* above) in visual representation ignores the
reality of women's work but emphasises their decorative role
(Spence, 1978/9). Women are also portrayed as virtuous and
modest. In fifteenth century society averted eyes were a sign of
chastity and obedience (Simons, 1988). In ballet too, women's virtue
is established by lowering eyes to the ground. Many photographs of
ballerinas dancing the role of Odette in *Swan Lake* illustrate them in
arabesque with demure downcast eyes (see Figure 11).

The reading of an image depends on who is looking at it. For
example, a black woman looking at an image of another black
woman is likely to assume some common identity because of the
construction of race. However, a white woman brings colonial
history to the images of a black woman, who can represent for
her the 'unknown, exciting, frightening, exotic, different' (Attille &
Blackwood, 1986, p. 207). The created image can say more about
the maker than those whom it supposedly represents.

Interventions by black artists have begun to change white
discourses. Parmar describes how there has been an 'emphasis on
"difference", on "otherness" and "plurality" [rejecting] the hege-
monic drive towards universality, which in the past has effectively
served to suppress "minority" voices and perspectives' (1988, p. 8).
When black dancers themselves control their own image they can
confront racist expectations. As Parmar (1988) points out, representation systems have created ideological frameworks which
distort black people's humanity. In a recent production of
Petrushka (first performed in 1911), the moor was made up to
look 'black' in an offensive manner. The movements of the moor in
Fokine's choreography are made to look simple. He is presented in
a stereotyped way with clumsy movements. At times he looks
lasciviously at the doll character, pretending to bite pieces of her
flesh. There is also a reference to jungle/tribal roots as he tosses a

coconut. Parody may well be intended, but this production is disturbingly open to racist connotations.

It is vital to understand images because of the role they play in defining the social and political power to which individuals and marginalised groups have access. 'The deeply ideological nature of imagery determines not only how other people think about us but how we think about ourselves' (Parmar, 1988, p. 9). This, of course, proves to be problematic in attempts to create new, challenging images as the doubts and inner voices urging reinforcment of the status quo, rather than challenging it, have to be quelled.

Empowerment and self-definition for groups with minority status lie in not being confined by dominant images. For example, it is not enough for there just to be images of black people. We also have to recognise the vast range of cultural differences and ethnic differences (Stuart Hall in Parmar, 1988). Moreover, as Parmar points out, there are difficulties with group identities and definitions which become exclusive. For example, funding policies often encourage fixed definitions of 'black' and 'ethnic' which mean that for people who do not conform to these definitions funding is unavailable.

Dominant images of women

Today we are surrounded by visual images and we are sophisticated in our ability to read visual signs. We read signs daily, for example, the picture of a man or woman on toilet doors. The mass media in the form of television, newspapers and magazines saturate us with images. This media are predominantly controlled and organised by men, offering images of women which are in the main passive, domestic and sexual. In a capitalist society these images are produced in order to increase consumption.

'Images of women', however, is not a simple term whereby we look at 'bad' images of women and simply replace them with 'good' ones. As Pollock (1977) suggests, the implication of this term is of a juxtaposition of two separate elements, 'woman as a gender or social group versus representations of women, or a real entity, woman, opposed to falsified, distorted male views of women' (p. 26). However, images are more complex than this, as they do not signify one generalised meaning. An image is composed of many, sometimes even conflicting meanings, which are internal to it and its context, rather than simply reflecting the world outside. There are a wide range of ideal concepts which the female form personifies (Warner, 1985).

In any image there are values which we take for granted and are, therefore, often hidden. Pollock suggests a way of revealing meanings attached to 'women' is by a process of male/female reversals. She cites a classic example from a soft porn print entitled 'Achtez de Pommes' in which a woman is carrying a tray of apples so that her breasts lay on the tray alongside the apples. Linda Nochlin juxtaposed this image with an image of a man carrying a tray of bananas at the level of his penis so that the fruit and penis were displayed together. What we take for granted in the image of the woman is the association of female sexuality, fruit and saleability. This is not so for the image of the man because there is no tradition or context and, therefore, some of the implications not previously clear are highlighted. Many of the images of women in the media and the arts present women as being sexually available (for men). This example can, of course, be applied to dance and is one which Jacky Lansley, a founding member of the X6 Collective (see Chapter Nine) has explored in some of her work.[2] There is a real difficulty, however, in attempting to transform images or to present them in a different context as an example of Pollock's illustrates:

> The appropriation of woman as body in all forms of representation has spawned within the women's movement a consistent attempt to decolonise the female body, a tendency which walks a tightrope between subversion and reappropriation, and often serves rather to consolidate the potency of the signification, rather than actually to rupture it. Much of this attempt has focussed on a kind of body imagery and an affirmative exposure of female sexuality through a celebratory imagery of female genitals (1977, p. 29).

That this is threatening is illustrated by the art book of vaginal imagery by Susanne Santora, removed from a travelling exhibition of art books by the Arts Council. It is disturbing, however, to recognise that similar imagery has since been reproduced in sex magazines (for example, *Penthouse*). This, Pollock (1977) suggests, indicates the limitation of the idea that women can create alternative imagery outside of existing ideological forms.

Advertising is one of the areas in which women's sexuality is exploited.[3] Within it there are set conventions governing how women are presented. There is a size relationship which is adhered to in order to reinforce the myth of superior male over female. Women in relation to men are usually smaller as a physical reminder of inferiority and men are seen to support women physically rather than the other way round (Goffman, 1979).[4]

These conventions are also frequently adhered to in dance choreography (see Chapter 2). In advertising, as in dance, conventions, style and ritual are drawn upon in order to create an ideal representation of the way things are. Our visual environment is pervaded by images of women's bodies (Ayalaha & Weinstock, 1979, p. 9). What we are offered for sale is the female body; the product is secondary. Women's bodies are frequently used to advertise goods which have no direct relationship with the image of the woman portrayed. The refusal of the Advertising Standards Board in England to take notice of the many objections to such images is one example of the refusal to take women seriously (Davis *et al.*, eds, 1987). These images of women perpetuate the ideology of the dominant culture. Women cease to be subjects with valid viewpoints and practices and become objects, 'the other' (de Beauvoir, 1972). One of women's expected roles is to be beautiful, and women in various parts of the world spend a great deal of money on cosmetics. Beauty contests elevate a particular notion of beauty which conforms to a white Western standard. The quest for beauty serves as a degradation and an escape from reality (Seager & Olson, 1986). If we are confronted daily by images which reinforce stereotypes of women as passive, domestic and sexual this will affect our perception of women in dance both as makers and as audience.

There is plenty of evidence in women's history of the manipulation and mutilation of our bodies to fit the idealised norm. Footbinding is a prime example, and whilst it is not so severe, the pain associated with pointe-work is another (for example see Dworkin 1974; Kirkland, 1986). Notions of beauty permeate social structures and reflect their values. This is because knowledge is not neutral but is constructed and validated by a particular society in the interests of the dominant class (Barrett, 1984). These standards are reflected in various arts such as ballet. Standards of beauty describe in precise terms the relationship that an individual should have to her own body. They prescribe her mobility, spontaneity, gait, posture, the uses to which she can put her body (for example see Wex, 1979). 'They define precisely the dimensions of her physical freedom'

(Dworkin, 1974, p. 113). Dworkin suggests that the relationship between physical freedom and creative potential is an umbilical one, so that creativity is correspondingly curtailed by physical restrictions. This, then, is the reason why female dancers who wish to challenge the idealised images they are supposed to aspire to have to find other ways of moving and other structures in which to create.

A first step in the process of the liberation of women is the radical redefining of the relationship between *women and our bodies*. Women within postmodern and new dance have begun this redefinition in their reworking of dance technique and in their attempts to subvert the display of women's bodies (see Chapters 7 and 9). However, most female dancers have internalised images of 'the feminine' and it is not easy to dismantle these. In traditional dance roles women present the ideal of femininity. So, for example, the sylphs of *La Sylphide* are light, delicate, attractive creatures epitomising some of the characteristics frequently associated with women. This ideal, which continues today in many modern ballets and contemporary dance, serves to hide women's strength and autonomy. To maintain the 'ideal' requires that the women do not display any 'unfeminine' characteristics to spoil the image. Women, therefore, frequently view our bodies as the matter which can be shaped, coloured and arranged to produce an object which will be both attractive and fashionable (Millum, 1975).

These restrictive notions of beauty have destructive effects on women and particularly for dancers. Female dancers are in a constant dilemma whilst training and performing. There is a deep conflict between their needs as human beings and their art. All Western dancers are 'or perceive the need to be thinner than the average person' (Vincent, 1979, p. 5). Female dancers are particularly susceptible to the pressure to achieve the idealised norm reflected in the images of women which surrounds them.

Absent or contradictory images of women

There is a prejudice against people with bodily characteristics different from the white Western standard. As it is white able-bodied men who hold the power, this prejudice is evident particularly towards black people, disabled people and all women. Almost any bodily deviation becomes a potential source of threat and a focus of hostility. The male admires and yet also fears and deprecates the female body. The current representation of women is problematic for all women because of the confined, stereotypical images used. However, this has particular implications for black and working class women. Women in these groups are often absent from images, reinforcing the idea that we are unimportant.

Inaccurate and restrictive representations are damaging, and being omitted from images creates a situation in which positive role models are unavailable (Davis *et al.*, 1987). For example, black ballet dancers in predominantly white companies are usually confined to character roles (see Chapter 8). In *Isadora* (1981) choreographed by MacMillan both Duncan and Loie Fuller, important influential early modern dancers, are portrayed in a derogatory fashion. The emphasis is on their personal relationships and their sexuality rather than their contributions as artists.

The absent images of women in dance are those which do not conform to 'the look'. The dance photographer is influenced by 'the look' which the company want to promote and by what is generally considered 'beautiful'. The companies then select a few photographs for publicity on the same basis. In this way the display of the female dancer's body is captured in the photographic image and her hard work or 'ugly' moments are absent.

Sometimes pictures are used which contradict or undermine the text. For example, Gelsey Kirkland, in *Dancing on my Grave* (1986), exposes the often damaging pressures of attempts to conform to the 'ballet look'. However, in an article about that book, the caption of the accompanying main photograph was 'Gelsey Kirkland in her prime – a rare beauty'. As a reader pointed out, this picture showed an emaciated young woman and perpetuated the very 'look' which Kirkland was attempting to expose (Sabbage, 1987). The practice of choreographers presenting women as art objects and photographers capturing 'the look' and duplicating it ignores the humanness of the dancer and her subjectivity.

Display

A central element of traditional dance performance is that of display. The dancer learns how to present her body for the pleasure of the audience. Initially, display was not so evident in modern dance but today contemporary dance techniques emphasise the presentation of the body, through body shape and line, costuming and the dancer's relationship to the audience. In this dance tradition 'the look' of the dancer is central. The accent is on woman as object rather than subject (see Figures 2, 3, 4 and 22).

The common experience of women dancers is evident in the words of an ex-Royal Ballet dancer who said:

> you are taught to deny your creativity, intellect and sexuality to conform to an exact, predetermined image. Severe dieting, for example, was common amongst ballet dancers . . . in some cases leading to total anorexia. We struggled to conform . . .
> You only have to look at the 'corps de ballet' to understand what this narcissistic struggle finally produces; rows of women with identical bodies and expression dancing as swans, nymphs and spirits in perfect harmony, driven and coerced by their ambition to become a 'swan queen' (Furse & Lansley, 1977, p. 6).

The context in which female dancers are viewed is one in which we are daily bombarded by idealised images of women. In dance the close fitting leotard, the tutu which displays the crotch and legs and the low cut tops emphasise the woman's 'to be looked-at-ness' (Mulvey, 1975, p. 418). (See Figure 12.) The audience is in the role of the voyeur in relationship to the dancer. The voyeur has power over the looked at, so that the dancer is displayed to gratify the audience's desire. Traditionally, in keeping with dualist notions, women have been portrayed stereotypically as either the 'virgin' or the 'whore'. In dance history a number of acclaimed ballerinas have been described by these two stereotypes. So that the 'virginal' qualities were attributed to Taglioni and Fonteyn whereas the 'whore' aspects of Elssler's and Seymour's performance were emphasised (See Chapter 5 for further details.) This is the male fantasy of women and 'femininity'. Women's experience in this context is rarely valued and usually invisible. There is a power imbalance in the relationship between the performer and the audience because the performer cannot control how she is looked at. Gelsey Kirkland (1986) makes clear the position of women in most ballet and contemporary dance companies. She says that Balanchine, choreographer for New York City Ballet, where she was principal ballerina, 'shaped each [ballerina] to fit his choreographic design' (p. 31). From this it can be seen that the relationships

2   Alla Michalchenko (Bolshoi Ballet Company) in *Raymonda*; choreographer Yuri Grigorovich.

3   The Bolshoi Ballet Company in rehearsal for *Raymonda*; choreographer Yuri Grigorovich.

4   London Contemporary Dance Theatre – 'Mantis'.

between the dancer, the choreographer and the audience all contribute to meanings of the dance work and the way the work is read.

Some new dance work resists mainstream dance practices. It emphasises the process, the performers' experiences and subjectivity, and chooses movements and costumes which do not emphasise the line of the body. In her early work with Martha Grogan and Dennis Greenwood, Miranda Tufnell emphasised the actions of walking, running and turning as illustrated in *Small Change* (1977). The dancers all wore loose fitting t-shirts and trousers and the focus was on the simplicity of the movement and the interaction between the dancers. In Pina Bausch's *Rite of Spring* (1975), women's experience of the world is expressed:

> This is clear throughout the work because there are many grounded, inward, focussed, womb-like movements; there's not the extension and exposure of the body that we are so used to seeing in many other dance works. The woman is subject. She clearly shows us her state by panting, heaving, sweating even, getting dirty. We see her from her point of view (Adair *et al.*, 1989, p. 30).

The gaze

In a discussion concerned with meaning we need to understand how the gaze operates. Initially, Laura Mulvey in 'Visual Pleasure and Narrative Cinema' (1975) argued that the pleasure for the audience of mainstream Hollywood cinema was derived from a structure in which the male gaze is active and the female provides 'to-be-looked-at-ness' (p. 418). The spectator then is invited to identify with a male gaze towards an objectified female. Dancers are, inevitably, conscious of this gaze both whilst practising and performing. This structure of active male/passive female mirrors the imbalance of power between men and women. Mulvey and other women theorists of the 1970s offered a rather puritanical solution to the problem, disrupting such pleasure in order to facilitate feminist art. This approach was reconsidered in the 1980s and 1990s.

Mulvey revised her original argument in her article 'On Duel in the Sun' (1981). She suggests that a female viewer may find 'masculinisation' of a film [dance] so much at odds with herself that her engagement with the text is broken. Or alternatively, she may enjoy the identification with the hero with its offer of action. So Mulvey offers a spectator position which is not fixed in relation to the text. Another important aspect she focusses on is that of contradictions within signification systems in patriarchal society. She argues that when woman is central to a text then the meanings shift. However, as Gamman (1988) points out, when women make work or play main characters, this does not necessarily produce the female gaze.

Dolan (1989) suggests that the female spectator, in relation to representation created by male desire, has two options. Either she can identify with the active male and be part of the female performer's objectification symbolically or she can identify with the objectified female performer which then positions her as an object. There is a challenge to male power when work is made with (explicit) male sexual representation because this power has always been linked to the act of looking rather than being looked at. One of the areas where this is evident is in the representation of gay men: 'the codification of men via male gay discourse enables a female erotic gaze' (p. 53). But, as already stated, this does not necessarily mean women then have power in this situation because of the dominant structures within which such representation is made and read. Also gay men's position is that of an oppressed group not least because of their acceptance of 'female' traits. They are viewed as not 'real' men and so suffer some of the stigma attached to women.

The understanding of how meanings are produced includes a recognition of active spectatorship. This offers particular cultural groups the opportunity of producing alternative readings of dominant images which are based on different shared codes, experiences and conventions (Stacey in Gamman & Marshment, eds, 1988). These alternative readings have certainly been offered in film (Weiss, 1988). However, there is little recognition of this possibility within theoretical discussions on dance although there have been one or two critical reworkings of classical dances. One example is *I Giselle* (1980), a production in which Fergus Early and Jacky Lansley (both founder members of X6 Collective; see Chapter 9) portrayed their own reading of the popular ballet *Giselle*.[5]

Dancers and dance makers have predominantly ignored or have only a limited understanding of separating images of women from dominant meanings and the example of performing naked in work underlines this. Mary Ann Doane (1981) questions the possibility of using the image of a naked woman. She suggests that the image of naked women can only be presented in a 'sexist and politically patriarchal way in this conjuncture'(p. 24). She develops her point by saying that the representation of the female body in the arts reinforces a hierarchy of sexual difference which is assumed to be natural. This construction defies a possibility of a 'nostalgic return to an unwritten body' (p. 24) and, therefore, if the female body is presented it must be within quotation marks.

In ballets such as *Mutations* (1971) choreographed by Glen Tetley, part of which was performed nude, the quotation marks were missing. Also, Johanna Boyce (in Daly & Martin, 1988) suggests that she has used 'female nudity but with a genderless, organic or animalistic stance' (p. 47). But in the light of the above discussion such a presentation is questionable.

Deconstructing images is a solution which can have more impact within dance. This approach of reading work so that the underlying ideology is revealed exposes the meanings and values usually attached to femininity as cultural constructions. Deconstruction is useful as a tool both for making work and for readings of choreography. This then brings us back to the problem of what is left after deconstruction because an uncoded body is not possible (Doane, 1981; see Chapter 2).

The hierarchical structure within which roles are located means that it is also difficult for women to appropriate 'the gaze' and 'the look'. Women cannot appropriate power by simply reversing these roles. Often there is an element of punishment for women who do break the rules and take the power of 'looking' (Doane, 1982, p. 10). The performers in Liz Aggiss/Billie Cowie's company Divas often 'use long moments of stillness to edge the performance into open confrontation, either cowering before us in harsh pools of light or snarling in frozen abuse' (Mackrell, 1987). This rule-breaking from Aggiss was met by critics' scathing sarcasm and her choreography was described by one critic as the 'horrors' (for further discussion of Aggiss' work see Chapter 10). In addition, for the female observer there is always the difficulty of her association with the image; 'she is the image' (Doane, 1982, p. 78).

The gaze as part of power relations is not a recent phenomenon. It has been used in earlier times as a means of supervising and controlling women, for example, the peepholes in nunnery and asylum doors (Simons, 1988, p. 23). Women internalise the gaze and live confined by a constant sense of surveillance. For dancers the constant checking of oneself in the actual or internal mirror means turning the gaze against oneself, for within the gaze one is always found wanting.

Irigaray puts the view that woman's relation to the visible is always problematic and that she is nearer to a sense of touch (in Doane, 1982). This is interesting in terms of the new and postmodern dance works which evolved in the late 1960s and early 1970s. Many of these works disregarded the visual aesthetic and concentrated more on the sensation and experience of the performer, with contact improvisation being a prime example. Obviously, ultimately, the visual aesthetic has to be considered for a performance art otherwise the dialogue with the audience is lost. However, it is important not to interpret such work in an 'essentialist' sense but to recognise the social construction of women's relationship to the tactile and visual senses.

Desire

Desire in film theory is usually discussed in terms of voyeurism or fetishism, 'a pleasure in seeing what is prohibited in relation to the female body' (Doane, 1982, p. 3). The emphasis in much of the writing about desire and pleasure in the 1970s focussed on male desire. The spectator was assumed to be male looking at a female object of his desire. The cinema, it was argued, was an ideological system, 'which created, maintained and regimented notions of desire in which the woman's primary role was to signify as the recipient of the male gaze, as the object, never the author of desire' (Myers, 1984, p. 35). As we have seen, this situation also exists within mainstream dance.

So why is it that woman, image and desire are so bound up together? Psychoanalysis has provided a major input into feminist theories attempting to extricate meaning from our cultural surroundings. It has been well established that the female body both in art and the media has traditionally been viewed as the site of desire (Kelly, 1984, p. 30).

Burgin points out that, whilst it is men's desire which frequently results in images which are oppressive to women and which continue the status quo, the images in themselves are not sexist. It is the images as signifiers in connection with others at a particular time which give us the meaning which may or may not be oppressive (1984, p. 32). An important aspect of desire is fetishism. 'The fetish is that fragment which allays the fetishist's castration anxiety by serving as a reassuring substitute for that which he construes as "missing" from the woman's body' (1984, p. 33). Mulvey has stated that there is a tendency for the woman's whole body to be fetishised in an attempt to make the whole make up for the 'lacking' part (in Burgin, 1984, p. 33).

Fetishism is evident in the female/male pas de deux in ballet. The male always lifts the woman who is required to appear to float effortlessly into position.

> The ballerina rises from the man's waist, from his crotch, above his shoulder, across his legs. He carries her erect, though her arms may soften the line, her legs remain stiff. An initial lift into one position is followed by him carrying her in another. Lifted he swoops and plunges with her, before bringing her down to earth so that the narrative can continue. He handles her as he would his own penis. Fondly he holds the phallus in his arms, longingly he looks into his princess' eyes, ecstatically he lifts her, his hands around her long, stiff tube of a body. Easily he holds and moves with her. Flying, she is his own (English, 1980, p. 18).

In many of the classic ballet stories the women are presented as fantasy creatures who either disappear offstage or die. English interprets these endings as representing orgasm after the masturbatory preparation of the pas de deux (English, 1980, p. 19).

Dance provides an ideal opportunity for the voyeur. Sitting in the dark of the auditorium the spectator is offered the body endlessly displayed to gratify the desire of the looker. The woman is not as remote as she might appear on the screen. She is there in the flesh constantly exposed.

So where does female desire fit in? Female desire has traditionally been viewed as absent. Marriage manuals spoke of women's role in meeting men's needs but assumed they had no desires of their own. More recently, women's desires have been seen as more legitimate but they are still linked to waiting and passivity rather than initiative and action. Desire is seen as an alternative to change so that 'ideology of romance or body culture fits within the acceptable parameters of female desire' (Myers, 1984, p. 35).

Rosalind Coward (1984) examines the ways in which female desire is expressed. She cites a number of categories which create desire but never fulfil it, for example romance, food, the home. It is the spaces between pleasure and desire, she suggests, which may break the bond to unfulfillment.

It was certainly my desire which was courted at performances of ballet and modern dance. My attention was frequently diverted from the choreography to the presentation of 'perfect' bodies with outstanding skills. I watched in the hope that I might be able to transfer that skill and 'perfect' body to myself. I frequently left performances transformed not so much by the communication of the choreographer's vision but rather by the feeding of my desire's dream for a 'perfect' body. This is part of the cruelty of dance in an oppressive society. Each dancer is constantly measuring herself against her own desires for perfection. She is always found wanting. So whilst the audience recognises and appreciates the performer's 'perfection' she considers herself as less than 'perfect'.

Pleasure

One of the reasons audiences watch dance is to satisfy visual pleasure. Pleasure may be derived differently for men and women. In order to create work which does not perpetuate the old stereotypes we need to understand the role pleasure has for those who watch such work. When film makers interrupted some of the expected conventions of cinema, audiences failed to receive the pleasure that films usually provided. Some feminists have argued that films should not necessarily be pleasurable and that audiences need to become familiar with new ways of looking. Whilst it is true that audiences may well need to detach themselves from old habits, to argue that pleasure too must go, is too harsh a position.

Questions such as 'What do women expect from dance?' and 'What dance offers pleasure?' are important beginnings to new work. However, as we saw earlier with the concept of 'recuperation' the media works hard at appropriating any changes women make. When women find pleasure in our subjectivity this is potentially disruptive to capitalist ideology because this is part of our power. For oppression to be perpetuated any sources of power within the culture of the oppressed must be corrupted. Audre Lorde (1978) in *Uses of the Erotic: The Erotic as Power*, suggests that for women a source of power, which can provide energy for change, is the erotic. She describes it as 'an assertion of the life-force of women; of that creative energy empowered, the knowledge and use of which we are now reclaiming in our language, our history, our dancing, our loving, our work, our lives' (pp. 3–4). Lorde distinguishes it from the pornographic which she says is a denial of the erotic. The pornographic suppresses feeling whereas the erotic is about experiencing our self and our strongest feelings. It is the power of the erotic which women choreographers, searching for expression of their own viewpoints, attempt to release (see Chapter 10). This is in contrast to the objectification of the female dancer's body which could be described as pornographic (Adair *et al.*, 1988).

Women's recent access to the role of producer offers the potential to create images from a subjective stance. Throughout the history of dance the main producers have been men. Women have this century taken the work into their own hands and created their own images but they are still frequently contextualised in a male world. The stage managers, technicians and funding bodies are still predominantly male. This creates conflict for women, so that whilst the potential is there it is not always easy to succeed without role models and adequate support. In addition, whilst it may be pleasurable to be able to see their ideas come to fruition, working with limited time schedules, small financial budgets and so on can be pressurising.

Some women, when making work, think of and create for a women's culture. They work from an expectation that women will be able to identify with the images and ideas of the dance. Others look for areas which have not been exploited by the dominant culture. There are many attempts to challenge the representations in the media which are an aspect of the patriarchal unconscious.

The domination of women by the male gaze is part of patriarchal strategy to contain the threat that the mother embodies, and to control the positive and negative impulses that memory traces of being mothered have left in the male unconscious. Women, in turn, have learned to associate their sexuality with the domination by the male gaze, a position involving a degree of masochism in finding their objectification erotic. We have participated in, and perpetuated, our domination by following the pleasure principle, which leaves us no options given our positioning. Everything thus revolves around the issue of pleasure, and it is here that patriarchal repression has been most negative (Kaplan, 1983, p. 205).

Conclusion

The context of an image, where, when, how and by whom it was made will affect the construction of an image. These aspects will also inform our viewing of it. Women working in dance who intend to establish their own viewpoint will be working against the status quo in which the male gaze, desire and pleasure is prioritised and constructs images. It was not, however, until the twentieth century that women had the opportunity to create their own visions. In ballet, the topic of the next chapter, men shaped the artform.

5

Titillating tutus – women in ballet

A predominant fantasy for many young girls is to become a ballerina (see Pascal in Heron, ed., 1985). As McRobbie (1984) points out, the many ballet stories which contribute to this fantasy offer girls a career option, an escape from women's domestic roles. These stories present an encouraging role model to girls with the message that hard work and talent will provide success. Whilst this message is founded on the capitalist work ethic it is, however, important for girls because they are so seldom encouraged to pursue their own dreams and to put relationships and motherhood second. My first experience of ballet was in a local dance school which offered tap and ballet classes. I loved the vigorous noisiness of tap, but felt constrained by ballet. Whilst I do not have any early memories of being entranced by a magical ballet performance or inspired by an unforgettable ballerina, I do remember being captivated by ballet stories. Now the appeal of the classic form draws me in and I admire the virtuosity of the dancers. Sometimes I am captivated by the choreography. Often, however, I feel detached, aware of the aristocratic heritage and the display of the women dancers. However, despite my objections to ballet, it is seductive; that is its power.

In this chapter I discuss some of the values of ballet which are evident both in the technique and in the choreography. In order to understand women's roles within Western theatre dance today it is necessary to look at its history. This provides a valuable context for the development of women's work in performance and choreography. The role of women in ballet is a Pandora's box of myths, fantasies and paradoxes. Female dancers have both colluded with and resisted the many stereotypes of women in ballet. In this chapter my aim is to reconsider women's achievements in ballet, through the development of technique, representation in choreography and the roles of some of the well-known dancers through the centuries. This choice, however, immediately places me in a dilemma. Ideally, I would prefer to discuss the conditions, and expectations of the majority of women dancers at any given time. However, these are not recorded in the dance scores and early dance writings. So, whilst I write about Camargo, Taglioni, Pavlova and Fonteyn, the famous names that automatically associate women with dance, it is important to remember that for each one of these there were many others who had their own inspirations, dreams and work structures.

Technique and training

Developments in technique, and the form and content of choreography are central to changes in theatre dance and hence to women's roles within ballet. The central aim of a technique is to improve bodily skill for performance. Dance students often strive for the end product of a particular image and forget the importance of the personal journey to that image. The dominance of technique in training may result in the training becoming an end in itself. Technique, as one of the major means of dance production, helps to determine the look of the dance but it can also be a barrier to the expression of the dance. Many of the values we see in dance are built into the various dance trainings. So by examining the history and purposes of the dance trainings the embodiment of the dominant ideology in ballet can be exposed. Those groups in society which are economically and politically dominant tend to dominate ideologically too. Although alternative ideologies either challenge or co-exist with the dominant ideology, ballet tends to uphold the dominant ideology. Consequently, many of the values and beliefs of the owning classes are reproduced within the ballet training institutions, the technique and the choreography.

Ballet technique evolved from European court life and was influenced by the ideas and theories of the educated classes. They were fascinated by the sense of beauty and the ideal human form evident in the classical sculpture of the Greeks and Romans. This beauty was sought after in ballet. The emphasis was on the body being portrayed in its most 'harmonious' and ideal form. A perfectly balanced pose depends on a central line of balance combined with particular proportions created by lines and angles of head, body and limbs (Lawson, 1979). The notion of *display* itself became endemic to the ballet style, so that a well turned-out body, in both senses, was valued.

Technical training became formalised in 1713 when a dance school was established at the Paris Opera. The strict rules of conduct and stylistic elegance from court dancing were taught to the first professional dancers. The opera ballet was the art form within which these professionals danced. However, female participation was restricted by the social conventions of the time. Women's clothes included long skirts, panniers and wigs, which inevitably limited their movement. (See Figure 5). It is not surprising therefore that men dominated the stage in the eighteenth century, not only because of tradition and patriarchal ideology, which gave them power and kept women in subordinate roles, but also because their clothes allowed a far greater range of movement.

Ballet technique was based on the turn out of the hip (emphasising the display of the body) and the five positions of the feet, established by Beauchamp, which are still retained today, together with the straight spine, the high held chest, the elegantly carried head and arms and the scrupulously arched feet of the French Courtier (Howard, 1974). The classical style is based on movement which conforms to rules established by long practice. The original steps from folk dances were refined first by courtiers and then by dancing masters. The latter taught their students both how to behave and how to display themselves in aristocratic society to the best advantage. Later, when professional dancers used the technique, even more attention was paid to the look and exact detail of each movement (Lawson, 1979).

From the seventeenth century on, with the establishment of dance as a profession, a pattern began to develop concerning the roles of the sexes in dance. The men were the organisers, teachers, thereoticians and choreographers (and stars in the eighteenth century). The women were stars, brilliant dancers who were noted for their 'good looks'. The dancers no longer came from the nobility but from poorer families and learnt their skills at the Academy (Kraus and Chapman, 1981). The audience, however, were still mostly aristocratic.

A Paris chez I.Mariette rue St Iacques aux Colonnes d'Hercules

Mademoiselle Moreau
Dansant a l'Opera

5 Mlle Moreau – a ballerina of the Paris Opera (*circa* 1700). From the collections of the Theatre Museum.

Two women who are famous from this time, **Marie Camargo** (1710–70) (see Figure 6) and **Marie Sallé** (1701–56), are known for their daring and their costume reforms. Without such reforms their dancing would have been severely limited. Camargo, who made her debut at the Paris Opera in 1726, was one of the first noted professional dancers. She was excellent technically, a virtuoso. To allow more freedom to execute the exacting steps and for these to be seen, she shortened her skirt nearly to the lower calf. Sallé is often cited as Camargo's rival and she was renowned for her dramatic and expressive style of dancing. In order to be true to her dance, she abandoned pannier, skirt and bodice and dared to appear in a simple muslin dress with her hair down when she danced *Pygmalion* (1734). It is significant that her costume reforms and her dramatic dancing are widely recognised but the fact that she was also a choreographer is far less well known (Au, 1988).

6   Marie Camargo – an engraving after the painting by Lancret.

Women attained a technique created by men and for men (the audiences were predominantly male). The ambivalent view men held of women, on the one hand as an ideal and on the other as a body to be used – evident in the literature and art of the nineteenth century, was epitomised both in the dances and the dancers.To perfect their technique and create the required images dancers spent hours training and rehearsing with their male teachers and choreographers. **Carlotta Grisi** (see Figure 10), a prominent dancer in the early nineteenth century, said:

> Jules [Perrot] stood on my hips like the Colossus of Rhodes while I lay face downwards on the floor – this was to strengthen my hips (Clarke & Crisp, 1987, p. 36).

Technique gradually became more complex and developed from steps for their own sake into an aspect of the dancer's expression. There were some tortuous methods used in training.

> Every morning my teacher imprisoned my feet in a grooved box. There, heel to heel, with knees pointing outwards, my martyred feet became used to remaining in a parallel line by themselves. They call this 'turning out' (Guest, 1980, p. 26).

'Turnout' was established to give the dancer maximum freedom to move in every direction; it also allows the body to be displayed to full advantage within the proscenium arch. The discovery of pointe work extended the ballerina's technique and enhanced the ethereal image of nineteenth-century choreography which was internalised by the performers. The illusion of effortlessness and weightlessness was sought both in the technique and with mechanical aids.

The training to be a ballet dancer today begins at an early age, maybe as young as three or four years old, and those considered talented have their whole lives organised to this end. The selection procedure for ballet training is rigorous. Only those with bodies which have no weakness and are structurally appropriate, are accepted. At the auditions for entrance to the Royal Ballet School, the selectors are searching for inborn talent for dancing combined with the right sort of body for classical ballet training (Jessel, 1985, p. 12).

The students

need to be good-looking and naturally slim, to have mobile, arched feet, flexible joints, efficient tendons, long limbs, a neat, beautifully held head (Jessel, 1985, p. 12).

The selection committee is, of course, searching for bodies that can be moulded into the classical ideal. Once accepted, there is no guarantee of success. Many are rejected each year as the training continues, because of injuries, not progressing well, putting on weight and so on (Furse & Early, 1979). This selection is particularly damaging to women, as the competition for places in training and in the companies mirrors that which women experience in wider society. The emphasis on the 'ideal' body is something which all women are subjected to in one way or another.

The main aim of the Royal Ballet School is to produce the best dancers possible. For women this means developing enough strength for pointe work which, through much pain and occasional deformity, gives the illusion of effortlessly defying gravity. The training reinforces rigid sex roles. The girls learn to move with lightness, grace and ease to create the Sylph-like images still popular today. A dancer learns to be constantly aware of her body as she checks and re-checks her image in the studio mirrors to ascertain whether she has created the correct look and the desired effect (see Figure 1). The look of the work has always been of paramount importance in ballet throughout its history. It is mostly girls who are attracted to ballet training, which is generally considered appropriate, as it provides attributes, such as poise and grace, which are valued for women in our society. Later, when they stop dancing, they then become the audience and in turn send their daughters to ballet lessons, and so the cycle is perpetuated.

In Britain the Royal Ballet is used as a vehicle for gaining international prestige. The wealth backing ballet and the role it can play in providing status ensures that it remains firmly in the control of the dominant classes. Ballet upholds the dominant ideology, for example, by continuing to select dancers on the basis of a classical ideal of beauty, by reinforcing traditional sex roles and by the hierarchical structures of both the training institutions and the ballet companies.

Ballet and politics

The issue of whether dance should be political or deal with political concerns is frequently debated.[1] However, overtly political motives were behind the early ballets, which were theatrical spectacles of dance and song with elaborate costumes of the courts of Italy and France. The arts played an important role in the lives of the aristocracy and dancing was considered a means of socialisation for the individual and a device for creating harmony with the group. The court ballets, a mixture of art, politics and entertainment, generally ended on a harmonious note and afterwards there was a ball in which everyone participated, 'symbolically drawing both spectators and performers into accord with the ideas expressed by the performance' (Au, 1988, p. 13).

The *Ballet Comique de la Reine* (1581) created by the Italian dancing master Belgiojoso has a story line which implies 'the eventual defeat of evil forces and the transfer of political power into the hands of the monarch' (Clarke & Crisp, 1981 p. 8).[2] From this time European monarchs included ballet in their entertainments and ballet de cour was the 'State in miniature' (Brinson, 1980). The sixteenth and seventeenth centuries were the greatest period of court ballet. It is clear that the ballets were used to reinforce the monarch's (male) power and to celebrate the (male) status quo. Louis XIV, 'Realising that art could be made to enhance his prestige as a monarch . . . chose men of real talent to produce the ballets which added so much to the brilliance of his court' (Guest, 1962, p. 21).

One of the few women to be named as having a role at this time was **Catherine de Medici**, Queen of France. She commissioned entertainments for the court, an example of which was, *Le Paradis d'Amour* (1572) on the occasion of the wedding of her daughter, Marguerite de Valois. Within the context of a mock combat the dance was performed by twelve 'ladies' costumed as nymphs (a role which was to be characteristic for women in the later Romantic ballet) (Au, 1988). Catherine de Medici remained true to her role of an aristocratic woman by ordering extravagant entertainments when her subjects would, no doubt, have been less than well fed.

Ballet as a profession

From the seventeenth century when Louis XIV added a dance school to the Académie Royale de Musique, there was a gradual change from amateur to professional dance. Initially, professional dancers had performed grotesque or acrobatic dances which were considered to lower a nobleman's dignity or were too technical.

Women professional dancers danced in the court ballets of Louis XIV. For example, **Mademoiselle Vertpré** danced opposite Louis XIV in the *Ballet de l'Impatience* (1661) (Au, 1988). As dance became professionalised, ballet became more technically skillful and was performed on a proscenium stage. The first principal ballerina of the Paris Opera was **Mademoiselle de Lafontaine** who was one of the first women to appear with the company in 1681. There was a difference in style between male and female, with the female performance being more restrained because of social conventions and restrictions of costume (see Figure 5). Although at first many of the steps were only performed by the male dancers, steps which we recognise today, for example, cabrioles, chassés, coupés, entrechats and sissones were already part of the dancer's technical vocabulary (Guest, 1962).[3]

The male documentation of dance began with the first dance treatise at the beginning of the fifteenth century (Domenico di Piacenza) continuing with treatises written by Arbeau (1588), Weaver (1712), Noverre (1760), Blasis (1820), and the manuals of dance notation by Feuillet (1699) and Stepanov (1891). The dancing masters, as the term indicates, were male, as were the choreographers and most of the dancers. It is, therefore, a male constructed vision of dance which makes up the ballet heritage. Many female dancers of the eighteenth and nineteenth centuries danced under the patronage of gentlemen of the court. Dancers, together with singers and actors[4], were generally thought to be available to men through charm or money. **Madeline Guimard** became wealthy from such patronage and was a powerful member of a group who managed to get Jean-Georges Noverre dismissed from his post as Director of the Paris Opera (Clarke & Crisp, 1987). This example highlights the paradox of women's position in society. Undoubtedly, Guimard was a powerful woman, but she was only in a position to exercise her power, within a structure in which men were dominant, because she was the mistress of a man with status. Despite ballerinas' achievements there was a social stigma attached to ballet because of the association with sexuality. During the nineteenth century The Paris Opera backstage was opened to privileged men so that they could mix with the dancers, many of whom were poor, and arrange sexual liaisons. Whilst the ballet patronage of the eighteenth century was royal and aristocratic the patronage of the nineteenth century (except in pre-revolutionary Russia which was still governed by the Tsars) was bourgeois and capitalist.

So, were there women challenging their roles at this time? Aphra Benn, a successful playwright, defended women's rights. Seventeen of her plays were produced in seventeen years at a time when London had only two theatres. In her first play, *The Forced Marriage* or *The Jealous Bridegroom*, which was performed in 1670, she presented women's experiences in a world ruled by men. She challenged the fact that women's work was rarely well received and that women's value was measured in primarily physical terms. Dale Spender (1983) illustrates the ways in which women's work is misrepresented or eradicated using Aphra Benn as a key example. She details the many ways the establishment use to discredit women and undermine our work.

A star of the Paris Opera who was interested in the possibilities for drama which dance offered was **Françoise Prévost** (1690–1741). In *Les Caractères de la Danse*, a famous solo of hers, she portrayed a series of lovers of both sexes and varying ages. This solo she taught to two of her students, Camargo and Sallé. When women succeed in areas previously assigned to men we are congratulated and compared with men, thus continuing the myth that the only standards which are applicable to achievements are associated with men. Camargo was, Voltaire said, 'the first ballerina to dance like a man' (i.e. by performing the steps usually associated with men; quoted in Guest, 1962, p. 29).

These ideas were questioned by women of the time. For example, Catherine Macaulay (1731–91) in her writing discusses the destructive practice of referring to creative and competent skills as masculine. Mary Astell in 1700 writes of the difference in power between men and women and how this is illustrated in marriage.

Mary Wollstonecraft (1759–97) encouraged women to affirm and articulate their personal experience so that they would discover the strength to protest against the injustices they experienced (Spender, 1983).

Revolution and romanticism

The nineteenth century was a time of social change with new ideas, particularly those of liberty and equality promoted by the French Revolution. There was the growth of a new middle class who gained wealth from the growth of commerce and industry. There was a need for reform within the arts; the emphasis on classicism meant that the form was frequently regarded as more important than the content, resulting in somewhat sterile work. The Romantic movement was partly a resistance to this preoccupation with form (Guest, 1962).

Ballet, like the other arts, revealed idealised worlds concerned with the supernatural and exotic, offering refuge from the rapidly growing, grimy, industrial world. After the revolution of 1830 in Paris the court patronage of the Paris Opera changed to commercial enterprise and more working- and middle-class people attended the theatre wanting entertainment. In 1831 when Dr Véron was made director of the Paris Opera, which was to be a subsidised private enterprise, he realised that the bourgeoisie was the audience he needed to appeal to, since their wealth, influence and new position in society made them ideal consumers of the Opera (Guest, 1980).

The female dancer is usually regarded as dominant in the Romantic ballet. However, this view is somewhat misleading. Undoubtedly, from this time male dancing declined and the female dancer's technique developed considerably. The increased skill of the ballerina's technique contributed to her central role in the Romantic ballets. Despite her apparently dominant role she was, nevertheless, interpreting rather than making the work. In addition, the ballet world was part of a social world in which, then as now, women were oppressed. The relationships they had with their male choreographers and the responses from the predominantly male audiences defined their roles as dancers. Indeed, the status of ballet did not have the high regard which it had enjoyed when male

University of Chester, Seaborne Library

Title: Choreographing difference : body and identity in contemporary dance / Ann Cooper Albright.
ID: 01115739
Due: 07-01-13

Title: Dancing identity : metaphysics in motion / Sondra Fraleigh.
ID: 01033382
Due: 07-01-13

Title: Women and dance : sylphs and sirens / Christy Adair ; foreword by Janet
ID: 36089591
Due: 07-01-13

Total items: 3
06/12/2012 10:45

Thank you for using Self Check

3

7   Mlle Zambelli and Mlle Sandini – Paris Opera (*circa* 1900).

dancers were dominant. As Margaret Mead (1970) observed, work done by women is considered less important.

The conditions of many dancers' lives seem harsh. They needed to make liaisons with wealthy men in order to pay for classes, practice clothes and other needs. The threat of an unwanted pregnancy must

8   Late nineteenth-century class in France.

have been a constant worry without adequate means of birth
control. Many dancers became pregnant and sometimes their
children travelled with them. Others, like **Fanny Elssler** (see
below) gave the child over to friends or relations whilst travelling.
Fanny's daughter was seven when she left for America and eleven
when she returned (Jowitt, 1988).

The cost of illusion

The introduction of gas lighting greatly assisted the creation of the
illusory settings. The sets were often quite dangerous and there were
a number of accidents. During a dress rehearsal **Marie Taglioni** fell
as she was disappearing up a chimney. She, however, avoided
injury. Carlotta Grisi was not so fortunate and injured herself
during a performance:

> The Opera stage was notoriously dangerous. 'Sometimes a scene comes
> toppling down . . . or an abyss is gaping beneath your feet, or jagged

nails are left unnoticed. What a hair-breadth escape had Carlotta, for the whole weight of her body fell on an upright nail, which, after having pierced through the chaussure, had its point bent in her foot, and was not extracted without a world of pain. (*Era*, 1846, quoted in Guest, 1980, p. 250).

The iron wires used to suspend ethereal creatures above the stage were also treacherous:

At the performance given for Mlle. Taglioni's benefit, two sylphides remained suspended in mid-air, it was impossible to pull them up or lower them down; people in the audience cried out in terror; at last a machinist risked his life and descended from the roof at the end of a rope and set them free. . . . It is not unlikely that another difficulty of this sort will recur (Gautier in Steinberg, ed., 1980, p. 84).

Another danger was that of fire. The combination of gas lighting and diaphanous costumes meant that this was ever present. **Clara Webster** died after her costume caught fire at the Drury Lane Theatre, London and **Emma Livry** died after months of pain following burns when her costume was set alight from a lamp. Taglioni had choreographed *Le Papillon* (1860) for Livry to show her skills. The management of the Opera had ordered all dancers to dip their costumes in fireproofing solution; however, Livry refused because she thought the tutus then looked dull (Anderson, 1987). She lost her life in her attempt to achieve an 'ideal' appearance.

Comments of the audience and critics

The dancers were exhorted by critics to strive harder for the right look.

Many of the dancers have put on too much flesh since we saw them last, and yet these girls have more opportunity than most to keep up their activity. Come, ladies, take some exercise! (*Journal des Théâtres*, 1821 quoted in Guest, 1980, p. 40).

The dance writings of the Romantic period frequently detailed the charms or shortcomings of the ballerinas rather than their interpretations of the role of Giselle and other characters. For example, Gautier wrote:

> La Cerrito is blonde; she has blue eyes which are very soft and tender, a gracious smile despite its too frequent appearance; her shoulders, her bosom do not have that scrawniness which is characteristic of female dancers (Gautier, 1846 in Cohen, 1974, p. 87).

His writing is that of the voyeur, obsessed with the looks of the woman dancer as though she is his possession. We learn nothing about her dancing roles or ability. When writing a review of Fanny Elssler's famous *Cachucha*, Charles de Boigne responds to its sensuous, erotic appeal:

> Those contortions, those movements of the hips, those arms which seem to seek and embrace an absent lover, that mouth crying out for a kiss, that thrilling, quivering, twisting body. (quoted in Jowitt, 1988, p. 62).

The writing of the nineteenth century makes evident that the paradox of an unattainable sylph being danced by a real woman who might well agree to make a sexual liaison was titillating. The myriad of souvenirs, including lithographs, placed ballerinas in a similar position to that of Hollywood movie stars (for example, Marilyn Monroe). Then and now, prints and pictures of ballerinas were and are sold for male pleasure and consumption. This seductive ballerina image also captivates women because it affirms their identity as 'successful' and 'desirable' women. The ideal image, however, changes as attitudes and fashions change, although it is still based on the classical ideals of the Greeks and Romans.

Marie Taglioni presented a new image of the female dancer at her first performance at the Paris Opera in 1827. Her dancing was characterised by its light and graceful quality (Clarke & Crisp, 1973). Taglioni created an ethereal vision. The development of technique meant that she could dance on pointe with apparent effortlessness. The loose fitting dresses enabled her to increase her range of movements, including sideways bending and freer movement of her thighs and hips and the stage machinery enhanced her supernatural image.

Her dancing brought a change in style which did not emphasise poses and tricks: 'she has completely reformed the ballet of her time' (*Journal des Débats*, 1832, quoted in Guest, 1980, p. 115). Undoubtedly, her influence was considerable and the change in dancers' styles was attributed to her work. Despite her success and influence she was not perceived by her critics to possess the looks expected of a dancer:

That this dancer, this great revolutionary, should have been an ill-made woman almost hump-backed, without beauty and without any of those striking exterior advantages that command success amounts to a miracle (author of Petits Mémoires de l'Opéra in Levinson, Steinberg, ed., 1980 p. 68).

She worked extremely hard, practising six hours a day under the exacting eye of her father. Her aim for perfection was such that she would sometimes collapse after her practice (Roslavleva, 1966). The training which Taglioni received from her father she passed on to her students, establishing the tradition. Her work was rewarded by her legendary fame. Her popularity was such that hairstyles were copied from her and '*taglioniser*' became a verb (Cohen, 1974). The comments of the audience and critics illustrate the male fantasy, the element of the male gaze observing the female displayed for his gratification. The writings of balletomanes, mainly male, are full of romantic illusions of female dancers with detailed descriptions of the dancers rather than the dance. For example, a writer in the *Illustrated London Life* (1843) observed:

We perfectly recollect . . . admiring the emotion of several ancient aristocrats in the stalls, on the recent appearance of the legs of Fanny Elssler. We thought that we observed one aged and respectable virtuoso shedding tears; another fainted in his satin breeks and diamond buckles; one appeared to go mad, and bit his neighbour's pig-tail in half in sheer ecstasy. Oh! the legs of Fanny displaced a vast deal of propriety, and frightened sober men from their prescribed complacency (quoted in Guest, 1972, p. 63).

The director of the Paris Opera realised that **Fanny Elssler**'s style would make a fascinating contrast to Taglioni's. Her skill was as a dancer/actor and in her execution of small quick steps. One of Elssler's key roles was in the *Cachucha* (1836), a titillating, balleticised Spanish dance (Au, 1988). Whilst it is the images of *La Sylphide* and *Giselle* which are usually associated with the Romantic ballet this very different image was another aspect of it. These contrasting choreographies resulted in Gautier, a leading figure of the Romantic movement, characterising Taglioni as a 'Christian dancer' and a 'woman's dancer' and Elssler as a 'pagan dancer' and a 'man's dancer'. Along with other opera dancers, Elssler attracted attacks from moralists and was called 'harlot Fanny'. The results of her diet, childbearing and the type of muscles she developed meant that Elssler's body was not the lean almost boyish shape of today's dancers.

Dr Véron, exploited the rivalry between the two women, promoting controversy and box-office receipts. These two approaches to dance and the sense of rivalry encouraged by their 'admirers' echoed Sallé and Camargo of an earlier generation and were followed by Pavlova and Karsavina and others later. This 'pairing' of ballerinas is another aspect of the false characterisation of women under the labels virgin/whore described in Chapter 4.

Whereas most of the women of the Romantic ballet were famous for their dancing, Thérèse Elssler, Fanny's sister, was also a choreographer. Her choreography for *La Volière* (1838) was praised but the plot was thought to be absurd, although aspects of it are interesting from a feminist perspective. The ballet is set in a sheltered garden on an island, where Thérèza (T. Elssler) who was deceived by her lover, has brought up her sister Zoe (F. Elssler) without any contact with men. However, a naval officer, Fernand, arrives and Zoe and the slave girls believe him to be an exotic bird similar to those in the large cage in the garden. At this point the women's autonomy ends and the plot follows the usual model of a happy heterosexual ending. Fernand's uncle arrives, who is Thérèza's former lover and they and Fernand and Zoe are united. Despite its ending it provides a number of positive images of women, illustrated by Gautier's depiction of a passage:

> the two sisters run, hand in hand, from the back of the stage, thrusting their legs forward in unison, which surpasses everything that can be imagined for its effect, correctness and precision. You might think that one is the other's shadow, and that each is advancing with a mirror at her side which follows and repeats her every movement (quoted in Guest, 1980, p. 169).

This description portrays an intimacy between the women which is striking and in contrast to the emphasis on male/female relationships, so frequently central to ballet.

The *Pas de Quatre* (1845) (see Figure 9) choreographed by Perrot was important because unlike many of the other ballets it did not follow a storyline, it emphasised the dancing (rather than dramatic performance) of four famous ballerinas, Taglioni, Grisi, Cerrito and Grahn. The newspapers of the time also focussed on the competitive

9 *Pas de Quatre* – Carlotta Grisi, Marie Taglioni, Fanny Cerrito, Lucile Grahn (1845).

behaviour between the women, as do many of the dance history books. Resistance to such behaviour and interpretations, and replacement by co-operative behaviour has been a key issue within the Women's Movements in this century. It is significant that much dance writing has been from a male perspective so that those details which have been passed on to us today are frequently anti-women.

Several women were writing of women and of rights for women, at this time, one of whom was Paulina Wright Davis (1813–76). She wanted women to know more about their own bodies and, through understanding, discard modesty and ignorance. She gave lectures on women's anatomy to this end; however, the widely held beliefs and unenlightened attitudes were such that many women fainted during her lectures (Spender, 1983).

Stories of ballets – re-readings

These enlightened views contrasted sharply with the popular images of ballet, which still have credence today and can be particularly attributed to the sylphs in *La Sylphide*, choreographed by Taglioni's father Filippo in 1832. The story is of James, a young farmer, who leaves his fiancée and the mortal world to pursue the sylph. Effie, the betrothed, appears to be the reliable wife and mother of the future with all the implications of boredom and restriction which these two roles hold in male fantasy. In contrast the sylph offers the lure of the unknown, the erotically charged adventure. She represents the 'ideal' woman.

There is potential for a feminist reading of this work. Madge, a soothsayer, during preparations for James' and Effie's wedding predicts that Effie will marry Gurn, also a farmer, instead. James throws Madge out but she curses him. The wedding festivities begin but James sees the sylph and leaves Effie in order to pursue her. Then Madge suggests that Gurn marry Effie, who agrees as she thinks James has disappeared forever. Later, James finds Madge alone and she suggests that if he binds the sylph with a bewitched scarf the sylph will always be his. This is, of course, a good example of the male desire to possess his 'ideal'. However, when James ties the scarf on the sylph her wings fall off and she dies. Madge triumphs over James' body. Although both the sylph and Effie have little power in relation to James' desires Madge directs his fate and is victorious in the end.

The ballet from the Romantic period which has most frequently been performed is *Giselle* (1841). (See Figure 10.) It was choreographed by Corelli, chief balletmaster of the Paris Opera, and Jules

10 Carlotta Grisi – '*Giselle*' drawn and lithographed by J. Brandard (*circa* 1842).

Perrot. In the first act, Giselle, a peasant girl, falls prey to the attentions of the romantic hero, Albrecht, an aristocrat who is disguised as the peasant Loys. Giselle loses her reason and commits suicide after Hilarion, a peasant also in love with her, reveals Loys' true identity, and Bathilde claims Albrecht as her fiancée. This ballet, in which class is a central theme, offers a reading of the exploitation of a working-class woman by an aristocratic man.

In Act Two, Giselle, after 'losing her reason' when betrayed, is transformed to an ethereal wili. The wilis are ghosts of young girls who were jilted and died before their wedding day. They seek their revenge by dancing to death any man they find during the darkness of the night. Myrtha, their Queen, has a powerful role. Her opening solo has many vigorous jumps, and bourées (fast little steps on pointe) in which she seems to glide through the space. Myrtha orders Giselle to entice Albrecht away from the cross on Giselle's grave but Giselle tries to support him in his dance of death. Morning comes and the ghosts fade away leaving the Count alive. Hilarion the honest peasant truly in love with Giselle succumbs to the wilis vengeance and dies, so that both the peasants pay for aristocratic dalliance. An alternative interpretation which supports the ideal of romantic love is that Giselle and Albrecht were meant for each other and the separation, inevitable because of their different class positions, is tragic.

There are many interpretations of this classic. Matz Ek choreographed a version of *Giselle* for the Culberg Ballet (1982) in which Act Two is set in an asylum. Ek points out that over half the patients in asylums today are women, underlining the social relevance of this setting. The central character of Giselle is one of a vulnerable, sensitive woman driven mad by Loys' deception. Myrtha is an authority figure with suggestions of nun and mother. When Giselle appears from under Myrtha's skirt, at one section in the act, it is reminiscent of the power of birth and the desire to go back to the womb where once it was safe. This work is a powerful interpretation.

Of the traditional versions of *Giselle*, 'the etherealization of the female body that is imaged in *Giselle* represents a particular moment within the general history of patriarchy in which the ascendancy of private economic relations called forth an image of woman as at once private and powerful, sacred and spectral, a figure of desire' (Alderson, 1987, p. 301).

Arthur Mitchell set his version of *Giselle* for the all black company, The Dance Theatre of Harlem, in Louisiana, in the nineteenth century. In *Creole Giselle* (1984), although the location has changed, the performance follows traditional interpretations through the choreography, set and costumes. In this ballet Mitchell succeeds (in his fight against racism), in proving that black ballet dancers can perform technically complex classical ballet. However, whilst it is necessary to dance within the tradition to make this point, Mitchell is then confined by a setting which does not lend itself to progressive representations for black people or women. Some of the characters appear stereotypical – for example, Giselle's mother is portrayed as a 'big fat mama'.

Jacky Lansley and Fergus Early collaborated on a production entitled *I Giselle* (1980). Their intention was to explore the gender roles and class backgrounds of the characters and to challenge the classical ballet tradition. Although *Giselle* is well known in the dance world, the varied venues to which *I Giselle* toured meant that the directors could not take knowledge of the story for granted. Therefore, they began with a short pantomime which told the story. They drew on the theatrical qualities of the work through use of film, slides, tapes and dialogue. There follows a re-defining process in which the positive links between the women, for example, Giselle and her mother and the strength of Myrtha are emphasised. The title was chosen to evoke the sense in which Giselle is defining her story in her own way. So for example, the mad scene is retained but the definition of madness is questioned (Lansley, 1980).

Russian ballet and its legacy

Ballet was imported into Russia in the second half of the nineteenth century during a time when many European fashions were popular. Unlike Europe, Russia had state-supported theatres whose directors were appointed by the Tsar. This led to a different attitude to dance as a career; it was respectable, whereas in Europe it was often regarded as morally dubious. This was particularly important for women because a dance career offered them a secure job and an independent life (Anderson, 1986). Karsavina went to the Imperial Ballet School partly because her mother thought that dance was a secure career for a girl (Montague, 1980). The legendary ballerina **Anna Pavlova** also trained at the School, which was described as a 'convent where frivolity is banned and merciless discipline reigns' (Kerensky, 1975, p. 7). This regime was established in order to fulfill the Tsar's pleasure in watching dance. The Imperial Ballet was characterised by its lavish display in terms of costume, set and choreography. The ballet reinforced the aristocratic values of the Tsars. Petipa and St Leon, both French choreographers and dancers, went to Russia after the French Revolution when ballet ceased to be supported by the court.

The work of French choreographer Petipa ensured that Russia became a leader rather than a follower in the world of ballet. His ballets, particularly *The Sleeping Beauty* and *Swan Lake*, are the epitome of 'classical ballet'. This term refers to a choreography which emphasises formal values including order, harmony, clarity and symmetry. The rules of academic ballet technique are essential and usually followed closely. An important part of the structure of classical ballets can be seen in the pas de deux. This takes the form of an adagio for the ballerina and her partner, followed by solo variations for each dancer, ending with a coda which is highly technical for both dancers. The main focus of this is the ballerina who is presented by her male partner to the audience.

The storylines of the ballets reinforce the aristocratic values of possession, wealth and power. Clearly, however, our reading of these works today will be affected by a number of complex factors. For example, *Sleeping Beauty* was first choreographed in 1892 in Tsarist Russia. Since then it has been performed countless times all over the world by many different ballet companies. Today, an English audience watching a performance of *Sleeping Beauty* choreographed by Frederick Ashton and performed by the Royal Ballet will be viewing a performance which embodies both the ideologies of its original context and those of the current context. The points I discuss here in terms of gender are, therefore only one part of the complexities of the interpretation of a dance work.

Sleeping Beauty has an extravagant set, costumes and choreography, reinforcing aristocratic values. The woman (the princess) too can be possessed by the all powerful prince. The court scenes celebrate the pomp and ceremony of royalty reaffirming its importance. The corps de ballet provides decoration, creating designs in space, so that the autonomy of the female dancer is subsumed for the overall effect. The Rose Adagio, in which the princess dances with each of her suitors in turn, is an excellent example of the woman on display.

She balances on pointe whilst they take turns to revolve her slowly on the spot. This dance is often performed separately as it demonstrates virtuosity, but this further emphasises the woman as object.

The ballet draws on the fairy tale tradition with which the audience will be familiar. When the prince arrives at the castle, his power is evident. He kisses the sleeping princess and immediately she moves. He is so supreme that he can banish one hundred years' sleep with the touch of his lips. The final scene portrays the good Lilac Fairy blessing the marriage of the united heterosexual couple at her feet. This, we remember, is how it is meant to be.

The long admired *Swan Lake* (1895), choreographed by Marius Petipa and Lev Ivanov, offers themes of ideal, eternal love, betrayal and the menace of death. There is a complex intertwine of issues concerned with gender, sexuality and class. The following outline briefly draws on one or two of these. During the celebrations for Prince Siegfried's birthday he dances with the peasant girls. This emphasises his importance; the women fulfill the role of playthings, subject to his charms. When he is given a chain by his mother, symbolising his future kingship we are drawn into empathising with the weight of his responsibilities. His dream is to find true love and when he meets Odette, who changes from a swan into an enchanting woman because she is under the evil magician Rothbart's spell, he is captivated and chooses to reach for this unattainable love.

In Act Three the patriarchal order is evident as Siegfried dances with each of his prospective fiancées. He has the power of rejection, which he exercises as he has already found his ideal love, the virginal Odette who is under Rothbart's spell. The spell can only be broken if a man promises to love her and be faithful which Siegfried does. Odile posing as Odette in order to lure Siegfried into breaking his promise to Odette dances with an outward, harsh gaze and a brashness of manner. When Siegfried chooses to marry Odile, Odette is betrayed and must die so she flings herself into the lake in despair, followed by Siegfried. She dies for love, just as Giselle did before her, reinforcing her role of woman as sacrifice.

Swan Lake has become synonymous with ballet. The major companies' productions of this ballet are performed to packed audiences and little-known ballet companies attract audiences when *Swan Lake* is in their programmes. For many people, the virginal Odette (see Figure 11) and the whorish Odile are the essence of ballet (see Figure 12). Undoubtedly the principal ballerina in

11 Odette, *Swan Lake*; dancer Monica Mason.

12 Odile, *Swan Lake*; dancer Monica Mason.

Swan Lake has a powerful role, not least because of the wide range of skill she displays. However, her power is undermined as her movements emphasise her fragility rather than her strength in her role as Odette, a delicate, pure white bird. Here is 'the woman on a pedestal' of male fantasy, whilst Odile provides the other extreme of male fantasy as 'a woman to be used'. Both roles are controlled and determined by men and lack autonomy.

Ballets Russes

At the beginining of the twentieth century, Russian ballet was revolutionised by the innovations of Diaghilev and his company, Ballets Russes, when artists worked together to achieve his visions of total theatre. Two company members, Fokine and Pavlova, clashed with the authorities when they led a group in support of revolutionary activities against the Tsar. Also Pavlova spoke against the army and the shooting of demonstrators at a ballet company meeting (Kerensky, 1975). Her working class background probably prompted her drive to share her dancing with the world. She toured for over twenty years, inspiring many future dancers and choreographers. One of her most famous roles was *The Dying Swan* (1907) (see Figure 13), choreographed for her by Fokine. Arlene Croce (1978), a dance critic, said that she was one of the few dancers who managed to combine the sacred/profane, Christian/pagan, virgin/whore stereotypes of Western dance (although usually she was contrasted to Karsarvina using the virgin/whore stereotype) – so that she was both Taglioni and Elssler. Pavlova thought the function of dancing was 'to give man a sight of an unreal world, beautiful, dazzling as his dreams' (Kerensky, 1975, p. 101).

Female dancers' desire to please is striking when reading their comments about the choreographers and impresarios for whom they worked. Their role as dancers mirrors exactly the expectations of women's behaviour (see Chapter 3). Diaghilev's power and influence were not only directed to the work but also to the personal lives of his dancers. Many of the dancers were young and impressionable. Markova said, 'When I joined Diaghilev I was in socks, and very naive and somehow he wanted to keep me that way' (in Coleman, 1989, p. 23). When Sokolova found she was pregnant Diaghilev tried to persuade her to have an abortion. Not

13 Anna Pavlova – '*The Swan*'.

willing to agree to this, yet determined to please him she danced all of her roles at six months pregnant. Later she found a woman to breastfeed her baby while she rehearsed, and persuaded her to travel with the company. This meant the woman had to leave her own eighteen-month-old son (Buckle, 1960).

The creators Diaghilev encouraged were mostly men, with **Bronislava Nijinska** the rare exception. Some of her dances can be interpreted as important social comments on women's roles. *Les Noces* (1923) (see Figure 14) is based on a traditional Russian peasant wedding ceremony where the marriage was an arranged one. Nijinska focusses her attention on the anxieties of the young bride, which are underlined by the high-pitched soprano voices of the score and the tension of the sharp pointe work of the choreography. There is a sense conveyed of two people 'trapped by fate and repressive social custom' (The Fine Arts Museum of San Francisco, 1986, p. 32). Her interpretation of the feelings of the bride and groom is shown through the movement:

14 *Les Noces* (1923).

In one of the ballet's central images, for example, the bride's hair is braided before being cut off to symbolize her loss of virginity . . . Nijinska had the young women surrounding the bride dance a small pas de bourée in which the toes, on pointe, stabbed the floor as the legs crossed and recrossed. In doing so, she evoked the rhythm and action of braiding, while intimating the ritual's chilling consequences (Fine Arts Museum of San Francisco, 1986, p. 34).

The wedding ritual is presented almost as a 'sacrifice', similar to the sacrifice of the virgin in the *Rite of Spring*. Nijinska focusses our attention on the lack of power the woman has in this situation.

In *Les Biches* (1924) Nijinska made two important comments. Firstly, she created a satirical sketch of a houseparty of fashionable Parisian society in the 1920's. Secondly, she showed a lesbian relationship between the Girls in Gray and an androgynous character, the Girl in Blue. As heterosexual relationships were central to virtually all ballets this was an important change. The Girl in Blue does not surrender to the male athlete, who attempts to seduce her, and despite the lift at the end of the pas de deux she never makes eye contact with him. The men in the ballet are presented as stereotyped studs whilst the women are more varied individuals. The Girls in Gray dance as one, maintaining physical contact and showing a warmth and ease which is lacking in the male/female partnerships in the ballet. It is noteworthy that in 1925 a London critic said that with *Les Biches*, 'feminism [has] at last tinged the ballet' (Fine Arts Museum of San Francisco, 1986, p. 40).

Nijinska's contribution to ballet has often been overlooked. She travelled internationally and was not attached to a particular company or country for any length of time so that those writing dance history often omitted her work. In addition, some of her work has been credited to others. She was also eclipsed by her famous brother Nijinsky. It is only recently that the importance of her choreographic work is being realised (Fine Arts Museum of San Francisco, 1986, p. 40). She was, of course, a woman in a male domain.

The ballet of today is built on the foundations of the traditions described above. The ideas of Noverre and Fokine are still relevant today and the traditions are continued at rehearsals from balletmaster to dancer and in class from teacher to student. There is, therefore, a direct link with the past through these personal contacts.

English ballet

The twentieth century has been a time of enormous social upheavals, two world wars and extremely fast changes in technological inventions. Lifestyles of today would have been unimaginable at the beginning of the century. The role of women has changed within this context and there have been two major Women's Movements in this century. The first, at the beginning of the century, was organised primarily around the suffrage campaign but there were many other aspects to it which have been ignored, misrepresented or hidden. An indication of the range of issues and discussions is well documented in Dale Spender's book *Time and Tide Wait for No Man* (1984), excerpts from a feminist political weekly in the 1920s.

It was during the 1920s that **Marie Rambert** and **Ninette de Valois** opened their dance schools and set the foundations for ballet and contemporary dance in this country. Whilst there is no documentation to suggest that de Valois or Rambert were connected with the Women's Movement, in fact from some of de Valois' comments it would seem to be highly unlikely, it is significant that this was the context in which women were able to take the lead within dance. The pioneering work of the early feminists did much to change attitudes and enable women to take on roles which in earlier times would have been more difficult.

The foundations on which Rambert and de Valois had to build were three hundred years of performance from visiting dancers and companies from Europe. The influence of Diaghilev's Ballets Russes and Pavlova was well established and in the 1920s the idea of an English ballet seemed extremely remote. De Valois was a soloist with Diaghilev's company and this gave her knowledge of the repertory of famous ballets and insight into how to direct and administer a ballet company. She was a skilled dancer, having trained with Cecchetti and Espinosa and learnt the principles of Italian and French techniques. She left the company in order to begin her school (Anglin in White, ed., 1985).

De Valois is a strong woman with clear determination and she succeeded in creating her vision of a national ballet company. This was, however, established in quite a dictatorial fashion. As Clarke (1955) points out, 'Her vision is so extraordinary and the future is so clear in her mind that she sometimes neglects to explain her plans fully to the people who carry them out' (1955, p. 8). For many years there was no state recognition but she went ahead with the project anyway.

De Valois' explanation for her success is that women are 'splendid pioneer workers' (1977, p. 188). She thinks they have a sense of dedication, detail, intuition and fanaticism. She, however, feels that this has to change as what is needed now is objectivity of outlook, logical reasoning and acceptance of reality.

> It is essential that we realise that the real history of ballet – and by this I mean the creative work, its organisation, its pedagogy – has been a history of great male choreographers, directors and teachers. We want the public to realise that once again the development of ballet is rapidly passing into the care of the male element (de Valois, 1977, p. 188).

She seems to be assuming here that it should be men in those roles and consequently denying her own success as a choreographer, director and teacher. It is true that she was a pioneer but her subsequent work as a director of a large company was also important and she surely did it as well as her male followers. That she should hold such a stereotyped view of male/female roles is, however, entirely in keeping with her background. Her ideas and her character are so interlinked with the Royal Ballet origins (as it is known today) that 'her origins have become part of its history' (Bland, 1981, p. 14). Ninette de Valois' family background was connected with the military and the landed gentry. In her book *Come Dance with Me* (1957) she describes the Irish environment in which she grew up and the influence of the Protestant owning-class virtues and traditions reaching back into the past. A bonfire had been built on the family hill for the expected male heir before her birth. When she arrived it was quickly dismantled, an action which hardly made her feel welcome when she later discovered it.

Her experience with Diaghilev and her technical and musical knowledge ensured she had the necessary expertise with which to start a school which would be the beginning of the company. Her meeting with Lilian Baylis, who established a repertory theatre for drama and opera at the Old Vic, South London, ensured that her dreams became reality. Baylis was insistent that the theatre was for the people and her ambitions paralleled those of de Valois. She wanted 'one great building which could house all the greatest achievements in art – of drama, of music, of dancing and painting' (Findlater, 1975, p. 174).

De Valois directed the Vic–Wells ballet company which bene-fitted from funds from The Camargo Society, which was formed to sponsor new ballet productions. Her vision and the dedication of the dancers ensured the company's success. In addition, de Valois was an effective choreographer using a dramatic style. Her ballets included *Job* (1931), *The Rake's Progress* (1935) and *Checkmate* (1937).

Alicia Markova and Anton Dolin were the leading dancers and when they left to form their own company a new era began, with dancers who were trained with the school becoming leading dancers. **Margot Fonteyn** was one of the first to go from the school to the company and she replaced Markova when she left. Fonteyn was considered to have a centred and proportionate body which was perfect for dancing (Montague, 1980). Frederick Ashton played a key role in her career; not only did he create major roles for her in his ballets but he also insisted that presenting herself well in terms of clothes and composure were part of the job and necessary for success (Percival, 1983). He said of her, 'She is my child' (Montague, 1980, p. 37). Ashton also described an incident in which he bullied her because he found her attitude superior. Eventually Fonteyn burst into tears and put her arms around him. At this point Ashton said he realised that she had conceded to him and that they would be able to work together. ('Dance on Four', May, 1989). These statements indicate the power relationship which often exists between male choreographers and the female ballerinas whom they develop as stars.

The ballet enterprise in England began in women's hands. However, de Valois administered the company true to her views so that men choreographed for the company once it was established and directed it (Ashton, MacMillan, Morrice, Dowell) once de Valois retired. Marie Rambert played a different role; although she too founded a school and a company, her particular ability was in encouraging and inspiring dancers and choreographers to realise their potential. For example, it was for the Rambert Dancers that Frederick Ashton created his first work *A Tragedy of Fashion* (1926) (see Figure 15). As with de Valois, Rambert started with a small group of dancers in a small theatre supported by the Ballet Club,

15 *A Tragedy of Fashion* – in demonstration Sir Frederick Ashton, choreographer, and dancer Sara Matthews.

which encouraged new choreographers, and developed audiences for ballet.

The majority of choreographers fostered by Rambert were men, **Andrée Howard** being a notable exception. She had danced with the Rambert company and she also made at least a dozen ballets for them. *Lady into Fox* (1939) was an important work of hers, about a young wife who escapes from her home when she turns into a fox and goes into the forest. **Sally Gilmour** who danced the part of the wife said that slowly through the ballet the woman becomes a wild thing wanting to get away (film by Margaret Dale of the Rambert Company, 1976). This could be interpreted as a stand against the conventions/restriction of the wife's role in marriage and for women's emancipation.

The company developed into a major classical company which put on some of the key classical ballets. In 1966 there was a significant change in the company and Norman Morrice worked with Rambert to build the company into a modern one. This was one of the first indications in this country of changes in the dance world (Mann in White, ed., 1988).

Conservative values

Many of the conservative values of ballet are evident from the writing of critics and comments of the choreographers and dancers. In an article about Jennifer Penney on her retirement from the Royal Ballet she is described as 'this dulcet ballerina of the grande valse . . . petite, precise, light and dainty . . . delectable, accomplished and classically pure' (Rigby, 1988, p. 22) She was also said to be the 'Vehicle of the choreographer's intention rather than of her own interpretation' (Rigby, 1988, p. 22). The oppression of women fulfilling prescribed roles to suit men's desires is evident in such writing – as it is in the numerous references to women as though they were food. For example, by the use of words such as the above 'delectable' (or 'delicious', Clarke, 1989, p. 25; see also Coward's discussion of this point, 1984). The myth of the genius is also alive and well within ballet. The statement that 'dancers are born not made' is constantly reiterated (Kane, 1989, p. 37; Collier quoted in Mackrell, 1989, p. 16).

As we have seen, the training reinforces many of these values. The stress on discipline and conformity does not make it very easy for the students to question what they are learning or to resist in any way. The girls are encouraged to develop qualities which are seen as 'feminine', and because of the competition for places they are undoubtedly encouraged to see themselves as special and part of an elite. The pictures in a book about the Royal Ballet school make evident the differences in expectations of girls' and boys' behaviour. Whilst the girls, all looking identical, carefully sew their ballet shoes, the boys are rushing through the woods having a good time (Jessel, 1985).

In ballet woman is first

Balanchine (1904–83) played a significant role in the development of ballet in the USA. He was a Russian choreographer and worked with Diaghilev before he established his own school and company in the States. His glorification of women is often held up as being in women's favour but he is hardly a supporter of women's liberation. When we consider his statements about his ideal woman familiar patriarchal themes are evident:

> Woman is naturally inferior in matters requiring action and imagination. Woman obligingly accepts her lowly place. Woman is an object of beauty and desire. Woman is first in ballet by default, because she is more beautiful than the opposite gender (quoted in Daly, 1986, p. 8).

In her analysis of Balanchine's *The Four Temperaments* (1946), Daly illustrates the ways in which the ballerina is displayed, manipulated and vulnerable to the control of her male partner. By asking how women are represented, whose desire is acted out and who has the power, we can begin to see that women in Balanchine's choreographies are not in privileged, dominant positions. Rather, the ballerina is displayed to be looked at, reinforcing 'feminine' passivity which does not have the status of active 'masculine' assertiveness. This follows the construction apparent in the media, sports and politics, in which 'men act and women appear. Men look at women. Women watch themselves being looked at' (Berger, 1972, p. 47). The Balanchine ballerina is unattainable as were the romantic sylphs and nymphs:

> She is specifically a white, heterosexual American Woman: fast, precise, impassive. These qualities, exemplified in her modern technical prowess, seduce the male gaze, but the titillating danger – the threat – of her self-sufficient virtuosity is tamed within the interaction . . . By arranging and rearranging the ballerina's body, the man (first the choreographer, then the partner, and voyeuristically, the male-constructed spectator) creates the beauty he longs for (Daly, 1986, pp. 13–14).

Ballet needs to be recognised as the cultural product it is rather than as natural. The image of a light, desirable being on pointe with man as her supporter ensures that women do not represent themselves in ballet. There is no biological reason why only women dance on pointe and the contact improvisation dancers have shown that weight has little to do with being able to lift someone (see Chapter Seven). How a dancer lifts and when, are the crucial factors in lifting. In addition, many ballerinas are anorexic and bulimic as a result of trying to attain a featherlight body (Daly, 1986).

Balanchine ruled his company in a totalitarian way in his search for perfection at the same time as he admired American democracy and refused to have a hierarchical structure of stars. His control of the company was such that Kriegsman observed 'I could actually feel their subordination to his will' (quoted in Hanna, 1988a, p. 129). Siegel (1972) described Balanchine's choreography as upgrading 'the pastime of girl watching to a classic art' (p. 17).

Gelsey Kirkland (1986), a ballerina for some years in Balanchine's company, describes the strains of her life as a dancer, including diets and plastic surgery in her efforts to achieve a perfect body. There was also the constant risk of injury as she distorted her body attempting to achieve a particular step. She also discusses the autocratic attitude of Balanchine which left no room for dissent. It is significant that her disclosure of the other side of the ideal was rejected vehemently. Some writers (e.g. McMahon, 1988) go so far as to suggest that the problems she discusses are of her own making – failing to recognise the issues she discusses of the power relationship between herself and Balanchine, the driving concern to achieve 'the look', and the danger to health of a number of practices to which dancers frequently resort.

A ballerina who has succeeded in presenting her own work is **Karole Armitage**. She was in Balanchine's company for a short time and also in the contemporary dance company of Merce Cunningham. She stresses the formal beauty, order and line of classicism but with a difference, using punk-style leather costumes, loud pop music and performing in a variety of venues. She uses pointe shoes like weapons and allows some of the struggle to keep on pointe to be revealed thus challenging the effortlessness previously considered essential. 'Armitage uses the drama of pointework to underscore the heroism of the female dancer' (Greskovic, 1985). The audience is not able to take the ballerina's skill for granted because of the way Armitage uses pointe work and the way she works with her partner, sometimes making it clear that she is sustaining her balance by clinging to him. Her work is usually classified as postmodern (see Chapter 7).

Conclusion

Most of ballet history has been male-dominated with some resistances from women. Twentieth-century ballet has its roots in the traditions and values of the courts of Italy, France and England in the sixteenth and seventeenth centuries with their emphasis on spectacle, where the male dancer reigned and the dance technique was carefully recorded with early notation and by the dancing masters. The professionalisation of ballet in the seventeenth century gave women more opportunity to dance though rarely to choreograph. It is from this period that the ballet we have today has developed. The eighteenth century brought significant developments in technique, costume reform and a call for ballet to be recognised as an expressive art, laying the foundations for the Romantic ballet of the nineteenth century in which the female dancer was central and the male role eclipsed. However, as we have seen, because of women's roles within society and the power of the male gaze, this was not the dominant position it is often considered to be.

By the end of the nineteenth century ballet had declined in the West. There had been no new choreographers to take the place of the well-known creators of ballet. The creative direction appeared lost and the public ceased to regard it as a serious art. It was largely the aristocracy of Russia which ensured the continuation of the art form. The twentieth century brought many changes in the aftermath of revolutions, industrialisation and technological inventions. Women's roles were challenged within society thus opening up new possibilities. De Valois and Rambert established ballet in England building on the innovations of Diaghilev. Balanchine established a school and company in the USA which was considered above criticism. Recently, however, feminist analysis is providing a different perspective for dance.

Women's main contribution to dance in this century began with the early modern dancers, for example Isadora Duncan, and continued with the establishment of modern dance of which Martha Graham's work is probably the best known. This work will be the subject of the next chapter.

6

Revolutionary women – modern dance

Modern dance was pioneered and developed, mainly by women, in both Europe and America. Initially it was created in opposition to the aristocratic ideals of European ballet. Modern dance was not a monolithic style or school; it was revolutionary by definition; unlike ballet, artists created their own movement forms and techniques necessary for their choreography. Choreographers were concerned with discovering their own sources of movements often using personal experiences and emotions as starting points. Modern dance was born in and of the twentieth century and sought to represent the attitudes and dreams of the time. The influences of Freud and Jung were evident in Martha Graham's work and often her characters became archetypes. In *Every Soul is a Circus* (1939) the Ideal Spectator must watch her own fickle behaviour as it is danced by the Empress of the Arena. The influence of Marx is evident in many of the 'social protest' dances which were made in the 1930s. Doris Humphrey's *The Trilogy – New Dance, Theatre Piece* and *With My Red Fires* (1935–6) derided worldly competition and commented on the complexities of human relationships.

Why was modern dance initiated by women? There were a number of contributory factors. From the early nineteenth century it became acceptable for women to dance but not men. The social construction of 'femininity' and 'masculinity' resulted in a divergence between what was considered acceptable female behaviour and what was considered acceptable male behaviour, although this was not necessarily the case for black dancers because of the integral place of dance in many black cultures. The women who created this new form, at a time when there was a strong upsurge in women's freedom, were from a variety of racial, national and religious backgrounds. They prepared the ground for modern dance to flourish at a time when there was a greater mobility in society. In this chapter, women dancers' and choreographers' contributions are discussed within the context of both the founding of modern dance and the development of the form within Europe and the USA. The dance practice has relevance to women's issues, including attitudes to the body and clothing, development of techniques and the subject matter and development of choreographic work.

The founders of modern dance

Two early pioneers of modern dance were Loie Fuller and Isadora Duncan. They were seen as rebels at a time when, despite the ideal of equality in the USA, women did not have the vote and were denied access to education and jobs. Although Fuller and Duncan were Americans they worked mainly in Europe.

Loie Fuller (1862–1928) (see Figure 16) was not a trained dancer but used new technological inventions, lighting effects and material to create spectacular designs, and she also established an all female company. By use of the recent inventions of electric light, yards of cloth and sticks, Fuller created images which had not been possible before. Duncan admired her and described one performance saying, 'Before our very eyes she turned to many coloured, shining orchids, to a wavering, flowing sea flower, and at length to a spiral-like lily, all the magic of Merlin, the sorcery of light, colour, flowing form' (Duncan, 1955, p. 95). In *The Serpentine* (1890) she captivated her audience by the variety of images she created through manipulation of her voluminous silks under different coloured lights. Fuller's work was certainly an inspiration for the later established modern dance. She led a so-called 'scandalous' life in that she did not attempt to conceal her lesbianism. Lesbians are usually quite hidden in dance and it is, therefore, significant that her sexual identity was not secret; she was defying convention and determining a woman's right to choose her own lifestyle (see Chapter 3). She appeared at the Metropolitan Opera House, New York in 1909, a time when America did not easily accept dancers with bare feet and no corsets.

16 Loie Fuller – San Francisco (*circa* 1900) *left*; New York (*circa* 1900) *right*.

In 1925 she appeared at The New York Hippodrome where 'she glorified the triumphs of her time . . . the dignity of women, the power of the machine' (Mazo, 1977, p. 34).

Isadora Duncan (1878–1927) (see Figure 17) created her own movement and her own images in a revolutionary way. She was dancing during an era of revolutionary activity which included the Russian Revolution and the Women's Movements in England and the USA. For example, the first big suffragists' parade in New York was in 1911. These events had a significant influence on her work. Duncan's stand against ballet demonstrates a clear feminist stance, as does her attitude towards her art in general. In the context of her time her feminist ideals led her to denounce ballet which she said deformed young bodies. She also objected to the stereotypes of women in ballet. Her rejection of these and of the corset enabled her to create a heroic figure which lives still in our imagination. Duncan emphasised her performance and teaching work more than her choreography. The tradition Duncan established was one in which stage work was considered inseparable from teaching and in which the individual approach was valued rather than being immersed in a mainstream method (Siegel, 1981). Her work has frequently been dismissed as having no established technique and no choreography. However, studies have proved that she had a

17 Isadora Duncan (*circa* 1900).

technique, if somewhat embryonic, and her works were choreographed rather than improvised (Layson, 1987).

Women had certainly questioned their roles before Duncan (see Chapter 5) and Wollstonecraft (1891, in Kramnick, ed., 1975) had analysed women's role within marriage. It was, however, still outrageous to put those ideas into practice and Duncan flaunted the views of the day by having a number of lovers and three children out of wedlock (a telling word). She was determined to fight for the right of every woman to control her own reproduction and lifestyle and rejected all conventions whether social, sexual or artistic. She was working at the beginning of the century over fifty years after the first 'Women's Rights Convention' (1848) held at Seneca Falls and she was very much at the forefront of a changing society.

The precedent for her dance was the work of François Delsarte (1811–71) who had analysed body postures and gestures used for expression and Jacques Dalcroze (1865–1950) who had connected movement to rhythm. Although Duncan rejected ballet, like many early modern dancers she did have ballet lessons. The few visiting ballerinas who came from Europe gave classes offering the opportunity for a partial ballet training (Kendall, 1979). Duncan's search for the source of movement and energy, had similarities in many Eastern forms, for example, T'ai Chi Chuan, Ki, Aikido and many dancers have returned to this initial search in order to dance from their own energy source rather than accept technical conventions.

Duncan was influenced by the Romantic movement in Europe, particularly its emphasis on nature, and by the aesthetics of ancient Greece, which are evident in the loose costumes she adopted. However, it was important to her that she should be regarded seriously and she refused to allow herself to be billed as a barefoot dancer when touring in Germany in 1902 (Duncan, 1955). Her actions did not always succeed in educating the audience. When she tried to convince a Boston audience that the human body was beautiful, by ripping her costume, baring one breast, she merely succeeded in shocking them. This response did not prevent her from telling her audience that her art was 'the symbolic freedom of woman' (Mazo, 1977, p. 58).

Duncan's objection to the corset and restrictive clothing stemmed from her wish to see women actively participating in society, their movement unhampered, living their lives to the fullest. She was born in the 1870s when women wore outer dresses with the waist tightly fastened over a tight-laced corset. Girls' bones and internal organs were threatened because of the restrictive clothes they wore at a young age, and after the American civil war the level of illness amongst women prompted a concern with health.

Her dances were created for the female body; 'they explore the range of womanhood, from the purity of girlhood to the coquetry of the gypsy to the violence of the Furies and Amazons' (McCarren, 1986, p. 47). An important factor was Duncan's physicality. When she was dancing in her twenties her body was sleek but after bearing three children by 1917 she was described as 'heroic in build' (Van Vechten in Layson, 1987, p. 284). For some (for example, Van Vechten in Padgette, ed., 1974) this was the key to her power but for others her body was criticised for its thickness and solidity. However, from audience reports it appears that Duncan's heroic physicality pushed her into the realms of uncharted expressiveness taking yet more risks (Layson, 1987). She provided an image of dance performance not confined by the 'ideal' body. Duncan's pride in her body led to a casual attitude towards accidental exposure of her own body during performance if her loose clothes were dislodged. These accidental revelations are different to the deliberate display of her breast to the audience in order to challenge assumptions that the body was 'shameful' (see above).

Unlike many of the modern dancers who were to follow her, Duncan used music for her inspiration. In addition to her dances which were mood based, interpreting the music of Beethoven, Brahms, Schubert and Chopin she also created narrative works, for example, *Iphigenia* (1908) and *Marche Slave* (*circa* 1909). As her career developed, Duncan made dances which commented on, for example, the first world war – *La Marseillaise* (performed at the Metropolitan Opera House, New York, 1915) – and the Russian Revolution. Motherhood was also an important influence on her choreography as was bereavement. Many of the dances she made after her children's deaths were dark, slow and weighty.[1] 'In the poignant *Mother* she didn't so much stand for a chorus of sorrowing women as for *every* mother who has lost a child' (Jowitt, 1988, p. 92). Divoire suggested that Duncan was an even more perceptive artist after this loss, tapping new sources in both her performance and choreography (in Layson, 1986).

Children were extremely important to Duncan and she had a vision of teaching them to move easily, spontaneously and freely. This was a particularly powerful dream for women as it offered an escape from the confinements of clothes and social conventions which restricted their movements. However, there was always the problem of raising money for tours and to establish her school. Duncan did manage to open a school in Russia which continued after her death until 1949 (Roslavleva, 1966). However, many of her efforts to open schools were frequently frustrated and she did not succeed in establishing one in the USA.

Ruth St Denis (1880–1968) did succeed in establishing a school, this was the Denishawn School created in 1915 in Los Angeles with her husband Ted Shawn. This school was the training ground for the founders of modern dance. In 1906 St Denis' first performance caused a sensation. *Rhada* was a sculptured goddess in her temple which St Denis created after researching the Indian mystics. If St Denis had wanted to learn Indian dancing she would not have been able to because the ancient temple dances had mainly become the domain of prostitutes. However, she did achieve an expressive solo form as the Bharata Natyam soloist does today (Jowitt, 1988). Another source of her inspirations were the Egyptian deities, which she researched after being inspired by an advert for cigarettes.

Part of St Denis' appeal was the sensual nature of her performance and her ability to entertain. So whilst she challenged women's social position by establishing her own school, presenting her own work and being financially successful, she exploited rather than challenged the power relationship between the female performer and the male gaze of the audience.

European modern dance

In the early part of this century European modern dance, located mainly in Germany, was established. The German dance was a decade older than the American and had greater technical solidity. **Mary Wigman** (1886–1973) was a major influence on modern dance in Europe for fifty years. She attempted to make a style of moving which was universal; part of her technique was a form of contraction and release. She also used space 'as a symbol of the forces of the universe which exert themselves upon individuals' (Mazo, 1977, p. 166).

It could be argued that Wigman's philosophy was reactionary because she believed dance to be a form and a language which everyone understands (Cohen, ed., 1974). Whilst it may be true that we can appreciate dance performances of any culture on a super-ficial level, it is not true that we can read the dance fully. For example, Westerners need to study or have explanations of classical Asian dance forms to be fully aware of the nuances.

Wigman believed dance to be more than just physical movement in space; 'it represents the internal experiences of the dancer' (Wigman in Cohen, ed., 1974, p. 150). It was through modern dance which she felt these experiences could be expressed. For Wigman, as for other modern dancers, the classical ballet had become so refined that it did not represent emotion and was defined by its virtuosity. When writing in 1927 she said, 'The longing for self-expression which is the characteristic of the age is driving the girls of today to seek satisfaction in dancing' (in Cohen, ed., 1974, p. 162).

Margaret Lloyd (1949) made an interesting comparison of Wigman with Duncan. She characterised Duncan as a dancer of light and ecstasy whereas she saw Wigman's ecstasy as that of gloom, dark and sombre. Their physical stature was, however, similar. Both were 'large, womanly, women' (p. 12) and the dance of their later years was concerned with womanhood. They were both impressive soloists: 'it was as if each in her majestic singleness, her capacious womanliness, contained humanity within herself' (p. 12). The dance of the future concerned them both.

Many of her dances explored a demonic and grotesque vision, allowing the powerful unconscious to come to the fore. The Ausdruckstanz (see below) laid the foundation for expressing the 'dark side' of human experience (Servos, 1987). Wigman certainly broke the expectations for women dancers by presenting images that were not 'beautiful'. Wigman did not fulfil our present day ideal of a dancer. She was stocky, muscular, not very young and danced in stark costumes, creating powerful, earthy, ugly images. In *The Witch Dance* (first version 1914) (see Figure 18), one of her most famous solos, from a sitting position she crawled, crept, dragging herself forward, creating an eerie effect with her masked face (Lloyd, 1949).

18 Mary Wigman – '*Witch Dance II*' (1926).

The sense of evil and animality that emanated from the grasping, clawlike gestures and the earthbound heaviness of the dancer's body were very remote indeed from the contemporary ballet's insubstantial prettiness, Duncan's emphasis on harmony or St. Denis' glamour (Au, 1988, p. 98).

The supposed emotions which Wigman discovered when choreographing this dance frightened her somewhat at the beginning. In her later dances Wigman dealt with many difficult or taboo subjects, including old age, death and the destruction of war. She made her first great choric work *Totenmal* in 1930 'in which a woman's chorus mourns their dead, who briefly return to life before being swallowed by death and oblivion' (Au, 1988, p. 99; see also Sorell, 1969). *Song of Fate* (1935) was 'a masked dance, [which] depicted a woman in youth, maturity and old age' (Au, 1988, p. 99). She also, however, made lyrical dances of which *Pastoral* (1929) is a good example.

Wigman's background was as a student of Laban whose explorations resulted in the form of expressive dance, Ausdruckstanz. This dance developed in a new age of scientific innovations, and psychological theories (Howe, 1985). Laban who directed dance productions in the 1920s and 1930s in Germany and Switzerland, was concerned with the spatial aspects and the flow of movement; his work was used widely in education, therapy, recreation and industry.

The development of German dance, however, was cut off by the Nazis. Wigman's school was taken over by them and it was not until 1945 that she was able to re-open it and continue to choreograph. Both Laban and Wigman co-operated with the Nazis' initially as there appeared some hope that the regime would support the German dance so dear to them (Müller, 1986). The emphasis on the community and the centrality of movement in people's lives are interests Wigman and Laban shared with the Nazis'. However, the Nazi control of culture swiftly began to limit Laban's and Wigman's work (Preston-Dunlop, 1988). The advances of feminism were seriously set back by the Nazis. Their main view of women was that of child bearers so that world domination could be achieved. This role was not seen as compatible with independent women artists (Stephenson, 1975).

Wigman's work ceased to be popular in the USA as many modern dancers suspected her connections with the Nazis because she did not leave Germany nor publicly detach herself from the regime (Sorell, 1969, p. 44). Her recognition of the importance of the personal in dance mirrored that of the Women's Movement, which also emphasised personal experience and politicised it by putting it into a social context. Many of her dances were solos for herself as the material was too personal for her to transfer to someone else. To take the dance out of its personal context and make it into a commodity would have been a violation of her view of dance (Gottschild, 1985). However, despite an initial challenge to rationalism through the 'dancing body', her choreography, which began as a powerful subversion of women's images in dance, eventually became a support for fascism.

The life drained out of Wigman's work as she tried to accommodate the contradictions of the Nazi regime. The images of women in the work were notably changed. In *Women's Dances* (1934) there was no longer an androgynous, asexual image of self-sufficient women. Instead, 'Wigman and her dancers retained overtly feminine personae throughout, impersonating various types of women rather than embodying visions of the self' (Manning, 1987). Her new presentation of woman as wife and mother corresponded to the Nazis' definition of women. As Manning points out:

> Whereas the 1926 solo . . . *Witch Dance* embodied an image of gender that defied the socio-cultural categories of masculinity and femininity, *Women's Dances* presents witches as one among a spectrum of images traditionally associated with women (Manning, 1987, p. 91).

A dancer who offered a different view to that of Wigman's was **Valeska Gert** (1900–78). Her work in some ways parallels that of Brecht's in the dramatic theatre. She scorned and commented on the forms she used, distancing herself from her performance with her deadpan expression. She was critical of the movement choir, a form developed by Laban, in which large groups of people moved harmoniously together, evoking a powerful, emotional experience. Gert's view was that through the movement choir there was an attempt to establish a sense of community when it did not exist (Manning, 1986).

Her performance style revealed her attraction for the extreme and outrageous. Her political awareness is evident in her statement that

'Since I didn't like the bourgeois, I danced those people dismissed by them, whores, procuresses, cast-offs, those who had slipped' (quoted de Keersmaeker, 1981, p. 58). She caused a scandal with *Canaille* (1920) in which she portrayed a streetwalker suggestively displaying herself until an imaginary customer appeared. She mimed intercourse, ending the dance differently, according to how she felt, at each performance. This was at a time when such acts were not seen on stage and in addition it expressed the degradation of prostitution. She was popular in Russia and her condemnation of capitalism was powerfully portrayed in her performances (in de Keersmaeker, 1981).

Hanya Holm (1898–) was both influenced by and influenced German and American modern dance. As a student of Wigman's she had set up a school in America in 1931 but the anti-Nazi mood made it impossible to continue with Wigman's name so, with Wigman's agreement, it became the Hanya Holm School. Holm's contribution to dance is primarily as a teacher. She travelled the college circuit and increased the following for dance. She believed that students needed to find their own inspiration for movement rather than copying other dancers (Sorell, 1969).

Some of her work took political themes but her concern was to probe deeper and look at 'human motivations of human power and suffering from it' (Sorell, 1969, p. 82), for example, in *They Too Are Exiles* (1940) inspired by the Spanish civil war. However, she also stated that there was no space for politics in art (Sorell, 1969). Her other successes were her musical choreographies including *Kiss Me Kate* (1948).

American modern dance

At the turn of the century, ballet in America and in Europe centred round virtuosity and was often part of extravaganzas. Much of the dancing became 'leg shows' and men who danced were generally considered effeminate. These factors resulted in dancers being viewed as outcasts from society (Weil, 1975a). It was from this background that women rebelled against the empty spectacle which ballet had become and pioneered the way towards a new dance form.

The modern dance pioneers of the 1920s, following Duncan and St Denis, were working in a time of social upheaval after the first world war. The USA advanced at such a rate that it became the richest and potentially the most powerful state in the world. This was a golden age for sports, arts, entertainment, exploration and finance. Clothes changed and women wore long tube like skirts just below the knees, and wore their hair bobbed, covered by a cloche hat. The change in emotional climate allowed people to re-evaluate their attitudes and beliefs so, for example, dancers began to ask 'What am I dancing about?' It was no longer enough to entertain the audience as St Denis had done. Ballet and Denishawn seemed escapist and not sufficiently relevant to twentieth-century America. This generation needed to express what it meant to be American. Whereas Duncan had been inspired by Greece, and St Denis by Egypt and India the new pioneers looked to their own culture for ideas.

The 1920s was a time in which social dance was extremely popular. American women took up dancing as a declaration of their independence in the jazz age at a time when the values of Puritanism were being eroded. These social factors influenced the new choreographers and the audiences of the time and the American college system provided a structure in which theatre dance could flourish. Women students at that time were expected to take exercise and find a creative outlet. There was also an active Women's Movement addressing many of the same issues which concern Women's Movements of today (Spender, 1984). This provided a context for women to define their own dance work.

The dancers did not initially get paid for their work. They were often middle-class women supported by their families for the time they were dancing, with teaching as another source of income. They did not look to the past for stimulus and they challenged the role of music so that dance was frequently unaccompanied. Costume and decor were reduced to a minimum. By the 1940s the major innovations had been established with distinctive artistic styles and work became more theatrical.

The early modern dancers had exceptional fluidity in their arms and legs, rhythmic sensitivity and feeling for the pulse and swing of their weight. Modern dance did not require the early training necessary for ballet so that for many dancers learning dance at college was the beginning of their dance career. Unfortunately, most of the work of the 1930s and 1940s has not survived as preservation of the work had a very low priority due to the expense involved as there was no funding for this fledgling art.

Martha Graham's (1894–1991) name is most commonly associated with modern dance and it is the Graham technique which has been widely studied. Films of her dancers in class and performing were inspiring for many students. Graham's achievements this century have been outstanding and she certainly presented strong women characters in her choreography. She studied and danced with Denishawn before breaking away, evolving her style by working solely with women. Her technique did not work as well for men because initially she did not take men's bodies into account. However, she was not afraid of dance looking ugly nor of showing women's power and strength. Graham evolved her technique as a structure for strong emotional power. This used the breath rhythm to contract the body; as the breath was expelled a strong energy source was created which was subsequently released, allowing the body to expand on the next breath. She recognised the dramatic potential of contraction. By working barefoot, a flexibility and use of the whole foot was possible in contrast to ballet in which the foot is encased in pointe-shoes.[2]

This technique, however, eventually became as codified and restricted as that of classical ballet. There are a set group of exercises which are gradually taught as the dancer's ability and strength increases in order to produce a specific body image. In training, students' body weights are monitored to make sure the desired limits are kept. The dancers train to produce an image of a Graham dancer in much the same way as ballet dancers train to produce an image of a classical dancer. There has also been a return to the use of mirrors in technique classes in recent years. Nonetheless, Graham established a dance technique in less than fifty years.

Graham was influenced by the Central European Expressionist dance which she read about when Louis Horst brought books back from Germany. She also saw pictures of Mary Wigman (McDonagh, 1976). Graham left Denishawn in order to create her own work and her first performance was in New York in 1926. Not only did Graham look for new movements but she also created costumes which lent a different appearance to the body. In *Lamentation* (1930) she used a tube of stretchy material within which one part of her body pulled against another. Her struggle and confinement created a dance which conveyed her grief in an extremely dynamic way. This dance, with its sense of grief, still has the power to move audiences today.

Graham and her dancers presented quite a different 'look' to that of ballet dancers. They gained strength from using gravity rather than defying it as in ballet. They were generally heavier than ballet dancers and tended to look stark, dressed in severe costumes, with dramatic make-up. In the early days her work was ridiculed. Instead of the chaste women characters of classical ballet who died of unrequited love or betrayal, Graham presented strong, autonomous women. Her dancers landed precisely on the beat giving a dynamic, aggressive effect. The female body in her work has power and force.

Through her dancing Graham explored her personal territory such as emotional life, her fears, angers as well as female archetypes drawn from mythologies. Works of the 1930s, such as *Primitive Mysteries* (1931) (see Figure 19) and *Frontier* (1935) can be interpreted as feminist statements establishing female autonomy and power. A reviewer in New York described *Primitive Mysteries* as having 'angular, cold stylised movement . . . Mellowness is no part of her. The freshness that is newness consumes her' (quoted in

19 Martha Graham – '*Primitive Mysteries*'.

Mazo, 1977, p. 163). In *Frontier* she 'celebrated the vigor, the tenacity, and the character of the settlers of the West who conquered an area of wilderness' (McDonagh, 1976, p. 106). There was a sense of nostalgia in the piece, of the early American life. The theme of conquering space was so appropriate to America, so central to the country's history. Isamu Noguchi's stunningly simple and effective set consisted of a section of fence with two ropes disappearing overhead, giving an illusion of a limitless plain. Graham undoubtedly provided very positive, active images of women. The strong American identity in her work was, however, entrenched in the white settler's viewpoint, ignoring the destruction of native Americans' culture and lifestyle.

Another theme in Graham's work was the redefinition of Greek myths from a female stance. In *Errand into the Maze* (1947), as in many other works, Graham (in the character of Ariadne) is working through a psychological dilemma. In the duet she struggles with a man who limits her actions. But

> what terrifies her is the man's sexual attraction and the knowledge that yielding to it will put her into a subordinate position. The loss of her own power represents an ultimate humiliation to her. Graham sees the woman who ends up in a subservient sexual relationship as either a pitiful victim, like Jocasta, or as one entitled to become an outlaw, who can violate the morals of society, like Medea or Clytemnestra (Siegel, 1981, p. 202).

The male bull-like creature in *Errand into the Maze* constantly looms over her. He seems absurdly muscle-bound, confined almost by his own dominance. At times he appears to conquer her but she throws him off. The woman's anguished state of mind vibrates through her persistent beating of the floor with her feet as she shudders and draws into herself. Despite the depth of her fear and the force of the battle she survives.

Graham's identification with female archetypes enabled her to create characters of great intensity. In *Night Journey* (1947), a reworking of the Oedipus myth, we see woman portrayed as lover, wife and mother. Graham reinterpreted these Greek myths making a female perspective central. In *Clytemnestra* (1958), thought to be one of her greatest works, she uses events from the *Oresteia* as well as from the *Iliad*. She explores the passions and violence of Clytemnestra, queen, murderess, mistress and mother who by accepting the burdens of guilt and lust is eventually freed.

The difference between the tragic but triumphant Graham heroines and the nineteenth-century ballet heroines of, for example, Giselle and Odette is that 'the Graham heroine possesses, herself, the key to her mystery. She does not entrust it to the hero; she herself must unlock the inner door' (Croce, 1978, p. 53). Graham's choreography so much depended on her dancing central roles that it was very hard for her to stop. She continued to perform until into her seventies.

As she gradually danced less and began to pass her work on it became more codified. Her recent work shows little evidence of the feminist stance of her early choreography. In *Rite of Spring* (1984) traditional stereotypes are reaffirmed with man as aggressor and woman as victim. She offers no resistance to patriarchal structures. Graham, the rebel against the establishment, is now very much part of it (Goldberg, 1986).

Doris Humphrey (1895–1958) was one of the key modern dancers. In 1913 when she saw Pavlova she decided to dance. She taught to support her family and then taught with Denishawn where she began to develop her own sequences, which provided material for her choreography. Her discoveries came from the wish to bring dance closer to people and their own lives. The other arts were moving away from idealised beauty and closer to life and she thought that was the direction in which dance needed to move. Fokine, Duncan, St Denis, Shawn all looked for deeper expression of the human spirit but stopped short of Humphrey's vision. She wanted to get to the root of the state of being human and she knew she needed to use her own experience (Lloyd, 1949).

> I wish my dance to reflect some experience of my own in relationship to the outside world; to be based on reality illumined by imagination, to be organic rather than synthetic; to call forth a definite reaction from my audience; and to make its contribution toward the drama of life (Stodelle, 1978, p. 28).

Some of her early work was based on nature, for example, *Water Study* (1928) and *Life of the Bee* (1929). In contrast, *The Shakers* (1929) was based on part of American history. The Shakers were a religious sect led by a woman and administered by female priests who achieved equality through renouncing sexuality. Humphrey's own struggles to retain some balance of conflicting demands within a patriarchal structure perhaps led her to appreciate the Shakers' solution (Siegel, 1981). This dance illustrates Humphrey's concern with social comment in her choreography. The form was of a strict symmetrical religious service against which the dancers leapt, spun and fell. Humphrey used authentic steps and patterns from the Shakers and managed to capture the religious fervour and frustrated sexual passion of the sect's ritual. The ensemble was dominant and the strongest and most important movements were given to the group.

Humphrey's concern with social comment is also evident in *Inquest* (1944). In this dance the speaker reads a newspaper report written in 1865 about a destitute family living in one room in a London slum. Their only income is from the father's boot selling. When he dies they refuse to go to the workhouse as they want to stay together (Denby, 1968).

Her choreographic skills were an important contribution to dance and her book on choreography, *The Art of Making Dances*, (1959) has proved to be a valuable reference book. Another contribution she made was her theory of all movement taking place between the arc of 'fall and recovery'. This was a pure movement idea and a dramatic concept which symbolised the human's eternal conflict of longing for security and yet the desire to risk.

> Falling and recovering is the very stuff of movement, the constant flux which is going on in every living body, in all its tiniest parts, all the time. Nor is this all, for the process has a psychological meaning as well. I recognised these emotional overtones very early and instinctively responded very strongly to the exciting danger of the fall, and the repose and peace of recovery (Humphrey quoted in Stodelle, 1978, p. 15).

She trained her dancers to feel whether they were correctly aligned or not. Hence in the studios there was only one mirror, behind the visitors' chairs, which was seldom used (Stodelle, 1978). There was much less dependence on the mirror than in ballet studios because the focus was on the internal feel or sensation of the movement rather than external display of the dancer's body.

Another dancer who made an important contribution to the establishment of American modern dance was **Helen Tamiris** (1905–66). Tamiris had directly benefitted from the early pioneers' work. She had worked with a teacher using some of Duncan's ideas, but unlike some of her contemporaries, she studied ballet and took classes with Fokine. In 1927 she gave a concert performance where her dances showed 'the spontaneous reactions of a dynamic personality to the world about her' (Martin, 1968, p. 245). She was influenced by black dance and in 1928 created *Negro Spirituals*.

Tamiris wanted her dance to reach a wide audience. She said that 'the validity of modern dance is rooted in its ability to express social problems' (quoted in Lloyd, 1949, p. 141). She valued working on Broadway and is particularly remembered for her choreography in *Annie Get Your Gun* (1946).

The early 1930s were the time of the Depression in America but even before this time most artists had difficulty surviving. However, Tamiris' determination to create an independent dance project, together with government funds for the Federal Theatre Project (1935) resulted in a forum for many of the modern dancers to show their work. Unfortunately, disagreements from within the project and criticisms both within and from outside led to its demise. It was merged with the Federal Theatre in 1937. In the short time in which it existed, however, it had made 'a substantial contribution to the entertainment and education of the public' (Thomas, 1986). This was a time of social protest in which artists, including some of the dance community, were active.

Tamiris had a box-office success with her work, *How Long Brethren?* (1937). It

> ran to standing-room-only houses for an unheard of forty-two performances. Its success gave the Federal Dance Project in New York respect both with the audience and administration; ironically it also gave Tamiris *Dance Magazine*'s first award for outstanding group choreography. The work illustrated her concern for social justice.

Conclusion

The issue of combining motherhood with a career was one of a number of concerns of the women dancers who created their own perspectives through their dance during the first half of the twentieth century. Women's issues were discussed at length in a number of women's periodicals in the 1920s and the movement for women's emancipation was well established. This context undoubtedly affected women choreographers working at the time, if only indirectly.

Isadora Duncan clearly linked some of her work with the revolutionary fervour in Russia in addition to making stands against puritanical attitudes to the body. Loie Fuller's innovatory stage techniques and lighting designs provided a significant model for women being involved in the technical aspects of a performance. She also broke with the tradition of mixed gender companies with her all-women company. The work of Duncan, Fuller and St Denis formed a basis from which Graham and Humphrey amongst others established a revolution in dance movement under the umbrella term of modern dance. This form enabled both women and black people (see Chapter 8) to present their own viewpoints unhindered by tradition.

The German expressionist dance of Mary Wigman influenced the early American modern dance and provided another means for women to explore and portray their perspectives. The development of this work was unfortunately stifled by the war. American modern dance, however, became sufficiently established to provoke rebellions, particularly against the expressive aspects of the form. The work which became labelled 'postmodern' dance is discussed in the next chapter.

7

We say no – postmodern dance

The term used for dance which developed in the USA in the 1960s is 'postmodern dance'. This label was first used to describe the work of The Judson Group whose work was regarded as both a progression from and reaction to modern dance. Between 1960 and 1973 in the USA there were a number of themes evident in postmodern dance of new uses of the body, time and space, and redefinitions of dance (Banes, 1987). There was a clear link between the political movements of, for example, black power, feminists, gays, students and anti-war protesters with some of the dance choreography between 1968 and 1973. After the early experimentations which Banes terms as 'breakaway postmodern dance', certain characteristics were associated with postmodern dance in the early 1970s. Functional clothing, silences, use of structural devices in choreography, a relaxed body and task-orientated movement are aspects of what Banes has termed 'analytic postmodern dance'. At the same time, an interest in non-Western dance and spiritual motivations for dance is defined by Banes as the 'metaphor and metaphysical' strands of postmodern dance. However, defining postmodern dance stylistically is problematic as this leads to confusion because much of the early postmodern dance was closer to modernist style in its emphasis on purity of the medium, stripping the dance back to basics and evolving a recognisable style. As with the term 'modern dance' used in the 1920s 'postmodern dance' has become an umbrella term, the boundaries of which are still being defined. The work included in this chapter is the work of the 1960s and 1970s which was labelled postmodern dance.

The 1960s

The 1960s were a time of important political change and they are remembered with nostalgia. For women, more control over our reproduction was made possible by the advent of the contraceptive pill and abortion law reforms. It was also an era of so-called sexual liberation although this notion was gradually challenged as women realised that the 'liberation' seemed to be mainly in men's favour. Betty Friedan wrote *The Feminine Mystique* (1963), describing 'the problem which had no name' of women's limited opportunities and internal conflicts. Many other feminist books followed and Simone de Beauvoir's classic *The Second Sex* (1949, reprint 1972) was widely re-read. The first National Women's Liberation Conference in Britain was held at Oxford in 1970.

The flourishing of feminism in Britain was part of a wider movement for change, of the student uprisings in France in 1968, the Civil Rights Movement in the USA and the Gay movements in the USA and Britain. It was in this decade also that Nelson Mandela was imprisoned, Martin Luther King was assassinated, John and Robert Kennedy were assassinated and British troops were mobilised in Northern Ireland. Cultural landmarks included the Beatles first single, the publication of *The L-Shaped Room* by Lynne Reid Banks (1960) and *The Golden Notebook* (1962) by Doris Lessing and the release of *Darling* starring Julie Christie (Maitland, 1988). The permissive and rebellious characteristics of the 1960s are sometimes described, excluding reference to the significant political changes which are still important now. I was a student in the late 1960s, but for me that decade was much more a starting point for the 1970s when I was involved with a variety of women's liberation groups and campaigns.

The meaning is in the movement

The 1960s offered new possibilities for women after the restrictive emphasis on domesticity of the 1950s designed to ensure that the world of work would again be the male province it had been before the war. As we have seen, Duncan's and Graham's challenges to the dance world were at times when women were campaigning for social change. However, although Graham and many other female modern dancers continued to work through the 1950s it is at this time that Merce Cunningham (a soloist with the Graham Company) provided another challenge for dance with his newly formed company at Black Mountain College (1953).

As Hanna (1988a) points out, when women successfully establish themselves in an area, men assert their own supremacy. It is not surprising, therefore, that men's work is now very evident in contemporary dance. In the ballet companies there has been a focus on the male dancer as superstar challenging the ballerina's central role. This can be read as a reaction to women's success so that powerful female work, which refuses to reinforce male dominance, sets off a backlash of stereotypical masculine roles to assuage male pride and status. This is not to deny the importance of the work of Cunningham and his contemporaries but rather to recognise the social factors at work in dance which contribute to the different ways in which male and female work is made and received.

Merce Cunningham was one of the main challengers to the view that dance needed to mean something. For him the meaning was in the movement, thereby assuming a classical position, i.e. emphasising form over content. He worked closely with the avant garde composer John Cage using chance methods of choreography to give more focus to the movement. The technique which he invented combined the upright posture and clear footwork of ballet with the flexible use of the spine and arms used by Graham and other modern dancers (Banes, 1987). Although Cunningham's work has been extremely innovatory, in the area of gender it has reinforced traditional stereotypes (see Figure 20). The pas de deux work which is often central to his choreography involves the man lifting and displaying the woman. This continues the tradition of classical ballet and the chance methods of his choreography do not alter this tradition as far as the representation of women is concerned. However, some of the dancers and choreographers who were influenced by or worked with Cunningham were also influenced by second wave feminism and began to question how they presented themselves as performers. They were labelled 'postmodern'.

20 Merce Cunningham Dance Company – '*Pictures*'.

Postmodernism and feminism

There has been much debate concerning the features of postmodernism. This theory reverses or modifies many of the features of modernism. It features a plurality of styles; quotations of old styles; ornamentation and decoration; multi-layered readings; and a concern with meaning (Walker, 1983). As Lyotard (1984) has pointed out, the postmodern artist is not governed by rules. However, a dilemma for postmodern theory is an inconsistency in a position which argues for the end of theory necessarily based on theory.

There has been resistance from feminist writers and critics to postmodernism. The pluralism of postmodernism is politically liberal, assuming that there is a harmonious co-existence between different groups. However, differences of, for example, class, race and gender ensure that some groups assert their supposed supremacy over others (Walker, 1983). Rosa Lee (1987) raises a number of important questions. Firstly, if the current climate allows for many options within the pluralism of postmodernism, what does this mean for women and our participation in making culture? Secondly, is the relative acceptance of women's art within postmodernism's plurality of styles positive and subversive or could the dominant values still continue with feminist art practice considered as just another style? She points out that feminist practice intervenes in artistic practice by an insistent questioning of patriarchal assumptions.

Feminist theories have analysed the patriarchal relations in society within which artists operate, refuting the myth that 'men create art; women merely have babies'. As Griselda Pollock points out this insidious myth has often been used to excuse the exclusion of women and the lack of recognition of women's work (in Lee, 1987). However, feminist art practice continues to be ignored or repressed within postmodern theory. Jameson (1984) is indifferent to it but Owens (in Foster, ed., 1985) attempts to overcome the problem by simply including work of feminist artists and writers dealing with sexual difference in the mainstream of ideas and theories of postmodernism. However, postmodern theory may be more indebted to feminism than is currently acknowledged. Indeed, whether postmodern pluralism is seen to offer more scope or is simply lacking in meaning feminism is *'the root cause* of the postmodern crisis of cultural authority, and *not merely a facet* of it' (Lee, 1987, p. 10).

McRobbie (1991) points out that the current debates concerned with postmodernism have reinforced a tendency in mainstream art of looking at the end product. This is problematic for feminist art work which has been concerned with process as much as product. Wolff (1990) however, suggests postmodernist art practice is a potentially critical and radical intervention into what is still predominantly a patriarchal culture. She states that the disillusion with modernism is the reason for optimism about postmodern cultural practices. It is seen as progressive, as outside the dominant academies of high modernism; it blurs the boundaries between high art and popular culture; the theories of Lyotard, Baudrillard and Derrida expose the impossibility of universalism. Postmodern discourses are 'deconstructive' seeking to distance us from and make us sceptical about beliefs concerning truth, knowledge, power, the self and language which are often taken for granted and used to legitimate contemporary Western culture (Flax, 1987).

This deconstruction of apparent truths is what Wolff (1990) suggests might be useful for feminist politics as it aims to expose and discredit dominant patriarchal discourses and can engage with dominant culture. Postmodern art practice is that 'work which self-consciously deconstructs tradition, by a variety of formal and other techniques (parody, juxtaposition, re-appropriation of images, irony, repetition and so on)' (p. 93).

Feminists have been involved in recreating their own artistic language subverting male desire. Some, for example Mary Kelly, have refused to represent directly the human body in their work because of the ways in which women's bodies in particular have been represented. Others, like Alexis Hunter, have produced positive images of women. In dance some of the women involved with the Judson Dance Theatre, a group of dancers and artists who redefined dance, created work which challenged female representation, such as Rainer's *Trio A*. As Frances Spalding (1986) argues, an exciting aspect of postmodernism has been the attempt to free the female image and female sexuality from male-dominated traditions.

There were a number of women who either worked with Rainer or were her contemporaries who contributed work which has significance for women in dance. I will discuss their work in terms of how it subverted the contemporary dance traditions and established new expectations, images and roles for women, highlighting those elements which contributed to the breaking of boundaries so that 'the dance of the freedom of women' which Duncan pioneered was brought into vision once more. In addition, where relevant, I will give examples of choreographers' work made in the 1970s and 1980s which illustrate the development of their earlier ideas.

The innovators – performers and choreographers

Anna Halprin is and has been an important influence for many dancers. She has run the San Francisco Dancers' Workshop, which is for dancers trained and untrained alike, for many years. She prefers to work with people, from a variety of backgrounds, who do not have traditional movement training. Her view of dance as a way of life has been influential with a number of people who were part of Grand Union (the group which evolved from the early experiments of the Judson Group and others, for example, Forti, Monk, Takei) (Hartmann, 1977–8).

Her concerns are with improvisation and the process of performance. She encourages dancers to sense the physical changes within themselves and to follow through any impulses they have. Technique, structure and rules are all challenged and frequently discarded. Her aim is to introduce dance to as many people as possible. Through her workshop intensives it is possible to make connections with one's body and feelings and to learn about the process of creativity. 'Her ability to stay in the moment, her vitality, sensitivity, and non-judgemental attitude immediately made her a striking role model' (Hartmann, 1977–8, p. 58). In order to establish a common ground for communication between people of various movement disciplines and others with no formal training, Halprin uses everyday movement. In a description of a workshop process some of the activities discussed were: active listening (i.e. listening to each other without pre-judgement or unnecessary advice); drawing self-portraits to enable participants to become more aware of their body images; other awareness techniques and also 'scores', sets of verbal or written directions or instructions that lead to performance.

Her approach to movement and her wish to generate creativity, Halprin sees as very female. She also regards the way in which she makes very public statements with her work and her use of scores as masculine elements. When she uses these terms female/feminine, male/masculine she is talking about the ways in which women and men tend to work and attitudes they may have. She does not, however, see this as static and suggests that it is for men and women to develop both sides of themselves into a balanced whole.

Halprin began to develop her approach to movement after attending an American dance festival and feeling that it was totally unconnected with her. 'After I realised that movement and feeling were intrinsically related and that each person was creating his [her] own experience, I discovered that your own personal growth will go hand in hand with your artistic growth' (Hartmann, 1977–8, p. 62). For Halprin creativity is central to her desire to create an environment in which each person is able to experience things for her/himself.

Halprin's decision to act as teacher and director rather than performer/choreographer is special. She was one of the first artists to dance in spaces other than theatres, using rural landscapes and urban settings (Luger & Laine, 1978, p. 63). She worked with multiracial groups, one of which was at Soledad Prison. More recently her work has developed in the areas of public rituals and self-healing. In 1987 she organised *Planetary Dance* in which thirty-five countries took part, creating their own scores.

The outstanding aspect of Halprin's work is the political nature of it and the connection with everyday life, which can of course be seen as political. Halprin says of herself that she always questioned the status quo. This attitude is one which is often missing in dance particularly with the insular training systems and the emphasis on star systems in the companies. She talks of training systems offending her because they ignore the uniqueness of the individual and just produce 'an army of clones' and she compares dance styles to fashion so that they are 'like skirts which go up and down'(1989, p. 71).

She has not only succeeded in transforming ideas of dance but also in involving her family in her work. This is a major achievement when women are often in the position of having to choose between career and family. One daughter introduced Gestalt work to the Dancers' Workshop when she became a therapist; the other contributed to Halprin's understanding of other cultures through her study of anthropology. Fritz Perls, the originator of Gestalt therapy, was invited to work with Halprin at the Dancers' Workshop after she became 'convinced that each performer could only essentially perform himself [herself]. Each person is his [her] own art. Whatever was being suppressed in the individual would become a severe limitation to an artist'. She thinks that in a climate of non-censorship or non-judgement, people are free to develop all aspects of themselves, otherwise they become defensive and hang on to one perspective (Luger & Laine, 1978, p. 65).

Anna Halprin and Meredith Monk are of different generations and working at opposite ends of the USA but they share many common concerns. They have both moved away from contemporary dance and chosen a form of expression which is more individual. They are both concerned with exploring the potentials of light, sound and space. They bring before the audience 'their own personal, female point of view' (Luger & Laine, 1978, p. 66). Halprin has, from her perspective, generated creative scores and Monk (her work is discussed more fully later in this chapter) has constructed theatre pieces that show various aspects of women's lives. They take themselves seriously as women artists and have had the courage to develop their own movement ideas for performance (Luger & Laine, 1978).

Halprin influenced some members of **The Judson Group**, which was the first co-operative venture in dance since the Workers Dance League of the 1930s. The Group evolved from Robert Dunn's composition classes and the founding members included Trisha Brown, Judith Dunn, David Gordon, Deborah and Alex Hay, Steve Paxton, Yvonne Rainer and James Waring. They performed in Judson Memorial Church in New York, hence the name (first performance 1962). They took Cunningham's aim to look at movement for its own sake one step further by abandoning technique and using pedestrian movement in a variety of settings. They applied Cage's philosophy of 'all sound is music' to dance and invited audiences to stop and look at everyday movements in a different context and recognise that 'all movement is dance'. Their main concern was creativity. The stage, repertory and technique did not interest them. Their important discoveries were made at a time when the divisions between ballet and modern dance were lessening. Dance students were studying both techniques, and modern dance choreographers were beginning to make works for ballet companies (Morrison Brown, 1980). There was a fusion of ideas between visual artists, dancers and choreographers in an atmosphere of acceptance and an understanding that all dances should be encouraged without censorship, so that some might develop and survive. There were very few resources and performances were informal. The audiences were mainly local people from Greenwich Village, many of whom were artists. It was a friendly audience which brought with it a sense of participation and identification with the performers (McDonagh, 1970).

The rejection of technique freed the body and made equality of participation more possible. At a time when the social controls of the body as discussed above were lessening, the Judson Group wanted to affirm the power of the 'lived body' and break down the, 'hegemony of mind over flesh' (Banes, 1981, p. 15). They asked, 'What is the nature of dancing?' and refused to be confined to virtuoso techniques and perfect dancers' bodies. One of the main forms to be developed during this time was contact improvisation, initiated by Steve Paxton (1981) who describes it as

> spontaneous mutual investigation of the energy and inertia paths created when two people engage actively – dancing freely, with their sensitivity to guide and safeguard them. Parts of the body may come to support weight which are unused to this, and several weeks of conditioning are essential to strengthen and communicate to the muscles what new stresses they may expect (p. 33).

It is significant that contact improvisation was given a descriptive name and not named after its founder as modern dance techniques were. It indicates the collaborative venture of much of the work and the challenge to star systems. Within the form there is an emphasis on equality between people and letting go of traditional role expectations. It is important that people take responsibility for themselves and only do fifty per cent of the work. 'Contact makes an important statement about relationships – about what is my responsibility, my territory, my decision making power, and what is yours' (Pritchard, 1981, p. 35). This form offers the possibility for dancers to be seen as human beings not as idealised images, thus offering great potential for women working. In addition women developed strength in their arms, learnt how to use their weight so that small women could lift large men, creating reversed roles that questioned the norm. This work was in contrast to work of the 1950s in which it was rare for women to touch each other or for men to touch each other. The Women's Movement and the Gay Movement broke down barriers which made it easier for casual physical contact and these changes were evident in the dance work of the 1960s and 1970s.

These developments introduced a new value system for dance. The practitioners were concerned to break down the artificial barriers between life and art, to work with untrained dancers as well as trained dancers and to work with a collective decision making process. This last factor was particularly important for women who were leaders in this movement. This was a structure in which they could choreograph and work out their own ideas unhindered by hierarchies and set techniques and in which sexual stereotypes could be challenged.

Yvonne Rainer played a central role in the Judson Dance Theatre through her controversial viewpoints and choreography. Her political stance and ways of working reflected feminist thinking of the 1960s and 1970s. The so called sexual liberation of this period was not welcomed with open arms by many women as there was a fear that this was not freedom for women but just another constraint on our behaviour. In the Victorian age women were expected to deny their sexual feelings; now this is not the case, instead we are expected to be sexually available to men. Reaction against this assumption was evident in many of the early postmodern dances. The dances did not display women sexually. Instead the emphasis was on the movement and through averted eyes and precise, complex patterns, the viewer's attention was drawn to the intricacies of the movement. 'The impoverishment of ideas, narcissism, and disguised sexual exhibitionism of most dancing' enraged Rainer (Copeland, 1982b, p. 50). Her dances had a quality of austerity, lacking sensuality and emphasising the cerebral. The costume of loose trousers, t-shirt and sneakers worn for many dances emphasised practicality and minimised display of the body. This too was the dress for many women during the 1960s and 1970s when feminists questioned fashionable clothes which stressed the display of the female body. Theatrical dance became suspect for many women because in dance women can be equated with their bodies. Through the introduction of spoken language and the emphasis on the complicated 'problems' which they set themselves in the choreography the choreographers questioned some of the assumptions concerned with display of the female in dance. Rainer also used a variety of movements mixing dance technique with 'quirky movements like twiddling the fingers in front of her face (The Bells, 1961), and drawing lines on her body with her finger (Three Satie Spoons, 1961)' (Banes, 1980, p. 42). Her work was like a stream of consciousness from her body, incorporating noises along with the gestures, such as grunts, shrieks and barks. She also used repetition within the structures.

Rainer formed the Grand Union, an improvisational dance company in 1970. The other members were, Becky Arnold, Barbara Dilley, Douglas Dunn, David Gordon, Nancy Lewis, Steve Paxton and Lincoln Scott (Banes, 1980). It was a collective of performers/choreographers who consistently broadened the boundaries of dance and redefined it during the six years they worked together.

Halprin's influence on Rainer is evident in her method of moving whilst holding objects. This was one of the methods, together with task-orientated movements and game structures, which she later created in order to remove the expressive qualities from the movements. With these structures, Rainer 'proposed a new dance that would recognize the objective presence of things, including movements and the human body' (Banes, 1980, p. 43). For Rainer, emotion, dramatic tension and storyline were not central to dance as had been the case with most of her predecessors in modern dance. After watching a good deal of Indian theatre and dance during a trip to India in 1971 she was able to reconsider dance and its content. She worked with a sense of detachment, objectifying emotions. In her most famous statement denying theatricality she said:

> No to spectacle no to virtuosity no to transformations and magic and make-believe no to the glamour and transcendency of the star image no to the heroic no to the anti-heroic no to trash imagery no to involvement of performer or spectator no to style no to camp no to seduction of spectator by the wiles of the performer no to eccentricity no to moving or being moved (Banes, 1980, p. 43).

In 1973 she made *This is the story of the woman who*. This was the last dance she made before becoming a film-maker. The content of this work consisted of a fight taking the form of slow-motion karate actions to the body together with screams and moans from the couple which were not quite synchronised with the action nor necessarily uttered by the person who had been attacked. The violence left a disturbing effect (Jowitt in Livet, 1978).

An important example of her choreography is *Trio A*. In this piece Rainer broke new ground and extended the boundaries of dance. Her concerns were phrasing, repetition and the distribution of energy. Her view of expression as irrelevant included her departure from traditional dance. It is possible now to regard dance as the 'presentation of objects themselves' (Banes, 1980, p. 49) rather than as the perfection of technique or expression. 'In the dance Rainer shows us ordinary movements as strange, at the same time making strange movements fall into place next to the extraordinary ordinary uses of the body' (Banes, 1980, p. 50). A straightforward delight in the ability of the body is communicated through dance. The emphasis on 'pure motion' of *Trio A* and the denial of expression and of style is what makes this dance so important. At the first performance (1966) it was entitled *The Mind is a Muscle, Part 1* and both the title and the dance illustrated the love Rainer has for the body; it is a dance which 'celebrates the body's capacity to be active' (Anderson, 1987). This, of course, provides a powerful contradiction to the traditional female role of woman as passive. Rainer also initially taught it to anyone who wanted to learn it whatever their experience, skill or age (Rainer, 1974).

In *Continuous Project Altered Daily* (1969) three couples simultaneously danced the same phrase. One couple knew it perfectly; one couple had learnt it a long time ago and been allowed to forget it; of the last couple, one person had never done the phrase before and the other knew it. By showing the work in this way the audience were able to see its development (Jowitt in Livet, 1978).

Trisha Brown made it clear in a recent discussion that she was not interested in reproducing stereotyped movements of men and women.[1] She was influenced by Halprin and worked with Rainer and Forti. She created many improvisation structures, one of which was called *Violent Contact* (1960). Ideas for this included running flat out, blocking a dancer, or speeding away from another dancer who was intent on collision (Banes, 1980, p. 78). This, of course, subverted any ideas of dance for women being pretty or delicate and emphasised action rather than emotion.

In 1960 Brown was showing work alongside other dancers and choreographers at Judson Church, experimenting with new concepts and collaborating with artists. In 1970 she formed her own company which has continued into the 1980s and 1990s. Her work has emphasised movement rather than expression and her power as a dancer and a choreographer is her ability to follow the natural pathways of the body. The thoroughness and skilfulness of her work can be appreciated by looking at some of the developments of her choreography. After the initial experiments in the 1960s she began making 'Equipment Pieces', using ropes and pullies such as *Man Walking down the Side of a Building* (1970).

In the early 1970s she began making 'Accumulation Pieces'. These were based on mathematical structures and simple gestures, which are gradually built on, like building blocks. *Accumulation with Talking plus Water Motor* (1978) is an excellent example of the demanding tasks and structures that Brown sets for herself. In this piece she told two stories interspersed with each other, while at the same time performing an exacting movement phrase. She had to remember where she left one story in order to begin at exactly the right place when she continued it after telling part of the other story. She was celebrating the ability of the dancer to think. She describes the standing *Accumulation* as feeling 'like I'm holding reins to about six horses, that they are going out from my body in a 360-degree angle on all sides, so I can't really see what I'm holding' (quoted in Banes, 1980, p. 34). In both the 'Equipment Pieces' and the 'Accumulation Pieces' Brown was defying some of the myths about women's interests and abilities. The pullies and ropes she used have strong links with mountain climbing which is usually seen as a male preserve and mathematics which is also traditionally viewed as a male area. She was also illustrating the complex, choreographed dance structures she used, which were not improvised, to critics and audiences unfamiliar with them who frequently assumed that they were.

The dancers' physical activity of changing clothes whilst they were supported by a rope gridwork above an actual rummage sale in *Rummage Sale and the Floor of the Forest* (1971) made evident the emptiness of consumerism and the search for clothes to fulfil the perfect look. Brown recognises the bankruptcy of consumerism in society and the overemphasis on the product in dance. For her the subjective experience of the dancer and the process have been more important than the product (Siegel, 1972). Subjectivity and process have been the emphasis of much feminist discussion and research and Brown's work adds yet another dimension to this. Another important aspect of her work is her lack of emphasis on sexual difference. Brown considered that such emphasis would inhibit her choreography. She, therefore, emphasised the similarities and gave men and women the same rules to play by. This approach freed the work from the fantasy love stories often evident in ballet and contemporary dance (McDonagh, 1970).

After eighteen years of running her own company Brown re-orientated her work for economic reasons. The lack of support for specific site and equipment pieces, and the audiences' lack of understanding of her multi-layered choreography left her financially unviable. She was determined not to de-radicalise the movement but decided to make it more accessible and popular. One of the main ways in which she did this was by collaborating with well-known visual artists and composers. In *Set and Reset* (1983) (see Figure 21) Robert Rauschenberg designed the set of three-dimensional shapes (a pyramid and two cubes) which were suspended above the performance space. A series of film images are projected onto these shapes, recognisable images from everyday life cut together and overlaid in unusual juxtapositions. The film prepares us for the unexpected. The surprise of seeing one of the dancers walking on the wall, supported by the others, heightens the anticipation. Laurie Anderson's powerful music *Long Time No See* is emphasised by the playful approach of the dancers appearing and disappearing from the wings or behind the transparent backdrop.

In *Set and Reset* we enter a world in which the body is like liquid, the energy coursing through it with a breathtaking quality. An impulse sent through a group of dancers fragments the initial shaping, only to catch the order in another form (Adair, 1988, p. 8).

Simone Forti's work is fascinating because of her investigations into early developmental human movement and the movements of animals. When she transfers her movement findings onto the adult body we are able to observe something quite unfamiliar. Her teacher was Anna Halprin who was working with a very open attitude towards finding any number of possible movements and

21 Trisha Brown Dance Company – '*Set and Reset*'.

combinations of them. Forti came to dance at the age of twenty-one, free of any of the restrictions of dance technique and she was able to work from imagery without judgement (Banes, 1980). Unlike the tension in ballet and contemporary dance her movement came from a relaxed state and was 'Very close to the holistic and generalized response of infants' (Forti in Banes, 1980, p. 22).

Forti was not part of the Grand Union at Judson Church as were most of the other women whose work was very influential at this time. She was, however, acknowledged as a primary influence upon the innovators of the 1960s although she rarely performed (Croce, 1978). McDonagh credits her with presenting one of the 'most influential concerts ever given by a dancer' in 1961 (1970, p. 171). Much of her work consisted of a series of 'Happenings'. One of these, *See-Saw* (1960) influenced Yvonne Rainer who performed in it. She was impressed by the structure of the piece which was a series of unconnected episodes. *Huddle* (*circa* 1960) is a kind of co-operative game in which the performers make a structure of themselves by linking arms around waists and shoulders whilst leaning forwards. One person then leaves the structure and finding hand and foot holds gradually hauls themselves over the human sculpture to the other side. The audience can walk round it and observe it from all angles. It is a wonderful way of demonstrating co-operation and playfulness.

In her work Forti is examining the basics of dance and exploring a whole range of movement. The game-playing, task-orientated aspects of movement fascinate her. In the 1970s she developed three main approaches, including animal movements, crawling and circling. Since 1974 nearly all of her dances have used these three ideas. Her work with animal movements began after close observations of animals in zoos. She talks about a 'dance state', almost like a meditational state with a strong sense of connectedness. Many of her concerns and investigations still have a freshness and power of the new about them and when I recently worked with her in a workshop I found it hard to believe that the ideas she was working with were twenty years old or more.

Deborah Hay's work is important in terms of directions for women's dance because she took the aspect of display away from her work when she introduced '*Circle Dances*'. It was important for Hay that her dances be accessible to anyone and she also wanted to communicate her own joy and understanding of dance. The '*Circle Dances*' are rooted in Hay's belief that ⌈breath is movement and movement is dance and anyone can dance⌉(Banes, 1980, p. 114). This approach is very much in line with feminist theory which stresses the importance of accessibility to information and resources for everyone and indeed many of the volatile debates within feminism have been concerned with putting these theories into practice. She worked with the idea that untrained performers could be as interesting to watch as trained dancers. The movement became the focus rather than the individual mover. She often worked with large groups and, as Banes (1980) points out, the grouping of people showed a democratic intention and matched the concerns of American society of the time. In the alternative culture groups there was a search for community and people organised groups for a variety of co-operative living, working and buying set-ups. Her interest in combating elitism is evident in the noncommittal manner in which the dancers, dressed in ordinary street clothes, performed *Group 1* (1967) (Jowitt, 1988).

Hay developed her own work after leaving the Cunningham Company in 1964. She abandoned dance training as she felt it was rather arbitrary with little meaning for her (McDonagh, 1970). As with some of her contemporaries, Hay was influenced by Eastern movement disciplines particularly T'ai Chi. She describes finding a way of transcendence through this movement form which she valued. Another aspect of her movement training is her use of the metaphor of a cellular consciousness. In each moment of the dance she expects every cell to be involved. The practice of this use of imagery means that all areas of the body are alert yet relaxed. The individuality of her dancers shines through supported by their skilled use of this technique (Foster, 1986). In the '*Circle Dances*' she has substituted the movements of T'ai Chi for more familiar movements and she uses a variety of music.

When she performs she works to evoke a feeling of belonging amongst the audience and her concerts may seem more like rituals than performances. Her work is very constructive, seeking to create more harmony and as with Duncan and Halprin she does not divide her art from her life. Her view is that 'Everyday the whole day from the minute you get up is potentially a dance' (quoted in Foster, 1986, p. 6).

Laura Dean's work gives us a visual impression of space through geometric patterns in her dances. An important aspect of her work is her concern with the individuality of the dancer. She recognises the importance of the uniqueness of the individual dancer and that it is through her that feeling and meaning are communicated in the dance. She presents dancers of a variety of shapes and sizes again challenging the notion of an ideal image. Her view of the body informs her work.

> What I know, I experience as multi-dimensional layers of body consciousness. The body is a symbol. To sense the reality within the form (body) requires an ability to shift levels of attention. Dance is the most immediate manifestation of this ability to project thoughts outward into physical form. It is in the imagination/image-in (Dean in Livet, 1978, p. 102).

Stamping Dance (1971) was her first group dance for four dancers. The dancers stamped down on the outside of the foot and pushed off with the inside of the foot. The counts were organised in progressive count cycles. The rhythms built so that dancers were stamping rhythms against each other. *Circle Dance* (1972) was for ten dancers organised in four concentric circles with a series of count cycles of 'shuffling steps'.

Changing (1974) was performed outside near a lake by three women dressed in vibrant satin dresses of red, yellow and blue. The dresses were huge and concealed the dancers' movement so that the audience gradually became aware of a changing relationship in the space as the dancers moved imperceptibly towards them away from the trees and the lake in the background. The dancers just appeared bigger and bigger until almost next to the audience when they fell on their faces, rolled over and then glided back to the lake. This dance gave the opportunity for the audience to look in different ways at their surroundings and it certainly presented images of women which were unusual. The image of increasing size is a very potent one because size is often equated with power and this expanding female presence reinforced a sense of women's importance.

For **Meredith Monk** art is about making people look at what they take for granted in other ways. Her synthesis of the arts is impressive and her work is an excellent example of the postmodernists' concern with breaking down boundaries between the arts. Monk now frequently refuses to categorise herself other than as an artist and occasionally speaks of herself as a musician. However, the movement base of her work is both compelling and influential. It is clear from the understated movements and costumes in her work that the glamour, sexual objectification and virtuosity so frequently associated with dance is of no interest or value for her.

Monk says that there is always some political aspect to her work, although she deals with themes rather than messages (Siegel, 1986). In *Quarry* (1979) she was interested in the forces of fascism and the events of the second world war. However, she was also concerned with the increasing interest in fascism in the present (in Kreemer, 1987). Monk counters the images of oppression and war in her work with kinship not just of the family but to all who respond to the plight of humanity (Foster, 1986). Another example, *Vessel* (1971), was about Joan of Arc but it also dealt with some contemporary issues (Briginshaw & Burt, 1987). As with other work in the 1970s, Monk did not confine this to the theatre instead the piece was performed in three parts in a loft, a theatre and a parking lot. In *16*

Millimeter Earrings (1964) Monk presented 'overlapping images of
the body as a medical phenomenon and a sensuous medium,
through the use of a complex technology' (Banes, 1980, p. 152).
The interactions of film, objects, sound and the performer create the
meanings in the work. There is a suggestion of both a young
woman's bedroom and her internal world. Her face is distorted in
the film images projected onto a drum which she is holding and as a
doll in the film burns, the young woman performer appears nude
from the flames (Croce, 1978). It is possible to read this as a
comment on the processes of female socialisation which emphasise
appearance and confinement.

Education of the Girlchild (1972) is the prime example of Monk's
work which can be read from a feminist perspective. It is an epic
and the female characters are archetypes. Each of the women
created their own personal characters which included elements of
her own personality (Steinman, 1986). Monk's solo of movement
and sound charts the journey of three stages in a woman's life.
Initially we see an old woman who seems to be remembering parts
of her life, then a middle-aged woman who, feet firmly planted on
the ground, makes a yodelling as though calling a child who is
playing outside. Lastly, Monk transforms herself into a young girl
who touches her body with a sense of discovery (Siegel, 1986). Her
work leaves room for interpretation at various levels. Her use of
images and history gives us glimpses of the future and reminds us to
reconsider the present. She offers us

> groups of strong individuals – often solely or predominantly women –
> whose social ties are unclear but whose emotional connections are
> obvious. Perhaps they could serve as models for feminist utopias, but
> they are not offered as political tracts or patent moral tales. They are
> descriptions of things as they could be (Banes, 1980, pp. 164–5).

Conclusion

The foundation on which much of the work of the 1970s was built
was the dance of Halprin, Rainer and the Judson Group. This era
was one of development of the political and artistic concerns of the
1960s. The feminist movement was well established and women's
arts practices were certainly influenced by it. A dance group which
emerged at this time was the Wallflower Order (1975). The

collective was formed to portray political perspectives of the Women's Movement through their personal stories and writing. They incorporated theatre, music, comedy, martial arts and sign language with the aim of creating a strong emotional impact. Their aim was to inspire social action through broadening political awareness. Their work incorporated international liberation struggles together with feminist issues (publicity information). Dance critic, Deborah Jowitt (1981), describes their dancing as distinctive with both strong, individual movement and harmonious group movement. She said, 'It's a long time since I've seen women dancers so luxuriantly at ease and yet so purposeful and daring with their bodies' (p. 55). Another critic, Marcia Siegel (1980), was impressed by their commitment to movement and their ability to use the potential of momentum and weight. Also evident, was their trust and responsiveness both of themselves and each other. Political issues are illustrated in the accompanying text: 'Have you ever held hands with a woman? Many times. I held the hand of a woman in childbirth, a woman who was lonely.' (p. 30). They make maximum use of the emotional impact of words accompanying movement. As one of the dancers says

> We want people to take control of their lives . . . We're pro-revolution. Following in the spirit of Emma Goldman, who once vowed that if she couldn't dance she didn't want to be part of the revolution. Wallflower dances the revolution – with a sense of humor (Fichter quoted in Retallick, 1981, p. 31).

In contrast to many dance groups working in the USA, in the 1970s the Wallflower Order were more interested in the political expressiveness of the 1930s modern dance. They viewed the formalism evident in much postmodern work as self-absorbed with little interest in content and social context. As well as dealing with issues of feminism the group dealt with issues of racism too. Many dancers in the 1960s and 1970s, despite the growth of political movements and awareness, ignored these issues and black people's contributions to dance, as in other eras, were not fully credited. In order to fully establish the significance and contribution of black dance, this will be dealt with separately in the following chapter.

8

Black power – black dance

Gender issues within dance are the primary focus of this book; however, in my research and writing, I have also questioned my white perspective. An understanding of oppression can accommodate an awareness that not only are we all connected as human beings but also we are painfully divided. It is important to know what the divisions are and to name them. Ignoring differences merely results in deeper oppression. The discussion of black dancers' and choreographers' work in the context of some of the debates concerned firstly, with feminism and secondly, with black dance raises the issue of racism in relation to dance practice. In this chapter I bring together black artists' work so that the social and political context within which they develop their work becomes clearer. When the work of black dancers/choreographers is discussed in the context of white artists its importance is often diluted and the destructive effects of racism minimised. Similarly, books which predominantly discuss men tokenise and depoliticise women's work when only one or two women are included. Black women, of course suffer a double oppression.

Feminism

In the late 1960s and early 1970s feminism again emerged in Britain amongst predominantly white women, having been underground for many years. Racism was unfortunately part of that feminism. White women often unawarely spoke of 'women' assuming that they spoke for all women. The Black Feminist Movement in Britain has challenged 'imperial feminism', recognising that, as in the USA, white feminists have often perpetuated racism (Amos & Parmar, 1984). Much feminist theory does not address black women's experience. As Angela Davis (1982) has made clear, white women's fight for the vote in the USA was often argued at the expense of black people. Similarly, there has frequently been a lack of awareness of the power relationship existing between white and black women within feminist research and it has been quite common for white researchers to study other cultures without questioning the validity of their task, methodology or their perspective. Moreover, the argument that development in economically poor countries will improve the situation for women needs to be questioned as this ignores the very complex, colonial history which has contributed to 'under-development' (Amos & Parmar, 1984). People from Africa, Asia and the Caribbean, continue to resist imperialism in many situations. This resistance is a central experience for black women and one that needs to be recognised and understood.

Black women were consciously debating feminist issues within the Civil Rights Movement well before discussions began within the, mainly white, Women's Movement. In their article, 'Challenging Imperial Feminism' (1984) Amos and Parmar discuss certain areas which have had prominence within feminist debates. They recognise the value of analysing the construction of female identity through domesticity, motherhood and relationships with men, but they question white academics' definitions of black women's role within the family. Such analysis has revealed stereotypes of, for example, the dominant African-Caribbean mother head of the household; the passive Asian woman victim of restrictive family practice. However, many white feminists have undoubtedly attempted to resist and undermine such stereotypes.

The second issue Amos and Parmar discuss is the importance of sexuality which is often overshadowed for black women by the more pressing demands involved in surviving in a racist society. Black women's sexuality has frequently been defined by others, but despite this, their resistance comes from a strong tradition of determining their own sexuality. Single-issue campaigns such as the National Abortion Campaign have had to reassess their actions because of black women's experiences. Black women are subjected to horrific abuse from some of the medical profession from dangerous drugs such as depo provera, unwanted sterilisations and abortions. Furthermore, the history of contraception was not the united success for women which it is often assumed to be. Instead many of the leading women were committed eugenists and, as many of the early feminists made clear, their concern for 'the race' (i.e. the white race) took priority over any concern for women (although clearly some white feminists recognised this for the oppression it was and challenged it).

Definitions of black dance

The reluctance of American and British society to take the contribution of black people seriously means that much information has been lost, particularly about black women (Alexander, *circa* 1988). There are very few well-known black female dancers or choreographers working within the Western theatre. This is hardly surprising given the very limited, stereotyped roles of comic stooge and 'exotic primitive' in which blacks could be successful on the stage.

Without racial equality or gender equality there is a case for autonomous black arts and for women's work to be acknowledged separately (although integration may well be a final goal). This may mean that some black women choose to work autonomously. As Williams sums up: 'As a cultural expression, an element of racial identity and a statement of strength against injustice and inequality, black dance is a viable entity . . . a vital art' (Williams, 1980, p. 63).

Black dance is used as a generic term and there are a number of problems associated with its usage. If there is black dance then there must be white dance and yet this term is rarely applied. There is also confusion in defining black dance. Is it to be defined by the dance origin, the dancers' origins, the dancers' skin colour? The debate, however, is not as simple as this. It has to be seen as a complex inter-relationship between the art, the people, aesthetics and dance in society (Semple, 1985). The concept of black arts (and black dance) has been defined both politically and culturally. A political definition specifies dance practiced by black people of African and Asian origin.[1]

> Black is a political term in relation to people, not a descriptive term for the skin colour of a person. It is a common term used to describe all people who have experienced and have a common history of imperialism,

colonialism, slavery, indentureship and racialism. Hence black people may be African, Caribbean, Chinese or South Asian in origin . . . (Gillian & Subham in Salmon, 1987, p. 12).

An opposition to such a definition has been made by Khan (1976). She emphasises the need for distinction between the political use of the word black and the cultural use of this word. She also questions the extent to which Asian arts may be designated as black art (Salmon, 1987). A definition of black dance

> as the western and non-western dance traditions practised by black people suggest . . . the cultural origin of black dancers has a profound effect on their perception and interpretation of a particular dance style, or a dance tradition (Salmon, 1987, p. 26).

Furthermore, black dance and black dancers may also encompass more than the cultural origin of the dancer.[2]

Funding policies to date have tended to discriminate against those black dancers working within the western European tradition because of narrow definitions of black dance (see Parry in Salmon, 1987). Indeed, the contentious nature of the definitions have resulted in some companies being reluctant to define themselves at all. The Arts Council Report, *Stepping Forward* (Devlin, 1989), recognised some of these problems and made some tentative moves to redress the balance. However, assessment is a key issue as black arts are often not funded because the Arts Council's criteria are inappropriate. Whilst it is important that definitions of black dance should not be confined to non-western dance, there is good reason for black people to identify with their African heritage since dance and music from this heritage have been a powerful uniting force for black people (Salmon, 1987). However, whereas in the 1960s the emphasis was on a celebration of being black (and/or a woman) and on the building of unity between groups, now there is a recognition of the diverse nature of black cultural experience. Indeed, 'A shared African origin is possibly the only common, unifying element' (Williams, 1980, p. 54). For many black dancers, the definition of black dance and its relevance is quite clear, but many white dancers have questioned the need for such a label. Lewis Williams researched the views of black artists in the 1960s and asked artists in the 1980s what had changed and what could be understood from such a label.

Rod Rodgers responded with some insightful comments:

> [whilst] our interpretation of our own experience is significantly different from the depictions of our heritage and culture by the establishment media and arts, there will be a justification for continuing to cultivate and support separate Afro-American arts generally and dance artists specifically' (Williams, 1980, p. 58).

All the respondents to Williams' questions recognised the value of black dance which gives, in its many varied forms, an expression to black experience and reaches beyond a selected elite to a wide range of people. Black dance also counters racism, making black work and artists visible. Joan Myers of the Philadelphia Dance Company defines black dance as not limited to the labels of ethnic, Caribbean or African but 'dance as the trained black dancer performs it'. She also points out how important black dance is for the continuation of black culture and the need not to be lost in European culture (quoted in Williams, 1980, p. 60).

History/roots of black dance

Dance has frequently played a central part in many black cultures. Black people managed to preserve their link with the past with dance despite its misuse by white slave owners to keep slaves exercised so that they were worth more and also for whites' entertainment. They maintained a strong connection with each other through drumming and dancing. The whites were afraid of this connection and the possibilities of rebellions and in some areas it appears that the drum was banned as early as 1700 (Emery, 1988).

The colonisation of Africa and the Caribbean resulted in an elevation of European activities and goods above African activities and goods, reinforcing the dominant Western ideology. However, European artists have often turned to African and Asian art for inspiration. Their work has then been acclaimed without sufficient recognition of the arts which stimulated the artists. For example, African sculpture has influenced the Cubists and African-American rhythms and instruments have influenced composers such as Debussy, Ravel and Stravinsky (Howard & O'Connor, 1988). The grounded earthiness which Wigman in Germany and Graham in the USA made central to their dance had long been part of black dance.

Professor Rex Nettleford, founder of the Jamaican National Dance Theatre Company which began in 1962, discussed black dance in a lecture in London (1989). He outlined some of the historical aspects, giving a context in which to understand the art form. The hierarchical structures of white society place black people and their culture at the base so reinforcing the assumptions that European art is superior and more sophisticated. Black people have set up patterns of resistance against the dominant cultures by, for example, keeping the rhythms and dances of Africa alive. This is a very different root from classical ballet which refined movement from peasant dances for the court.

In classical technique and some contemporary techniques the line and form of the movement are emphasised. However, some African dance styles emphasise the ground and the different body shapes create a different aesthetic. As Professor Nettleford asked, 'Why should the deer dance of Mexico and the animal dances of Africa be inferior to the dying swan of England?' Such a question challenges the dominant aesthetic of the dominant culture. Another effect of this dominance is the internalisation of a white European 'look' so that some black women aspire to this 'look'. In order to understand black dance we need to understand that ballet is also from an ethnic group. Nettleford suggested that the critics should stop seeing black dance as a form without thought or reason and begin to understand the points of reference within the dance.

In the USA, by the mid-nineteenth century, black minstrels (rather than white minstrels made up to black) were performing the degrading stereotypes which whites had created of blacks. One of the myths which minstrelsy created was that of the contented slave. Whites appropriated black music and dance so that there was no place for representation of black experience.

In the twentieth century, black dance moved from the dance hall to the theatre. Two of the women stars in the 1920s were Florence Mills and Josephine Baker who both began their careers as chorus-line dancers. **Florence Mills** (1892–1927) became a star in *Shuffle Along* with 'Her eccentric dancing, with its comedy streak and jocose tricks' (Emery, 1988, p. 224). It is from this work that tap dancing began to gain real popularity and that chorus dancers began to learn jazz. From the 1920s to the 1940s the focus of Black

American dance was Harlem and white people began to arrive to watch black dancers in bars and cabarets (Emery, 1988).

Despite a number of attempts, **Josephine Baker** (1906–75) did not become a star in the USA until 1951 but she was a very notable star in Europe from 1926. She was credited with creating the lasting fashion for jazz music in France (Emery, 1988). She combined her performing career with her role of mother to twelve adopted children. After spending the last of her resources on establishing a home for them in a château in the Dordogne she was faced with bankruptcy and forced to abandon it, moving with her family to a tiny apartment in Paris.

Baker was brought up in St Louis, where the race riots made a deep impression on her. Black people were killed indiscriminately but neither the city nor government officials condemned these atrocities; rather, they were reluctant to act at all, therefore condoning the racism (Howard & O'Connor, 1988). Unsurprisingly, she internalised some of the racist values by for example, using lemon juice on her skin in an attempt to lighten it, and joking about using milk also to lighten her skin. She experienced racism on tour and in France on one occasion she was asked to leave a hotel because two Americans were not prepared to share it with a black. Such experiences were common place for black people.

She was, by all accounts, an outstanding performer. Colette, in a review of her performance, wrote 'Paris is going to see, on the stage of the Folies, how Josephine Baker, in the nude, shows all other nude dancers the meaning of modesty' (quoted in Howard & O'Connor, 1988, p. 143). However, some of her appeal for white audiences is likely to have been rooted in notions of 'the exotic' and racist myths of uninhibited black sexuality. The songs, full of innuendoes, often composed by and largely for whites emphasised this view and continued the minstrelsy tradition.

Katherine Dunham thought her an exceptional performer in total theatre, excelling as she did in dancing, singing and acting. However, Josephine Baker did not see herself as exceptional. She said:

> I do not like people to say when they see an outstanding Negro performer 'Why, she is an exception'. There are few exceptions, but lots of people with talent who never get the opportunity to display it . . . We are the greatest race in the world . . . More is achieved by love than hate. Hate is the downfall of any race and nation (quoted in Howard & O'Connor, 1988, p. 160).

An important stand she made against racism in 1950 was in Miami. She was invited to perform in a club there at a time when strict segregation was enforced. She agreed to perform on condition that the club was open to blacks and whites and this was finally accepted (Thorpe, 1989).

Ballet

Ballet, which upholds the white, male aristocratic values of its roots, has not been very accessible to black people although this is slowly changing. There is very little documentation concerned with black people's involvement in ballet but there is a history which relates both to individual dancers' experiences and the establishment of black ballet companies. In the following discussion of ballet and modern dance, male choreographers' work and comments are included in order to context the issues of race which affect black women dancers/choreographers.

The performance roles open to black dancers are usually limited and one prejudice black ballet dancers have had to overcome is the view that black bodies cannot do ballet. The ballet dancers from integrated companies and all black companies have disproved that myth. However, the myth is about an aesthetic which has general acceptance. There is a widely accepted concept of beauty within the Western world which is based on being white, blond and blue-eyed with black being seen in contrast as ugly. Ballet is based on symmetry and harmony and it is comparatively recently that London Festival Ballet's (now English National Ballet) administration told the press that one black swan in the corps would look odd and that was the reason for not accepting blacks into the company (Onwurah, 1986). In Britain in 1986 the Royal Ballet School had three black students out of two hundred and thirty, the London Festival Ballet Company had two black dancers in a company of sixty-five whilst the other major companies with a total of one hundred and forty dancers had no black dancers (Onwurah, 1986). In 1980 Anna Benn Sims was the first black woman dancer in the American Ballet Theatre (Adamczyk, 1989). It is important to note that those black ballet dancers who have succeeded in ballet in the USA conform to a look which is appreciated by whites (Emery, 1988).

The experience of **Syvilla Fort** (a dancer in Katherine Dunham's company) must be typical of many black dancers who faced rejection from ballet classes because the teachers were frightened of losing white students (Allen, 1976). Her choreography drew on a range of dance techniques but she never received the funds to enable her to pursue her artistic concerns properly. She decided to concentrate more on teaching than performing although many people wanted her to be a celebrity. 'Her significance as a teacher left an indelible print on successive generations of black dance-artists' (Chenzira, 1979).

It was not until the 1950s that the Ballet Russe de Monte Carlo took on its first black ballerina, **Raven Wilkinson**. Her appointment followed two years of discussion between her teachers and the company director! There were many times whilst touring in the South when she could not dance in certain theatres, or stay in certain hotels and there were confrontations with the Ku Klux Klan (Allen, 1976).

It is a popularly held belief that the Dance Theatre of Harlem was the first black ballet company. However, this is not the case. In the 1930s there was Baron Eugene von Grona's American Negro Ballet Company (Allen, 1976). He began the company by training thirty students, few of whom had danced before, for three years. The work was closer to German modern dance than it was to classical ballet. Despite the early success and the tremendous effort which had gone into the company it folded from lack of support. After that there was the New York Negro Ballet Company which was a classical ballet company. This company operated from 1955–58 but had to disband after a tour of Britain because of lack of funds. Such a company would have offered black dancers performance opportunities other than the exotic character roles offered by the white companies (Rodgers, 1967).

In the 1940s Berto Pasuka, from Jamaica, formed Les Ballet Negres, the first black ballet company in Europe. Despite its French name, all the dancers were British or African-Caribbean. The work was different from conventional ballet in both its use of the body and music. There was more emphasis placed on head, shoulder and hip movements and the dancers were given more room for spontaneity as the musicians followed them. The company closed in 1952 as whites began to feel threatened by people immigrating from the Caribbean, and bookings ceased. An Arts Council documentary film, *Ballet Black*, was made about the company in 1986 but, unfortunately, the social and political context of the company's work is not explored and the racism of the time is ignored. The dances were misinterpreted by the audiences as exotic and erotic entertainment rather than art (Onwurah, 1986).

Whilst some of Pasuka's choreography seems idealistic, the ballet *They Came* (*circa* 1946) based on the colonisation of Africa still appears vibrant and relevant, a clear indication of the importance of this company's place in ballet history; also of the short-sightedness of the funding bodies which did not give the company support.

The Dance Theatre of Harlem (see Figure 22), an all-black ballet company directed by Arthur Mitchell, a black principal dancer with the New York City Ballet, performed for the first time in 1971. Marcia Siegel (1972), in some of the articles she wrote at the time, clearly highlights some of the issues for black ballet dancers and for an all-black ballet company including, separatism, black heritage and discrimination.

22 Dance Theatre of Harlem – '*Firebird*'; choreographer John Taras; dancers Donald Williams and Stephanie Dabney.

In the 1990s it is easier for black students to gain access to the New York City Ballet's School of American Ballet and to the Royal Ballet School (that is black students are accepted). This is not the end of the story, however; once accepted by a company black dancers still have to overcome prejudice. Arthur Mitchell's goals were to disprove the idea that classical ballet cannot be danced by black dancers and to give an opportunity for black performers. His company, the Dance Theatre of Harlem, obviously achieves those goals. Although he has been asked many times to integrate the company he has decided to keep the company for black dancers until there are enough jobs available for them. He has also been asked by black militants why the company does not perform black dance (i.e. African-Caribbean) but, as he says, his expertise is ballet (in Siegel, 1972). He started the company partly because he was frustrated by the limited opportunities for him in ballet because he was black. George Balanchine created a pas de deux role for Mitchell in *Agon* but it was not re-created for television because the Southern stations would refuse to show it. The prejudiced minority frequently has dictatorial power (Emery, 1988). Certainly, having a black separatist ballet company has meant that black dancers have had the opportunity to perform and a good deal of prejudice has been challenged in the process. The debate concerning issues of separatism has had coverage within the dance press at different times. In a commentary in *Dance and Dancers* (July, 1984) it was stated that The Cuban National Ballet disproves the argument that a mixed cast looks wrong and argued that the policy of elitism is endangering ballet's future.

Undoubtedly, there is a lack of role models for black ballet dancers.[3] **Janet Collins** (première danseuse, Metropolitan Opera Ballet 1950–54) was auditioned for the Ballets Russes but not accepted because she was black. Also many black dancers have trained in ballet but then not danced in ballet companies. **Judith Jamison**, a principal dancer with the Martha Graham Company for many years, is an excellent example. Not only is she black but, at 5′ 10″ she is considered too tall so she breaks the ballet aesthetic on two counts. However, her performance of *Cry* (1971), a solo choreographed for her by Alvin Ailey, has received wide acclaim. The solo is dedicated to black women and 'moves from oppression through sorrow and pain to a kind of anguished liberation' (Siegel, 1972, p. 161).

Modern dance

There is obviously a wide range of black dance companies, mostly established in the USA, since the 1940s, the majority of which are directed by men. As with the white companies discussed (see Chapter 6), the political viewpoint of the director and choreographer will influence whether there are positive openings for women within the companies. Whilst Mitchell's ballet company and Alvin Ailey's modern company offer much needed opportunities for black male and female performers, they do little to counter stereotypes of women (Constanti, 1986; Siegel, 1972). The discussions in the 1960s at a time when there was much radical questioning concentrated on men's perceptions of black dance. Rod Rodgers in an article entitled 'For the Celebration of Our Blackness' (1967) outlined some of the difficulties still facing the black dancer, including access to dance training and gaining acceptance as performers and choreographers. The integration which existed in the 1960s when Rodgers was writing was minimal. Rodgers recognised the importance of emphasising differences between black and white as a precondition for integration and pointed out that, 'Since the instrument of dance is the human body, it is this art which can deal directly with our distinctive physical racial identity' (1967, p. 8). However, it is harder for black women who are up against the Western standards of beauty and 'ideal' proportions and the sexism and racism which those standards illustrate. In a video programme made in 1984, *Dance Black America*, a range of black dance was shown but the only work by women was *Shango* (1945), choreographed by Katherine Dunham and a group called the Jazzy Jumpers.[4]

In Britain in 1977 when modern dance had become relatively established, the Arts Council and Greater London Arts Association provided a small amount of funds for a black dance company MAAS Movers. The Minority Arts Advisory Service[5] supported the venture, hence the name. The company were divided about whether they should concentrate on being a contemporary dance company using Graham technique or whether they should utilise their black heritage for their movement vocabulary. This issue, of a company identity and how much to incorporate their roots and/or European techniques, together with inadequate funds, ensured the company did not develop. Modern dancers use their experiences and backgrounds to inform their practice. European attitudes to art have tended to emphasise individual achievement and the product but traditional African arts serve a multifarious function within the religious, social, political and economic organisation of the society. In this context there has been a tendency to emphasise the communal aspect of art and its process. Black dancers are able to draw on an attitude to art which places creativity as central to life and a number of Black performers/choreographers look to their black heritage for dance (Semple, 1985).

Katherine Dunham is a prime example of someone dedicated to creating dance which was relevant to her own background. She faced enormous difficulties attempting to establish a serious art form in the 1930s when African-American movements were frequently used and associated with social dance and musical comedy (Aschenbrenner, 1980). There were many popular misconceptions to overcome – for example, the assumption that black Americans did not need training because they were 'natural' performers. Dunham challenged such misconceptions and insisted on the need for thorough training in order to gain excellence in dance. Her approach was authoritative and successful. She founded a school in which she trained dancers and established a company offering dancers the opportunity to perform in reasonable conditions (de Mille, 1963).

Dunham managed to tour widely with her company despite receiving very little financial support. Her focus on mixing art and politics did not endear her to the funding bodies. Indeed, without her European touring she stated the company would not have survived (Aschenbrenner, 1980). Black dancers left America in order to have a chance of performance. Whilst white dancers like Tamiris were influenced by African and African-Caribbean movement and rhythm, black dancers had to fight discrimination in order to dance.

Dunham set out to achieve her goal of a company despite the obstacles. To succeed as a black woman she had to be exceptionally good. Not only was she a choreographer but also an anthropologist. Her research informed her dance, as for example in *L'Ag'Ya* (1944), based on a Martinique fighting dance, set in a fishing village. This dance included authentic African-Caribbean movements, from her research, performed by a variety of people with different body types. One of Dunham's best choreographies was *Shango* (1945) in which, as part of a group ritual, someone, believing himself to be possessed by a snake spirit, slithers and twitches in an apparent trance (Dance Black America, Channel 4 television, 1984). She succeeded because of her technique, performance ability and choreography, in which she demonstrated the inherent beauty of the folk arts which she studied. Dunham and her Company believed 'in the value of their own culture, arts and traditions as a medium of artistic expression and they refuse[d] to pander to the audience' (Pierre, 1947, in Aschenbrenner, 1980, p. 46).

Dunham created her own technique which combined classical ballet with central European, Caribbean and African elements. Throughout her early career her company was the target for racial prejudice and had to survive discrimination. For example, in Las Vegas in the 1940s blacks could entertain in hotels but not sleep in them. It must have been a relief for her to train Senegal's National Ballet in Africa, where her students recognised the cultural, social, artistic and political significance of her work (Beckford, 1979).

One of the many public stands she made against racism was in Kentucky when the management of the theatre which had booked the company tried to enforce a rule that blacks should only be allowed to sit in the balcony. Dunham came on stage and said,

> Right now war is being fought. People the color such as we are going without question to fight the war, giving our lives, and we come to a city like this and find that we cannot have our people seated among you because of color. I will have to say that it is impossible for us to return to you, or appear for you again. . . . But we cannot appear where people such as ourselves cannot sit next to people such as you (Beckford, 1979, p. 69).

This powerful statement received an emotional, supportive response from the audience. Her company never appeared without at least one black person sitting in what had previously been a segregated part of the audience.

Pearl Primus was also a choreographer and anthropologist. (see Figure 23) She helped to destroy the stereotypes associated with black people and build a pride amongst American blacks in their roots. She said, 'The dance has been my teacher, ever patiently revealing to me the dignity, beauty and strength in the cultural heritage of my people as a vital part of the great heritage of *all* mankind' (Emery, 1988, p. 266).

African Ceremonial (performed 1943), a solo, was one of the African dances which she learnt from books. She checked their

23 Pearl Primus.

authenticity with friends. Primus had never been to Africa but as a result of a performance in 1948 which included a re-choreographed group version of *African Ceremonial* she was offered a Rosenwald

Fellowship. She then travelled, studied and performed in many parts of Africa.

Her dances, concerned with the African-American experience, were ones of protest. They were designed to draw attention to the injustices black Americans suffered. *Strange Fruit* (1943), initially performed with the accompaniment of a poem by Lewis Allen but later performed to sounds of Primus' feet thudding on the ground, the swish of her costume and her fists beating the earth, evoked the aftermath of a lynching (Lloyd, 1949).

Hard Time Blues (*circa* 1945) was a protest against sharecropping (a practice which forced the farmer to share the profits from his crop with the landlord). In this dance Primus performed some amazing defiant or perhaps despairing jumps, in which she 'lands in an upper corner and sits there' (Lloyd, 1949, p. 271). After her debut on Broadway in 1944 when these two dances were performed, Edith Segal, critic of the *Daily Worker* wrote 'Miss Primus has wisely gone to the rich heritage of her people and has brought us treasures of great beauty, enhanced by her own enormous talent. Pearl Primus reaches her greatest moments in her dances of protest' (quoted in Thorpe, 1989, p. 121).

Postmodern and new dance

Postmodern Dance in the USA and New Dance in England have involved predominantly white artists. The concerns for most black choreographers in the 1960s and 1970s focussed on black identity. They did not share the questioning of technique and the nature of dance itself which were the focus of most of the white postmodern dancers. In addition, the connection between music and dance in African-American dance is central but the modern dancers and the postmodern dancers frequently excluded music. Whereas many black dancers looked to Africa for inspiration, many of the white modern and postmodern dancers were drawn to Asian dance forms.

There has been a shift in the 1980s with white postmodern dancers making works with musicians and designers (for example, Trisha Brown) and political expression evident in some works. In addition there have been a number of dance festivals and programmes organised with specific political themes, for example a black postmodern series in the USA (Banes, 1980) and *Salut* (1989) in England.

When Parallels in Black, a group of six independent black American artists, visited Britain in 1987 audiences had the opportunity to see some of the black performers who had chosen to work within postmodern dance. Whilst they are very individual choreographers there are some aspects which they share in common. They are all interested in multi-media approaches, particularly including the use of text with movement. Their work draws on their black heritage and they have a tendency to work collaboratively, respectfully using the skills of the performers they work with. The three women from the group are Blondell Cummings, Bebe Miller and Jawole Willa Jo Zollar (Zimmer, 1987).

Blondell Cummings joined Meredith Monk's Company in the late 1960s and began her own choreography in 1978. The content of several recent pieces has been the relationship between food and people. Obviously, such subject matter has a number of political implications. There is the unequal availability of food throughout the world and within individual countries. Food and eating are frequently central concerns for women whose prescribed role is preparing food and nurturing others. In the Western world there is over-emphasis on dieting for women to achieve the prescribed look.

Two other pieces which make evident Cummings political awareness are *In the Dark* (from *Talking Diaries*, 1985) which is danced almost in blackout accompanied by her commentary about being driven to dancing in the dark by 'tenement life in Harlem' and shyness. *Aerobics USA* (from *Talking Diaries*, 1985) is based on gymnastic workout movements and has many references to 'the narcissistic and sexual frustrations of being less than physically perfect in a society which sets such store on health, vigor, and a perfect set of teeth' (Powell, 1987).

Bebe Miller started her own company in 1984 after dancing with Nina Weiner and Dana Reitz. Her work clearly offers alternatives to the black male/female stereotypes in dance perpetuated by, for example, the Alvin Ailey Company and Phoenix Dance Company in which the men are often exaggeratedly virile and athletic and the women overly sensuous. In *Two* (1986), which she choreographed with Ralph Lemmon, the conventional courting gestures have no neat resolution. Instead, there is potent conflict. The roles in the relationship are questioned but the answers are not supplied. Miller says of her work, 'I don't think I need to reflect on black experience, other than my own. If you look closely, it's there' (quoted in Zimmer, 1987, p. 5).

Jawole Willa Jo Zollar was first taught by a member of the Dunham Company and began performing when she was six or seven years old. She also had a background of African dance and Graham technique. She credits her grounding in African technique for her ability to resist the pressure to diet and be self-critical of her looks. In an interview in *New Dance* (No 41, 1987) she describes how her understanding of her African roots, and the strengths of the women dancers in her company have influenced her thinking and her work.

Her current Company Urban Bush Women (see Figure 24) is all female, although this was not initially intended, but she now finds that the group is central to the creative process. Deborah Jowitt said that her work seems to be 'about a community of women working

24 Urban Bush Women – '*Bitter Tongue*'; Choreographer Jawole Willa Jo Zollar; dancers (*l* to *r*) Christine King, Marlies Yearby, Grisha Coleman, Jawole Willa Jo Zollar, Terri Cousar, Christina Jones and Viola Sheely.

together to keep the world turning' (Zimmer, 1987, p. 7; see also Chapter 10).

Black dance has yet to become established. Although black people have been living in Britain for five hundred years, it was not until the end of the second world war that black people emigrated in significant numbers to England from Africa and the Caribbean (Fryer, 1984). Also, it was only in the mid-1960s that Ballet Rambert (now Rambert Dance Company), which had been a classical company, changed to a contemporary company. It was at this time too that members of Graham's Company, notably Robert Cohan, came to establish what became London Contemporary Dance Theatre. These contemporary companies, like others which were established later, began to hire black dancers.

Beverley Glean has created a company which attempts to avoid many of the stereotypes and to provide positive images of black men and women. Her company Irie! (a greeting word used throughout the Caribbean) was formed in 1984. Glean studied European techniques and realised that jazz and African-Caribbean techniques were not viewed as sufficient training for a serious dancer. When she finished her training in the early 1980s, she found there was no outlet for her as a black dancer as there was very little black dance at that time and little or no access for black dancers in white dance. Eventually she went to a summer school in Jamaica in which she was exposed to a society which was proud of its cultural heritage. When she returned she felt the time was right to establish a company and so Irie!, which fuses European and African-Caribbean dance forms, began.

She wanted a black company because there was not enough exposure for black dancers. She decided to have men and women in the company because many of the Caribbean dance forms require men and women in them. However, in 1985 at The Albany Empire, London, which is the company's base, there was an evening devoted to female black choreographers' work. Many black dancers are told they will not make a dancer because they are the wrong shape but fortunately, Beverley Glean did not let that stop her. In her choreography she consciously subverts images of women as frail; instead she rather reinforces their power. She deliberately has very few male/female duos because of the stereotypes which are some-times difficult to avoid.[6]

Hints of Afrikha (1989), as the title suggests, is inspired by traditional African dance but also incorporates contemporary techniques. The energy and enjoyment of the dancers is infectious. Like many women, Glean manages to combine her work of directing and choreographing for the company, with her role as mother of two small children. There is constant financial pressure as the company is small scale, but it is an extremely important development, particularly for black women dancers in England since it provides employment and role models (see also Chapter 10).

The initial image in *Breaking the Mould* (1989), a television programme about issues for black dancers is a picture of Margot Fonteyn dancing amidst tall, classical, white columns with a male announcer's voice informing us that she was one of the greatest dancers of our time, the image shatters like a plastercast and a black dancer emerges.

The programme also features **Carol Straker**'s company, which she began in order to encourage black dancers to stay in England and dance rather than go abroad. She is interested in the dance being initiated from the dancer's movements rather than a specific aesthetic. In the conversations between dancers in the programme the prejudice and discrimination which they face is still only too evident.[7] The first public performance at the Hackney Empire in 1988 was enthusiastically received by the audience.

Audiences and critics

There appears to be a black and a white audience for dance. Many white people do not fully appreciate black expression in dance and many black people are alienated by white dance. The choreographic expression is inevitably different in the two groups because of the different social experiences. Williams suggests that whereas black companies, such as the Dance Theatre of Harlem, the Alvin Ailey American Dance Theater and the Pearl Primus Company attract some white members in the audience the white companies, for example, the Merce Cunningham Company, the Louis Falco Company or the Murray Louis Company attract fewer black members in their audiences. For some postmodern dance performances she states that she was the only black member of the audience (Williams, 1980). Having fought to gain entrance to classes and dance training, established their own techniques and companies, and created work which offers strong statements of black female experience what response do black performers, particularly women, receive from the critics and the funding bodies?

In 'The Critical Response', a paper in the 1980 *Dance Research Annual*, Joyce Aschenbrenner discusses whether black dancers are judged according to their skills of technique and interpretation as other dancers or whether they are assumed to be 'natural performers' and seen as exotic. In addition, she asks, 'are the artistic traditions within which they work recognised as producing valid art forms in their own right?' (1980, p. 41).

Whilst there have been racial biases, generally American critics have been favourable towards African-American dance for two main reasons. Firstly, African-American dance has been of a reliably high standard and innovative once on the professional stage. Secondly, it has the backing of influential people and groups once it has reached professionalism. Critics have managed to praise good work despite the conservatism of the town leadership in which performance takes place (Aschenbrenner, 1980).

In an overview of reviews of black performances, Aschenbrenner picks out some typical responses to work. There are many comments about innate ability rather than applied work, about mysterious qualities of performers and an over-emphasis on the physicality of dancers. Dancers have to fight these stereotypes in order to establish themselves as serious creative artists using their rich African-American heritage.

Some dancers chose to excel in European forms whilst others concentrated on African-American traditions and some artists used both. The critics' attitudes to Dunham's work over the years makes clear the struggle for white critics to appreciate appropriately black creativity (see reviews in Aschenbrenner, 1980). William Moore (1977) in an article about white critics reviewing black dance held the view that the critics had been destructive to the new creativeness.

Barbara Smith (1986) in her article, 'Towards a Black Feminist Criticism', details some of the many ways in which black women's work has been rendered invisible, and in particular that of black lesbians. Although she is specifically discussing literature many of her points are equally appropriate to dance. Smith calls for a radical reconsideration of feminist culture. She also makes a strong case for black feminist criticism which would offer an innovative approach together with an awareness of the political implications of criticism. Such a criticism would, of course, be useful for dance.

Conclusion

The political awareness of both race and gender has changed significantly from the 1960s to the 1990s. Whereas in the 1960s there was a sense of discovering differences and there was much hopefulness about change, after more than twenty years of struggle for change many gains have been made but there needs to be more understanding of the extent to which many of the concepts and structures are deeply rooted.

Jawole Willa Jo Zollar and Beverley Glean are two examples of black women using their background to form the type of companies they want, challenging sexist and racist assumptions. For black women performers and choreographers, decisions of whether to work in all-black companies, to work with men, to work within companies or to form their own, all confront issues of race and gender. As we have seen, black women have taken all those paths, joining established predominantly white ballet companies, performing with black ballet companies, beginning their own companies based on their black heritage and/or developing their own approaches. Black women have shared their experiences and created significant performances and companies overcoming barriers. Their work continues to break through racist and sexist stereotypes. Black women's performance work is on the frontline. Breaking through stereotypes and redefining dance were also concerns of the X6 Collective and the new dance movement which are the focus of the next chapter.

9

Beginning again – new dance

New dance in England developed from the early classes, performances and writing of the X6 Collective and those who worked with
them or at the same time. They were concerned to form new ideas,
theories and practices for dance. They also aimed to recognise and
challenge oppressive behaviour, action and patterns in themselves
and others, and to begin to develop a dance practice that
contributed usefully to the development of a just, rational and
humane society. Their aims were radical and indicate some of the
changes evident in society and in certain art practices during the
1970s and early 1980s.

Some of the concerns of X6 were mirrored by and overlapped
those of the Women's Liberation Movement. 'For many women,
theatrical dancing of any sort became suspect; for dance is a
physical art in which women are most fully reduced to and equated
with their bodies' (Copeland, 1982a). Through their questioning
and personal experiences, the women in X6 produced work giving
their views of the world as women. The influence of feminism is
illustrated in the way they were re-evaluating their bodies, their
training and their performances.

The majority of new dance performers and choreographers
during this time were women, including Emilyn Claid, Maedée
Duprès, Jacky Lansley and Mary Prestidge from X6, the American
Mary Fulkerson, Head of Dance at Dartington College of Arts,
who also organised the yearly International Dance Festivals held
there, and Rosemary Butcher who has been a formative influence
for many young dancers today. However, some men were also
questioning gender roles and reassessing their dance work including
Fergus Early from X6, Dennis Greenwood who danced in

Rosemary Butcher's company as well as doing his own work and Steve Paxton, an American, who was a visiting lecturer at Dartington College and taught many of today's new dancers.

Significant challenges to gender roles in dance were evident in the 1970s in England within the work of the new dance movement. Reassessment of technique, working away from the proscenium arch (see Figure 25), using functional clothing rather than costume which displayed the body, finding non-hierarchical ways of working, all contributed to new images of women and men in dance which were connected with the social realities of the time.

The group, which later became the X6 Collective, initially met through contact at The Place, the home of the new London Contemporary Dance School, in the early 1970s, where there was much experimentation and visits from dance groups from different countries.[1] Some of the students at the school were mature students who were already experienced in other disciplines and this added to the richness of the experimentation. This was at a time of much political activity in London, including the early Women's Movement.

25 '*Dance on the Roof*' – London.

Strider dance company was formed in 1971 by Richard Alston (now artistic director of Rambert Dance Company) together with other students from the School including Christopher Banner, Di Davies, Sally Potter, Jacky Lansley and Wendy Levett.[2] By 1974 Jacky Lansley and Sally Potter formed Limited Dance Company which combined feminist politics with artistic innovation. One of their artistic strategies was to place female stereotypes in absurd situations. Lansley describes one performance for the Edinburgh Arts '74 programme at Lochilpaed in Scotland:

> two women emerged from the sea in black evening dresses with flippers on their feet into a moving tableaux previously set up around the swings, paddling pool, and public benches on the sea front, and were met in the pool by two corresponding white figures who had moved down the main street gathering litter. This piece was performed in this small coastal town in Scotland as the tide was coming in and related to the natural symmetry of the landscape (1988, p. 10).

The roots of this work were in the early 1960s. **Teresa Early** set up Balletmakers in 1962 and for the next five or six years it provided a base from which dancers, choreographers, designers and composers could make and perform dance work. It was important because it provided an alternative to the ballet establishment in that it allowed artists to get together to make work in their own way (Hutchinson, 1967).

In 1975, under the name Dance Organisation, a group, most of whom later formed the X6 Collective, performed at the International Contemporary Music Festival in France. The performers were, Emilyn Claid, Maedée Duprès, Fergus Early, Tom Jobe, Janet Krengel and Jacky Lansley together with musicians Michael Finnissy, Martyn Hill, Jon Keliehor and Nigel Osborne. As Early (1987) describes, 'The performance was noteworthy for provoking, literally a riot. Audience members fell to blows over their opinion of the work, and for the only time in my life I actually had eggs thrown at me on stage!' (p. 12). Such were the perils for daring to create new work!

Some of the group continued to work collaboratively making environmental work but tired of enduring inhospitable rehearsal conditions. The need to find a space to work in was the initial impetus for the X6 Collective. Space is always a crucial dilemma for any dancer who is not a part of a company or institution. It is difficult to find and often expensive. Yet dancers need space in order to create work, and to share ideas.

The group, Emilyn Claid, Maedée Duprès, Fergus Early, Jacky Lansley and Mary Prestidge[3] wanted a space of their own: one where they could explore their dance trainings and find alternative ways of working, both in teaching and performing. The organisation was a collective one, very different from the usual hierarchical dance institutions. Everyone was responsible for all administration of the space. It was not, however, a 'dance group', that is they did not necessarily dance with each other or make work for each other (although that did happen occasionally). The space made it possible for them to work on their own dance forms and to experiment; and give support to each other.

X6 Collective

At the beginning of 1975 the five members of the collective searched for a space and eventually were offered the top floor of an old warehouse building in X block, hence the name. X6 was the only independent dance space in London. It was used as rehearsal space for the members of the group's own projects; for classes and workshops taught by members of the Collective and visiting teachers; for performances by members of the Collective and others; as a base for New Dance Magazine; for general meetings and conferences about dance.

It was certainly an inspiring dance space, close to the river with a beautiful wooden floor and large beams. However, it was located in a derelict area of dockland, which meant that it was relatively inaccessible and performances were attended mainly by the dance community and other artists. There were other artists in the area with studios in adjoining blocks who supported performances. However, as a performance space, it was limited, being most appropriate for small-scale work often involving direct contact with the audience. There was an emphasis in the performances on new work, both by individuals and groups who wanted to share work with an audience for the first time; and by artists who were more established but who wanted to break away from old patterns and find new ways. There was certainly a sense of the unexpected created through the performances. I remember at one performance sitting waiting expectantly, when the performer, Emilyn Claid, arrived through a trapdoor in the roof.

As people chatted in the informal atmosphere after the shows a network of understanding was formed which supported these new ideas. The classes too were important with their emphasis on encouraging people to succeed and breaking down the mystification of dance technique. One of the inspiring aspects of the workshops held both at X6 and at the Dartington Festival (see below) was the mixture of very experienced performers and artists with very little dance experience, or people who had just discovered the exhilaration of improvisation.

The Collective was concerned with changing dance practice. Members were concerned with the fundamental or root aspects of the dance aesthetic, activity and experience. Baxandall (1972) suggests, that, for the first time since the Industrial Revolution, it is now possible for artists to define themselves against the values of capitalist society and yet attract an audience. This audience, a large subgroup of the population, also defines itself in opposition to the dominant culture. A central concern of the work of X6 was to bring art back into everyday life away from its isolated position. The X6 Collective also wanted to counter oppressive attitudes and change roles for both men and women in dance and society.

It is not common for dancers to be interested in and involved in political concerns. The nature of the training and lifestyle make such involvement difficult. However, for X6 this was an important focus of their work. **Emilyn Claid** questioned her training and dance background. She thought that there must be another way for dancers to learn their skills which was less harmful. From her personal explorations and her contact with Lansley and Early, she became concerned with performing, choreographing and teaching in a way which was not oppressive to her as a woman. One of her performances which clearly illustrates the 'personal is political' is *Making a Baby* (1979). This was performed whilst Claid was seven months pregnant. By exploring her own movements and thoughts and connecting her history as a dancer with her movements whilst pregnant she confronted some of the misconceptions about pregnant women as fragile, ungainly or set apart. In one section of the dance, set aside for the baby, Claid lay on her back, balancing a dish of water, in which floated a plastic swan, on her stomach. As the baby began to kick the swan rocked on the water. This was a very powerful way of sharing the reality of carrying a baby which unfortunately, is so often hidden or denied. The final section involved the audience participating in the movements and child-birth customs from other cultures. From this it was clear that the Western medical model of the woman surrounded by strangers whilst lying on her back, is at odds with the more woman-centred approach in which the woman squats or kneels encouraged by loving supporters (Green, 1979).

In *A Dance Score* (1978) Maedée Duprès provided an opportu-nity for both experienced dancers and dancers from her beginners' class to perform together and the audience were invited to participate at the end. This work was political in the sense that it made dance more accessible and challenged the dancer's role as suitable only for those with long trainings.[4] There was also an attempt to breakdown the division between performers and audience.[5]

Fergus Early was concerned to improve dancers' employment conditions. This led him to encourage dancers of the Royal Ballet to join the union when he was a member of the company. The explicit political focus of *I Giselle* (1980) which he co-directed with Jacky Lansley, is also evident in *Are you right there Michael, are you right?* (1983). This performance exposes men's vulnerability and con-sciously denies dance conventions. In this society, men are discour-aged from expressing many emotions and any challenge to this has political force.[6]

Jacky Lansley was involved with women's consciousness-raising groups and political study groups in the early 1970s whilst at the Place. Her feminist consciousness informs her work, she ran women's creative workshops at X6 and from these *The Fast Supper* (1979) was created. It used the theme of under/overcon-sumption of food and ritualisation to explore body image, religion and paternalism. In the future developments of the workshop the group was named Helen Jives. Consideration was given to their presentation as a women's performance group, individual and collective ways of working and the balance between script and improvisation. Helen Jives also created *Edge City* (1979) which 'was the space where they could play around with their own past, their personal poetry, the way they perceive things. A mobile framework allowing changing patterns in performance, a catalyst sparking off different reactions within the group' (Furse *et al.*, 1979, p. 14).

Mary Prestidge reached a point in her dance career, whilst dancing with Ballet Rambert (now Rambert Dance Company), when she did not know whether she wanted to continue or not. She was no longer satisfied as a dancer, striving to be the perfect image and interpreting someone else's ideas. She went to New York and on her return joined the X6 Collective. She had realised at Ballet Rambert that, whilst the choreographic workshops were open for both men and women, that was not enough. The socialisation processes, the dance training, the assumptions and expectations within the dance institutions and dance companies, make it very much harder for women than for men, to feel confident about their creativity and to succeed. However, the supportive structure, which the Collective established, enabled all of the artists to explore their experience and abilities in fresh ways.

In *Around Rolling* (1978), Mary Prestidge together with Sarah Green had another look at the competition they had been subjected to in gymnastics. 'It is towards the competition that one is encouraged to build suppleness and strength, diet and manipulate one's body in order to cut the correct figure' (Prestidge, *circa* 1983, unpub. paper). In the final section of the performance when they ran and flipped over enjoying the sheer sensation of moving they offered an alternative to competition.[7]

Whilst the X6 Collective continually discussed ways of producing work that was relevant to the social context, they recognised the dangers of presenting a line or being too literal. They were committed to producing work from their own explorations and backgrounds. Claid, Lansley and Prestidge used the topic of menstruation as a part of a theme for a performance entitled *Bleeding Fairies* (1977) performed as part of a women's festival at Action Space in London. In this they took tableaux of romantic ballet poses which they gradually destroyed with karate moves and wild gestures. They improvised and worked with pas de deux and lifts. The song they wrote to sing during the performance was printed on the cover of *New Dance* (No. 5, 1978) emphasising the reality of women's lives rather than the ideal image of the ballerina:

> If I had known about the blood when I first saw a fairy,
> I would have made her dew drops red instead of pearly white.
> I would have dreamt her all with tits,
> And made her wand of tampons.
> She would not have been a fantasy, but very much more like me.

CHORUS
Who invented fairies first, were they bleeders first,
Do we need a fairy, or will a bleeder do.

If I had known about the cramps when I first saw a fairy,
I would have allowed her a frown now and then,
Instead of delicate smiles.
I would have allowed her to squat on her heels,
And given her hot water bottles.
She would have had some real feelings,
Very much more like me.

CHORUS

If I had known about my body when I first saw a fairy,
I would not have allowed her to float in white dresses,
But given her a pair of knickers.
I'd get rid of her image of eternal perfection,
And let her grow lumps wherever she liked.
In fact, she could grow and change and bleed,
Very much more like me.

CHORUS

In addition to making performances together there were several
other advantages to working in a collective. Being with other
dancers/choreographers with similar concerns, freed from designated roles, was supportive. The pressure to make work was absent and
talking time was available, something dancers often lack. There were
discussions about the male/female balance of the group. Other men
were invited to join, but for various reasons, this did not happen. As
a mixed collective they may have been taken more seriously than if
they had been a women's collective. Women's activities are often not
taken as seriously as men's, therefore it might have been easier to
dismiss a women's collective. The group were, however, united in
their determination to overcome sexism and strictly defined sex roles.
   Their challenge was to some of the widely accepted values and
attitudes in dance. As we have seen, the structure of most dance
companies is a hierarchical one. The choreographer has the vision
and the dancers are often used as instruments to fulfill that vision.
By choreographing their own work and occasionally collaborating
together the group challenged this structure. Also for the women
this was going against the expectation that it should be men who
create work. They were interested in the concept of the 'thinking

body' rather than the dancer as object. Jacky Lansley created a solo which was a consideration of her own role as woman/dancer/artist, called *Dance Object* (1977). In this work a recording of Lansley's voice which described her creative process and source material accompanied her performance. The audience was able to both hear her intellectual process and see her performance simultaneously. This device cut through the traditional image of the silent dancer and also curtailed voyeurism.

By working collectively X6 also provided an alternative to the dance structure which relies on directors. Through their commitment to share their experiences and discoveries with others and to make their work accessible, they countered the belief that to dance one has to be 'born great'. Their emphasis on exploring their individual backgrounds and working out how they wanted to present themselves in their work, rather than fitting an established image, was radical.

Jacky Lansley (1977) discusses some of the ways in which dance can explore political ideas. This can be through the way dancers organise themselves, where they work, how they relate as men and women and using accessible everyday movement. Other aspects include finding one's own way of moving; using a variety of places in which to perform; using different costumes – for example, wearing loose functional clothing which does not restrict the body rather than leotards and costumes which display the legs. Women can demonstrate an alternative image through the silent means of dancing; however, it is important to make a connection with what is happening to women in a wider social context 'or else there's a danger of simply regarding the work as a new vogue aesthetic of what the "modern" dancer should look like' (p. 8).

As the X6 Dance Collective became established, they began to see that they could provide a focus for discussion in the community of alternative dance activity, which was growing. A conference held at the X6 dance space in August 1976, on experimental dance was a beginning. Some of the issues discussed included technique and ways of working. The group thought that,

> new dance needs a new language, it is time we began to define ourselves and our work . . . Writing is necessary . . . as a creative extension of our work, in order to project outwards, receive feedback and communicate in depth to others (Lansley, 1977, p. 3).

New Dance

The Collective issued *New Dance* magazine No 1 in the new year of 1977 and entered the world of alternative publications, particularly those concerned with art and politics. After this first issue there was an editorial collective which changed with each issue. This allowed for a wider range of ideas and also for people to have a break from time to time. Initially, the emphasis was on dancers having a voice and writing about their own work. Gradually, wider issues emerged with links made to aspects of dance other than performance.[8] So from the initial aim of the dancers having a voice, the issues broadened to considering dance from many aspects in its social context. It was the only magazine which dealt with new dance and social issues.[9]

New dance is an umbrella term applicable to experimental work which began in England in the 1970s and continues into the 1990s. The term was originally used for the title of the magazine. It then became convenient to use it as a label when applying for funding. The label highlighted the inadequate funding of a whole area of work. In addition to the issue of funding, gender roles in dance and technique were other areas frequently discussed in the Collective, and occasionally aired in the magazine. New dancers were interested in ways of training, which allowed the dancer autonomy over her body and life; ways to find her own motivations to move, rather than trying to create a particular look. They were concerned to find ways of learning which were not full of pressure and forcing of the body, as in the ballet and contemporary classes that they had attended. They considered the training systems, particularly ballet, to be oppressive and uneconomic. That is, people were damaged physically, emotionally and psychologically, through the training process. Part of the problem is that it is difficult to divorce the training from the end product.[10] Because of the social contexts in which these trainings were established there are real limitations to the ways in which they can be used for dances concerned with present day issues. Any movement presents an image and it is necessary to think where it comes from and the possible meanings which it conveys. It is important to use technique in one's own way.[11] Ballet and contemporary dance were taught at X6 but from an emphasis on imagery, the source of the movement and body structure. This approach was informed by the work of Mabel Todd (1975) and Barbara Clark (1977)) which Mary Fulkerson, an American choreographer at Dartington College, England, was teaching. X6 provided a space for her to share some of her work so that more people came into contact with it.

Mary Fulkerson (1982) (see Figure 26) describes her work as an

attempt to take charge of my thoughts and actions in such a way that the politics of belief in the individual voice are reaffirmed. For this reason I include in my work reference to the working process, its thoughts and actions. I want to share the process of making and sharing work which is related to the thoughtful and personal state taught by stillness. My work has been about a redefinition of consciousness which allows this to occur – the move to stillness (p. 26).

Mary Fulkerson also organised the Dartington International Dance Festival which ran for ten years until 1987. This provided the opportunity to explore some of the diverse, radical paths of new dance and for emerging choreographers to show their work in an informal atmosphere.

Rosemary Butcher had connections with Dartington College, as this was where she trained in 1965 and after studying in America with amongst others Yvonne Rainer and Anna Halprin, she also taught there in the 1970s. She was an important influence on many of the new dancers, including Gaby Agis, Sue MacLennan and Miranda Tufnell. Her first choreography was *Uneven Time* (1974) which was based on everyday movements including walking, running, falling and gestures such as running fingers through the hair (Jordan, 1986). Her use and understanding of improvisation has been important in the development of her work as has her minimalist approach and her spatial focus.[12]

Butcher has frequently taken her work into the environment away from the confines of the proscenium arch. Her view of choreography is that it is

basically a teaching art. It's about finding a language through which you can allow other people to say what you want to say that is not at odds with the body or at odds with that personality. That's true choreography. It's allowing their body to say it in their sort of way (in interview with Burt, 1988, p. 13).

26 Mary Fulkerson – '*Real Life Adventures*'.

Although her way of working encourages the dancers to find their own ways she also has a very clear vision of what she wants the piece to look like. When the dancers begin work she gives them instructions which will lead them to movement which will fit with her overall vision.[13] In much of her work men and women are interchangeable in that there are not specific roles for men and women, she is solely concerned with the movement qualities the individual dancer uses (see Chapter 10).

Dancers in Butcher's company, and other new dancers, studied a number of movement techniques including T'ai Chi and Alexander Technique. Mary Prestidge describes the effects of both practices as very powerful, creating 'space for energy to flow by means of gentle persuasion and by following the simplest of directions' (*circa* 1983, p. 4). The emphasis in movement was placed more on the process than the final form. Whilst not all members of the Collective studied these forms, they shared their information through classes, workshops and discussions. Contact improvisation was another form which was practised. Steve Paxton introduced this when he taught at Dartington College of Arts. This form together with other examples of new dance, allows a far greater range of body images and sizes. People training used different movement forms to create alternative body shapes.[14]

New dance came out of and was in direct contact with, the social issues of the time, for example, the questioning of gender roles of early feminism. Moreover, new dance is in a constant state of flux and development. As with the early modern dance, there is a wide range of work and it is difficult to locate a style. Some of the aspects of new dance were: a use of many different movement forms as discussed above; consciously working to make dance which challenged the dance stereotypes; use of mixed media; use of different performance spaces; and encouraging audience participation.

'Thinking bodies'

New dance and postmodern dance were very much influenced by women. The women who were in the forefront of postmodern dance and new dance were determined to show that they were 'thinking bodies' and presenting an alternative to the established view.

Some of the issues concerned with new work which they had to consider are discussed by Kaplan (1983) in relation to film but which are also relevant to dance. Firstly, a great deal of work is often demanded of the spectator. Secondly, pleasure is linked to a particular kind of structure. For example, through romance recognition/identification mechanisms, we are kept fixed in established positions in patriarchal culture. In *Bleeding Fairies* the disturbance of ballet poses which have specific associations challenged such established positions. Thirdly, much new work deliberately denies the pleasure people are used to. These are certainly some of the problems choreographers in X6 were tackling.

The women in the X6 Collective, through their questioning and personal experiences, produced work giving their viewpoints, as women, of the world. Some of the performances were made consciously as feminist work whereas others were not. However, a consideration of the way these dancers were re-evaluating their bodies, their training and their performances illustrates the influence of feminism.

Some women have recognised the benefits of working in an all women dance group – although it is frequently assumed that dance is a favourable profession to women and, therefore, the need to work separately should not arise. However, the issues are complex and it is necessary for women to work separately, 'in order to understand the specific psychology of professional dance and how it oppresses us as women' (Lansley, 1977, p. 8). Whilst there have been different projects with all women's groups there has not been a specifically professional dance company as there was in America, for example, The Wallflower Order (now two companies, Crowsfeet and the Dance Brigade; see Chapter 10). This group's aim was 'to express political perspectives of the feminist movement through expression of their own personal stories and contemporary writing' (publicity, *circa* 1982). A diversity of work was shown at the X6 space and in order to encourage dance to be looked at in a wider artistic context and making collaboration more possible, informality was a key to the performances there. However, a danger with performances in a form other than the traditional one and with the use of a variety of spaces, is that they may end up being more exclusive than the traditional performances. This can occur because there are no accepted rules to follow. People often feel threatened in such situations and they are not able to be sufficiently open to appreciate what is going on.

The early work of X6 and the performers/choreographers/ teachers at Dartington created new audiences and paved the way for the next generation of dancers and choreographers. For example **Gaby Agis**'s *Shouting Out Loud* (1984) was full of forceful images, showing many women's strengths which are often overlooked in mainstream dance works. Thirteen women ran into the space, weaving in and out of each other, kicking off shoes and boots. At another point in the dance the women in small groups softly gave and took each other's weight. Later the women spread across the space, stood still and clearly looked into the audience. These images reflected, respectively, fun and energy, supportiveness and strength. It was a beautifully constructed dance and a powerful challenge to the usual received images. The way Agis worked was different also. She said in her programme note that a lot of the material came from the performers themselves and that that was the only process of working which she was interested in at that time.[15]

Claire Hayes worked with a number of women's issues. After reading *The Wise Wound* (Shuttle and Redgrove, 1978) she took the female cycle as the starting point for a dance, *Dark* (1981) She revealed this cycle to be purposeful, joyful and vital, rather than the shameful secret it is often viewed to be.[16] In *Sphinx* (1980) rape was the issue.

> The emotional depth of this performance gathered momentum, as the audience watched the performer strike out definitely against this victim role, demonstrating a tremendous physical power let loose in a series of harmonious and athletic gestures, informed by Aikido and other skills (Lansley, 1981, p. 18).

This performance was part of an evening at the Women's Arts Alliance in London. In *Under* (1980) **Anna Furse** framed some of the everyday experiences of Arab women and drew attention to the parallels she perceived between Western women's experiences and Arab women's experiences.

> Dance does not easily lend itself to social statement as so much of its history has been bound up with pure formalism and the aesthetic objectification of women, and yet dance as a tool for the liberation of women is obvious, and was particularly clear in these performances.

Their work involved a dynamic interaction of ideas and movement, and dealt explicitly with issues concerning women's role in present day society. For women to reclaim the power and health of their bodies is an important step towards freedom (Lansley, 1980, p. 18).

These performances illustrate the development of feminist ideas in dance performance in the late 1970s and early 1980s. They portray some of the issues which were central then, some of which are still significant now, for example, rape.

Conclusion

The X6 Dance Collective and other new dancers achieved a number of breakthroughs in dance. The development of extended boundaries for dance with the use of a variety of other media, use of different environments and breaking down the performer/audience barrier have meant that definitions for dance have been called into question once again. In this way, together with the introduction of new movement forms and a variety of collaborations of various artists, the dancers in X6 and others who worked with them challenged the established norms for dance.

Their performance work and teaching, together with *New Dance* magazine gave this alternative dance a focus. The X6 dance space and the writing in the magazine provided a focus for dance artists and interested others to share their political ideas and concerns for dance to be linked with its social context in a radical way. The X6 Collective named this process and work and broke through the isolation which had previously existed. This development was very similar to the process which Betty Friedan (1963), a feminist writer, describes as the 'problem which had no name' of women's isolation, limited opportunities and internal conflicts. In both situations, naming the difficulties and joining forces with others was an important aspect of improving conditions. The X6 Collective's concern with working from their position as women and in Early's case a commitment to working with non-oppressive imagery, meant that they questioned their sex roles in their performances, their teaching and the day to day running of the Collective. The Association of Dance and Mime Festivals, the performances at Action Space and the sharing of work at Dartington all provided outlets for this work and provided encouragement for other artists to question their work and that of others from this point of view. Three issues of New Dance magazine focussed on sexual politics (Nos 14, 15, 41).

The X6 space also provided a place for the exposure of new work from other countries which enabled people to see what parallel experiments were happening abroad. The magazine realised some of its aims. There has been communication of new ideas, themes and practices for dance. There has also been a move to locate dance in its social context and to challenge oppressive ideas. This can be seen by looking at the areas the magazine covers.

Dancers writing about their own work and reviewing each other's work provide an alternative to the traditional critics, many of whom had difficulty in knowing how to look at new dance. The discussion of dance criticism and improvements which were needed were given detailed consideration both at conferences and in the magazine. The magazine also provided an important forum for new dance writers.[17]

The postmodern dance work in the USA in the 1960s and the new dance work in Britain in the 1970s established a new consciousness of the possibilities in dance. Women particularly created new ways of working, new images, and political statements. The celebration of dance together with a sense of solidarity amongst dancers of creating non-oppressive forms of dance was the tentative beginning of a dance identity. In the 1980s, however, with the increase of reactionary values in both Britain and the USA avant-garde dance became more diffuse and fragmented, and political concerns have tended to disappear. Despite all difficulties, powerful dance is being created and women continue to take the space for themselves and their work. The work of the founder members of the X6 Collective and of Mary Fulkerson and Rosemary Butcher has continued to develop in many different ways and their dynamic influences can be seen in current new work which is the focus of the next chapter.

10

The subversives – women's dance practice

The discussion of gender issues in dance offers the opportunity to extend or reassess perceptions. The issues raised in the first half of this book give a context in which to consider some of the issues and practices of women in Western theatre dance history. The training process, the critics' practices and funding policies all contribute to the production and reception of dance located as one of a number of cultural practices clearly influenced by factors such as class, race and gender. In this context the oppression of women is a part of dance practice; however, as illustrated, many women have consistently resisted oppression whenever possible. More recently there has been a growing recognition that the oppression of women cannot be separated from issues of race, class, sexual orientation, age and religion.

The concept of the social construction of the body opposes biological determinism and essentialism. As the body is central to dance training and practice, recognition that that which is socially constructed can be deconstructed offers a challenge to traditional practices. Deconstruction of the representations of women in dance enables rejection of restrictive, offensive images of women, because it involves analysis of images in terms of the differences and multiplicities of representations. Creating new images and an awareness for viewing comes from asking questions such as 'How can women present themselves on stage when woman equals sexuality?'

Undoubtedly, women will work both within and outside of the mainstream to create the dance they want. For some women, working within the major companies will mean that whilst they may make enormous contributions and achieve great success they are often, intentionally or otherwise, reinforcing the status quo rather than undermining it as is illustrated by the case of Ninette de Valois (see Chapter 5). In addition, what may begin as radical work may eventually become part of established modes as was the case with Martha Graham's technique and later choreography.

Female directors and choreographers in ballet and contemporary dance are likely to reinforce dominant practices as they are working within the mainstream. Although women's work in these dance forms is important because, simply by the act of directing and/or choreographing they are challenging male supremacy, this is not where subversive images/dance practice are likely to emerge. The subversives are likely to be the 'independents', the dance workers in small- to middle-scale companies, the choreographers/ performers/ directors working with limited budgets.

In this chapter I am concerned with women's work which does not accept restrictive views of women but which subverts the dominant gender stereotypes of Western culture, and expands boundaries of women's dance work. The examples used illustrate the themes raised throughout the book, including body image and 'the look', autonomy and relationships, similarities and differences and sexuality. The act of selecting work has presented a dilemma as discussion of individual women's work elevates it at the expense of other women's work. The choreography has been chosen for the issues of gender which it raises, which may or may not have been the conscious intention of the choreographer. It is not my intention either to reinforce any notions of genius of the individual artist, nor to highlight some dance works as more important or more 'feminist' than others, but rather to discuss women's work which subverts dance traditions and gender expectations.

Women working outside the mainstream, on limited budgets, frequently receive little comment from critics. This results in their work being lost and unavailable to future audiences and the distant researcher who cannot glean information at source. However, it is also likely that the lack of adequate funding in the 1980s and 1990s, particularly in the USA and England, has resulted in less radical work. Yet with so many obstacles to overcome, women's resilient determination to shape their own world comes through in the following examples of independent artists. One woman artist, when asked what this term meant to her replied, ' "Freedom to do the kind of work I want to do" but . . . it [also] means lack of funding, no support systems, casual work in between a tight rehearsal schedule, no union and little recognition' (Adair *et al.*, 1989, p. 28). In this country in contrast for example, with Holland and France, small-scale companies struggle for survival and artists frequently cannot develop their work in the ways they want to because the money is absent. It is no coincidence that this is where most women's work is concentrated. As we have seen in the classical and contemporary companies which are better funded and have some security, men predominate in positions of power. Women who do have positions as directors or choreographers in these structures suffer because they are in the minority and because of negative social attitudes to women in power. The 1970s emphasised collective politics of which the X6 Collective is a good example. The 1980s and 1990s, however, have emphasised consumer individualism and this has been evident in women's dance work. The emphasis on the image of the work has been as strong if not stronger than the emphasis on the action. The Cholmondeleys, for example, have collaborated with a photographer to produce distilled images of their work which is very effective but is removed from the dance context. The image is separated ready to be consumed (see Figure 27). This approach could be problematic, because to change attitudes, conditions and dance, work requires a collective support and strength rather than isolated, individualist stances.

It is significant that often when people think about women's work which they like or about opportunities for women dancers in this country they think in terms of numbers rather than power structures. So the fact that they can think of a number of women choreographing effectively indicates to them that women have equal opportunities to men. From the previous chapters it is evident that this is not the case, yet the myth persists. This was apparent from the responses to a festival of women's work entitled 'Danger! Women at Work!' (1988) at a prestigious London venue. The entire week of performances was sold out, indicating the popularity of such a festival. The Artistic Director, **Emilyn Claid**, was intent on presenting a range of women's performance work from dance and mime through to performance art, bringing together work from both established creators and newcomers.

27 The Cholmondeleys – '*Flag*'.

While covering a great range of skills and ideas, the work explores and expresses, in many ways, women's full power as creators and directors of the performing arts. I see it as a chance to state loud and clear that we are, and always have been, at the front line in the world of creative entertainment (Claid, press release, 1988).

In her introduction to the programme Claid made clear statements about some of the issues facing women artists. These statements were provocative and out of line with the views of the dance establishment, but they very much echo the themes which I have developed in this book. For example, she said:

In the white, male, heterosexual, middle-class system woman's role has inevitably been that of victim, waiting woman or cunning witch. If the woman artist no longer wishes to occupy that role, she must work outside the dominant structures of the system that created it (Claid, programme notes, 1988).

Women making their own work, like Claid, look for new structures and tactics with which to inform their practice. She outlines three examples. Firstly, women choreographers can make use of information they have concerned with relationships, emotions, sexuality and reproduction as source material for their work. These powerful sources of imagery are interconnected with issues of class and race. Secondly, by creating positive images of women performers our differences and our experiences will be highlighted in contrast to the 'ideal' woman. Thirdly, the performers can be involved in the creative process in a collaborative way rather than using a hierarchical model with which to work. There is a need, Claid emphasises, for all women in the arts to support each other's work in order for it to be recognised and clearly documented.

The festival was discussed by the critics in terms of politics rather than content so that some were concerned to correct Claid's 'mistaken' comments whilst others gave statistical backing to her points. For example, Jann Parry writing in *The Observer* (September 14, 1988) says, 'it is a misrepresentation of history to pretend that dance, of all the arts, has been dominated by heterosexual men, either as creators or administrators'. Mary Clarke writing in the *The Guardian* (2 September 1988) attacks Claid's statements by saying that whilst "the white, male, heterosexual, middle-class system" which relegates women to being "victim, waiting woman or cunning witch" may be so for much of society this is not the case for dance. Yet, as Nadine Meisner points out in *The Sunday Times* (4 September 1988), in the larger dance companies in Britain women's work is barely evident. For example, London Contemporary Dance Theatre between 1986 and 1988 performed only five works by women out of a total of twenty-seven (18.5%) and the Rambert Dance Company four out of twenty-two (18.2%). These figures are only a little better than those for the Birmingham Royal Ballet with four out of twenty-four (16.6%). However, out of twenty-nine ballets that the Royal Ballet Company staged and thirty-two from the English National Ballet none were by women (although the latter included two classical stagings by Natalia Makarova).

With deliberate intent

For some women choreographers gender issues are a primary concern. This leads them to question the way they work, the images they create and the politics of the dance work. In England, Emilyn Claid became Artistic Director of Extemporary Dance Theatre, a middle-scale touring dance company funded by the Arts Council, shortly after the X6 Collective disbanded. Claid sees a direct connection between the work which she did at X6 and that with Extemporary. It was an opportunity for Claid to put some of her ideas into practice in a middle-scale company rather than with a small-scale group, despite the restrictions of such a position.

She views her work as feminist and choreographs from a position which values the working process and draws out the performer's attributes, allowing emotional experiences, together with physical skills and awareness to shape the work.[1] *Grace and Glitter* (1987) (see Figure 28) co-directed with Maggie Semple, created a collective women's voice through a production which was designed, composed and performed by women. Tasha Fairbanks recorded text speaks of 'the tidal flood of women down the years'. For Claid and Semple, dance and politics are inseparable; the presentation of images which do not question race, class and gender and which continue to perpetuate oppressive images is unacceptable. Rather, dance can liberate through questioning hierarchical ways of working, making dances from real experiences, of real dancers, rather than idealised

28 Extemporary Dance Company – '*Grace & Glitter*'; directors Emilyn
Claid and Maggie Semple; dancers Chantal Donaldson and Kaye
Brown.

images, and contribute work which is meaningful in terms of
current issues.

Fundamental to women changing structures predominantly
controlled by men, has been the understanding that the personal
is political. That is, our feelings and personal lives are crucial to
political change. Sharing experiences of gender, race and class, is a
valuable way of making connections between, and challenging,
some of the oppressive economic and ideological structures.

Throughout the creative process of *Grace and Glitter* the dancers
read, took notes and talked about their own experiences of these
issues, and from this starting point created dance phrases and
theatrical scenes which were later structured. Through this way of
working the dancers retained their power and had a voice. The work
also had repercussions in their own lives. Ideas and theory began to
make a different kind of sense and became practice. The directors'

commitment to the process as well as the product was evident. By inviting me to record the process it was made visible (Adair, 1987). When the process as well as the product is made available, art is less mystifying.

Jacky Lansley, who was Artistic Director for English New Dance Theatre (also a founder member of X6 Collective), used her experience as a mother to create *Small Chair* (1986). The motivation for this piece she said came from her wish to integrate this experience.

> I worked with my own early physical memories and experiences, with Ursula's [her daughter] movements, and with the movements we made together. Juxtaposed with that I used ballet [she was a member of the Royal Ballet Company for two years], as a very stylised, rarefied form of movement. But within that very heightened physical form, you can actually find the same source and centre as in that early, beginning, grass roots movement (1987, p. 19).

Lansley developed the solo of *Small Chair* into a group piece *A Child's Play* (1987), 'drawing on the qualities children have, their constant sense of physicality and exploration' (1987, p. 20). Lansley described wanting to form a group of

> strange and bizarre characters who demand the right to creative freedom . . . It's interesting how rarely people deal with the relationships between adults and children, and how marginal children and their carers are in this society. That's why I want to do the piece. There are just so few interesting images of children around. So its's quite a political piece in a way. I want to attract an audience's attention by making a piece that's highly imaginative and creative; so many people assume that anything relating to children is boring and domestic. So this piece will be really sharp – not at all sentimental (Lansley, 1987, p. 20).

After a time directing and choreographing in mainstream theatre Lansley made a piece inspired by Shakespeare's *Richard II*.

> The piece isn't a remake of *Richard II*, I'm using material from the play to talk about other issues, such as the role of women in traditional theatre . . . In *The Breath of Kings* (1987) the women take control of the language . . . The women are involved in a conspiracy to take over the play and use it for their own ends – there's a kind of onstage and offstage form to the piece. It parallels the reality in our society, where women are often relegated to a 'backstage' position, where the only kind of power they can have is a hidden, conspiratorial one. The men take centre stage (Lansley, 1987, p. 20).

Lansley first presented this piece at the Dartington International Dance Festival which frequently provided a supportive setting within which to show work in progress. She then went on to develop it into a much longer piece. It is crucial that artists have opportunities to experiment, take risks and challenge the norms. This is particularly important for women because, as we have seen, it is the women performers and choreographers who usually have less access to the necessary funds and spaces.

Pina Bausch is one of the few women choreographers/directors to have both funds and space. The art form she works with is Tanztheater which has replaced ballet in some of the West German opera houses. In 1973 Bausch took over the somewhat obscure Wuppertal Dance Theater and introduced expression of reality rather than the illusion of ballet. The roots of her dance are from the Weimar Republic German dance and theatre traditions. She studied with Kurt Jooss, later teaching Ausdruckstanz, a modern expressionist style. Bausch's work is unique and ranges over fifteen years. The performers contribute extensively to the work and in a recent retrospective (1987) the point was made that without the original performers the pieces may be weaker (Schmidt, 1987).

Bausch's work is inspiring in a number of ways. Frequently, activities within the performance are simultaneous so that as the audience you create your own performance by choosing where and when to look at actions on the stage. The references to everyday activities and events are powerful. By framing familiar images within the proscenium arch or the confines of the camera (she works both with live performance and with film) we are presented with the opportunity of reflecting on images which we take for granted. Images re-occur throughout her work in a non-linear fashion and the intensity and unexpectedness of them ensures that they live on long after we have ceased to watch them. She is very much a choreographer dealing with contemporary issues of which a central concern is gender. In each of her pieces she works with the struggle between men and women and there is no neat end to the choreographies; instead we are left with a sense of going on and on . . .

An insight into how Bausch creates her work is given by Renate Klett (1984) in an article about the rehearsals for *Kontakthof*. In one section Bausch asks the company to show what they don't like about their bodies, they continue to add new 'complexes' until they can hardly move trying to hide their imperfections. On stage she is concerned with, 'recounting the universal history of the body'[2] (Kaplan, 1987, p. 5), but at the same time the audience is offered something of the real life of the people performing and there is no attempt to conceal the effort involved in the work, either physical or emotional. Bausch's work is important for the insights it affords us of human emotions and actions together with the exploitative nature of male/female relationships. Servos (1987) credits Bausch with making effective social comment. Kaplan (1987), however, challenges this view and sees Bausch's work as biologically determined feminism which is cynical and humourless. She states that Bausch presents women as 'victims, deprived of any meaningful agency' (p. 77).

It is true that Bausch's characters are not placed in specific social settings, thus lending strength to the idea of them as universal representations, but she does more than present women as victims. She shows their power, for example, as mothers, even if this power is limited by social constructions. By indicating male isolation as the cause of violence, she is making an important social comment because frequently such violence is reported without any attempt to connect it with social conditions.

Her portrayal of the legend of *Bluebeard – While Listening to a Tape Recording of Béla Bartók's Opera 'Duke Bluebeard's Castle*'[3] is of a relentless sexual struggle between women and men which is full of the inescapable pain of guilt and loneliness. One of the opening images is of Bluebeard lying curled in a foetal position, on top of Judith, inertly hanging on to her as she writhes underneath him across the floor. He is both adopting a male-dominant position on top of a woman and a helpless, passive baby position at the same time. She appears to be struggling for her very existence as she might when being born, or when being attacked. Or her pushing might be interpreted as giving birth. Fascination with Bausch's work is centred on her ability to create these images with multi-layered meanings which encourage a new perception of familiar experiences. There is a section in which Bluebeard stands with arms outstretched and Judith attempts to fall into them but he stands passively, letting her fall or leaving her to choose to fall repeatedly. This is an image which Bausch has used in other works including *Cafe Müller* (1978). The use of this type of image is extremely thought-provoking and can raise questions for the audience about male/female images, passivity and dependence. There is also a good deal of reference to violence within male/female relationships. Judith kneels in front of Bluebeard, reaching up to his face, but he forces her head down with his hands repeatedly even when she stands.

So many of Bausch's images comment vividly on the apparently insoluble problems between men and women and their different social roles and expectations. In *1980* (1980) one couple stand facing each other, the woman applies lipstick to her male partner's mouth and then kisses his face, this is repeated again and again until he looks scarred. In another section of *1980* a man walks in front of a line of women commanding them to jump in turn. He also gives them numbers. The references to the degradation of beauty contests are further reinforced when a woman comes forward and gives a lengthy list of an absurd collection of hobbies.[4] There are further references to display as the men and women line up alternately and display their legs in profile to the audience. The actors take it in turn to describe and indicate their real scars and how they got them. This is a very powerful contradiction to the myth of performers being perfect and having beautiful bodies.

Sexuality

Sexuality in dance is frequently explored in terms of women's relationships with men, which are presented, usually, from a male perspective. The choreography of the women in this chapter is a refreshing departure from that tradition either because it is performed by companies of women or where the work is performed by mixed companies another perspective is provided of male/female relationships. Both Boyce (see below) and Claid intentionally explore issues of sexuality in their work. Other choreographers for example, Glean, Jeyasingh (see below) and Lansley subvert traditional expectations making women's roles more central and powerful.

Sexuality is also central to much of Bausch's work. In *Bluebeard* one woman thrusts her pelvis at her male partner as she advances crab like towards him. At one point the women surround Bluebeard and holding their hair like a weapon hit him with it, then walk away individually examining their hair. At another point the women repeatedly pull the men's legs as they sit with their backs to the wall.

Immediately the women let go of their legs the men resume their original sitting position. The women seem to be urging men on to express more feelings and the men seem to be resisting. An impression is also formed of mothers with recalcitrant adolescents. Bausch creates a number of situations where the women's relationship to the men appears maternal. There is no easy solution in these images; instead we are left to grapple with the negative aspects of female experiences.

In Bausch's *Rite of Spring* (1975) woman is the subject rather than the object, experiencing her feelings from the inside, intent on her own events. The initial image is of a woman on the ground with her focus inward not looking out towards the audience; she is self-contained. No attempt is made to display the body, and although the costume is a sensuous silky slip it does not emphasise the line of the body. When the women are gathered together for unified group movement they retain individual identities by doing movements in their own ways. These movements are from a contained central point. The women begin the dance from their viewpoint and they introduce some of the key movements. Many of the movements collapse and curve rather than straighten in the phallic manner of the ballerina as a fetish (see Chapter 4). There is an integrity in the moments of exposure; for example, when one of the men stands behind a woman and feels her breasts, there is a reverent respect for her body evoking the wonder of a first sexual experience. The sacrifice of the woman is symbolised as loss rather than portraying her as a victim. Bausch's emphasis is different in this respect to other choreographies of the *Rite of Spring*. The energy of the piece is raw with a sense of task rather than display.

Although this is one interpretation, because of the dominant culture and the way in which women's bodies are usually viewed members of the audience could objectify the women performers and interpret the work differently. The interpretation is dependent not only on the work but also on the audience. This work is a good example of the erotic in Lorde's terms, the presentation of women's autonomous sexual power (see Chapter 4).

Sexuality was amongst several themes in Bausch's *Lament of the Empress* (made as a video production, 1989) which also included the decay of civilisation, mothering, and an almost Alice Millerish type comment on our attitude to children (1985).[5] Bausch also connected personal concerns with the wider issue of a global crisis in future terms. One of the most profound images which emerges throughout the piece is that of a wandering bunny girl staggering through squidgy mud. There is a sense of death as we watch the girl, who is undoubtedly a woman lost and betrayed, at odds with her home the earth and the landscape. The non-linear structure of Bausch's work allows the audience to make connections in unexpected ways. At one point we see the bunny girl digging in the mud, perhaps looking for what she has lost by such a confined, degrading role. The next scene is of a male, mud-covered body gyrating to music. It is as though Bausch challenges the myths of sexuality and presents them in their nakedness with the lights on. The closing image of an older woman dancing alone to some band music in a corridor with absorption and enjoyment is a powerful image of female autonomy.

In New York, **Crowsfeet Dance Collective** are also concerned with female autonomy. 'Crowsfeet' is used to describe the lines at the corner of the eyes and it is often seen as a negative aspect of women's ageing, but for the company, those lines symbolise experience, wisdom and humour. They describe themselves as 'a multicultural dance company' (publicity information) which formed in 1984 when Wallflower Order disbanded. Their aim is to use the tools of dance, theatre, song and humour for social change. They use a variety of dance and movement styles and each member's heritage (Black, Latin, Jewish and Asian) informs the collective's work.

Disappeared (1984) is a vibrant, deeply politicised dance.

> As the name indicates, [it] pays tribute to the tens of thousands of Latin American victims of right-wing regimes from Chile to El Salvador. Midway through the piece, the dancers put on masks that have the odd effect of simultaneously depersonalizing and unifying them, as if, in losing themselves, they become everyone (Mutnick, 1988 pp. 18–20).

Barbie's Revenge (1985) is a comment on the effects on women caught in the web of consumerism. Crowsfeet's intention in this dance is to 'speak of the danger that something as simple as a plastic doll can represent to the values of future generations' (Torres, 1986, p. 6).

Dance Brigade has also evolved from the Wallflower Order and is based in California. They say:

our dance style deliberately breaks with the traditional stereotype of female dancers – we use broad strong techniques that require physical strength as well as grace, and our movements, influenced by the martial arts and gymnastics, are expansive rather than constrained (publicity information, 1988).

They don't have typical dancers' bodies which they view positively. Also, their work does not separate art from politics.

Krissy Keefer, co-director of the company with Nina Fichter, says, 'We owe our life's breath to the women's movement and a huge proportion of them are lesbian women. Since the beginning of Wallflower, we've included lesbians, bi-women and heterosexuals in the collective. And we always perform at least one piece in every concert that celebrates women together' (publicity information, 1988).

Bring the War Home (1984) 'was a long, riveting, and sometimes hilarious account of a woman's personal growth and change in the 60's. It included lots of body contact (lifts, counterbalances) even our worst youthful fears of acne!' (Carroll-Smith, 1988).

Personal/political issues

It can be a political statement to work from the personal. Claid, Lansley and Bausch as described above all incorporated some personal experience or viewpoint in their way of working. **Johanna Boyce** working in the USA has also effectively used autobiographical material in her choreography. In talking about her work she says that she gets tired of the narrow American understanding of female and the ways in which women are frequently viewed and she is interested in presenting herself and her experiences differently. She says, 'Its hard to find advice about how to run your own life. I feel art can address those issues by presenting situational experiences. It's information for living' (Smith, 1985, p. 52). In *Only connect . . .* (1981), the first overtly autobiographical piece which Boyce made, she weaves the story of her younger brother's accidental death with the disappearance of a friend from El Salvador forming a 'moving, controlled meditation on memory and loss' (Smith, 1985, p. 50).

Boyce has not been through the traditional dance training, sealed off within the dance world. She is able to use some of the postmodern dance techniques in a new way because she does not have the originators' concerns of rebelling against restricting techniques. For Boyce the relationship of the individual to the group is important as is the focus of feminist concerns also. Boyce works with untrained dancers. Their attitude is task-orientated rather than seeking audience approval. The look we see in the work is different from mainstream dance because these performers have not spent years using their bodies as instruments. As Boyce points out, 'I've always wanted to subvert a certain way of looking at women and the easiest way is to use really unusual body types'. (in Goldberg and Albright, 1987/88, p. 46). The dancers have a more casual approach but one which is based on an ease with themselves which allows them to take risks within performance. They are mostly her friends so a supportive trust is established.

In *Ties That Bind 2* (1984) Boyce wanted to investigate love relationships between women.

> I felt that if I could select moments from each of the women's histories that anybody could empathize with, people would come to understand their position. I was particularly interested in seeing whether or not lesbianism is nature or nurture. I thought that in exploring the background of the two women, some of that would come out. I was confused at the end. Both women come from matriarchal families with strong grandmothers – liberal environments that gave them freedom to choose their partners. I deliberately incorporated that information in the text they spoke while they danced (quoted in Goldberg and Albright, 1987–8, p. 49).

'The look' – body image

In Western society there is an obsession with visual images and recording them (Coward, 1984). For women, this means being reduced to and equated with our bodies. To present an image which challenges that expectation in an art form which uses the body is not an easy task. The perpetuation of ideal physical standards leads to an over-emphasis on 'looking right', which results in women frequently feeling alienated from our bodies. The way we look has been, and still is, crucially important to the way we feel about ourselves as women.

The work of **Liz Aggiss**, an English choreographer, has its roots in the German expressionist dance tradition. Aggiss' study with Hanya Holm encouraged her to work with her experience and to be concerned with the initiation of ideas rather than an over-emphasis on the external image. This is part of the appeal of Aggiss' work, which has much in common with the work of Pina Bausch. Parallels which are evident are the use of a number of performing skills (dancing, singing, mime), powerful theatricality (use of costume, lighting and props are all central), creating a definite relationship with the audience often in a challenging way and an integration of music with the total idea of the piece (Briginshaw, 1988).

Whilst the images of women Aggiss presents are a strong contrast to what we usually see on stage, there are also many ambivalences in her work. There is always a tight-rope to be walked when attempting to subvert the accepted conventions. There is the risk the work will be misunderstood. Unfortunately, some of her work does lend itself to voyeuristic viewing. For example, in *Dead Steps* (1988) there is a female solo in which the dancer, on the floor, interweaves her legs and arms in a masturbatory fashion. Whilst this could be read as a woman strongly focussing attention on herself and establishing her autonomy, the fact that the dancer looks out in a suggestive manner, the display of her crotch during the sequence and the similarity of such imagery with that used in pornography means that it is much more likely to be viewed in a voyeuristic manner.

Although the critics frequently talk about the choreography as solely that of Liz Aggiss, Aggiss herself is adamant that her male collaborator Billie Cowie is completely involved in the creative process to such an extent that they are never sure who has created specific elements in the work. However, Aggiss' background is dance and Cowie's is music. Aggiss is aware of and challenges our preconceptions of women performers, and gender is a conscious focus of the work which is at times blatant at others more subtle. *Die Orchidee im Plastik-Karton* (1988) was a comment on some of the ridiculous phrases in a BBC German language course. Sexual stereotyping is sharply satirised. As the women scuttle backwards and forwards on hands and feet, pelvises thrust upwards, the endless repetition of domestic work which is usually done by women is made apparent to the background recital of the phrase '*dann geht sie Einkaufen – Hausfrau und Mutter*' (then she goes shopping – housewife and mother).

The descriptions the critics use of Aggiss' work indicate the subversive nature of much of it. Their reactions to her work have varied from incomprehension and sarcasm[6] to enthusiasm and understanding of a new approach[7]. In terms of challenging the expectations of mainstream dance her work is uncompromising. Aggiss is concerned with making pieces which are relevant to today's audiences. Human feelings and sexuality are themes which she confronts with a shocking starkness. As Aggiss says, 'It's good to make works that assail you, involve you, make you think about what you believe in' (quoted in Tawn, 1989, p. 73).

Aggiss'/Cowie's performance group The Divas are a group of six women with different dance experiences and occupations and they vary in age. The very composition of the group, as they step on stage, is a challenge to the tradition of dance because they do not conform to accepted standards of aesthetics for women performers. This in itself is a political statement. Aggiss further emphasises this with the costumes, such as vests and y fronts, which emphasise the different body shapes and the vulnerability of the performers. She is constantly searching for a new female aesthetic, a fresh way to look at the body and other ways to move. Also make-up is used for grotesque effects rather than its usual use to beautify. The dancers often have stark white faces, eyes rimmed with black and blood-red lips.

In *Grotesque Dancer* (1986) (see Figure 29), a solo by Aggiss, there are many ambiguities and contradictions which force the audience to think about their own reactions and perceptions. Using a German cabaret style of the 1920s and 1930s it combines a tremendous power and strength with painful vulnerability. The images of relentless physical exercises and body building to militaristic rhythms convey the harsh fanaticism of the Hitler Youth Movement. This work comments on the precarious exposure with which a performer works. Also apparent is male surveillance of women. When Aggiss, facing away from the audience, bends and reaches between her legs, feeling her buttocks, woman's colonised body, devoured by the voyeurism of the audience, is portrayed. Later Aggiss takes off her wig to reveal a shaved head; she shockingly defies the conventional ideas of female beauty. She is transformed from an ambivalent character in black bloomers, white socks and top to a frighteningly vulnerable creature with shaven head in long, black satin gown. She limps off, one shoe in hand leaving the audience to make sense of the issues of power, oppression, female experience and imagery which have been encountered.

29 Liz Aggiss – '*Grotesque Dancer*'.

30 Molissa Fenley – Dance Umbrella, Riverside Studios

Molissa Fenley (see Figure 30), an American, presents an alternative female image quite differently to the women discussed so far. She has been described as 'The Human Tornado' (Moszynska, 1983). Her work is extremely athletic, and relentlessly dynamic. She is adamantly independent and the focus in her work is very much dance itself. Her influences include her early childhood experiences in Africa, and she sees a ritualistic quality in her work. One of the appeals of her choreography is the energy the audience pick up from performers dancing at their peak, almost confronting them. This approach to dance is very popular and complements the body perfection and fitness trends. Very fit, powerful, energetic women challenge the stereotype of women as passive and submissive; but if the superfit, superwoman image merely becomes another stereotype that too becomes limiting.

Although training is important, Fenley thinks there is too much focus on her methods which detract from the work itself. In *State of Darkness* (1988) set to Stravinsky's music *Le Sacre du Printemps*, she creates an amazing feat of both expression and sheer energy. It is powerful in delivery and also because there is no reference to woman as victim. Through repetition of large, circular arm gestures, space-eating, skipping jumps together with fluttering stomach movements and criss-crossing arms, the dance accumulates power. Fenley dances in black tights, leaving her torso bare so that her movements are clearly visible. The physical demands of the piece and emphasis on the task detract from voyeuristic perception.

Lea Anderson is forthright about the images she creates and the stereotypes she is challenging. She formed an all-female group in 1984 which she named the Cholmondeleys after her first piece *The Cholmondeley Sisters*, which, in turn, was named after a seventeenth-century painting. The group toured a variety of non-dance venues, from crowded bars to foot tunnels under a river. This provided an excellent training ground for making the work dynamic, with immediate impact. One of the key features of Anderson's work is her use of gesture and communication of another 'language'. She is interested in tackling political issues but not head on; as she describes it, 'rather like assuming there's been a sex-war and we've won'.[8]

Her background in ballet allows her to use it as a starting point and then subvert the tradition as in *Marina* (1987). Balletic vocabulary is combined with silent gaping mouths, wide-eyed stares and fishy undulations. Anderson's use of unconventional gestures puts balletic references and movements into a different context.

Perhaps because of this background she says that she is obsessed with body image in a negative way, so that if a dancer has a 'dancerly' body she is prejudiced against her. She wants her audience to identify with the people on stage and that means choosing performers who do not fit the dancer stereotype. However, the dancers need to be highly skilled so that the audience recognise that they have been mistaken in their narrow image of what a dancer should look like. She is concerned with her dancers' welfare so that she would not put them in a costume in which they did not feel both comfortable and confident. However, this can cause problems with such a mixed group of body shapes when the intention is for the group to wear the same style costume.[9] The visual impact of Anderson's work is central and the images she creates retain a lasting impression.

Dragon (1985) presents us with striding, heroic women who fill the space, glaring, gesticulating fiercely to the pounding music. The rush of almost manic movement builds through the simple structure of presenting the material first as a solo, then a duo and finally as a trio. It is intense, moving and left me wanting the dance to go on. This is no mean achievement, when many dances do not get the pruning they need for impact.

The conscious choice to work with an all women company was used to good effect in *No Joy* (1987). Anderson used the idea of making contact between people through touch in a matter of fact way after being influenced by people with visual disabilities. Some dancers stand facing the audience whilst others manipulate their faces, whilst there is a sensual quality to the movement, the focus is on the contact between the people in a way which would not be possible if it was a mixed group. Interpretations of such movements and gestures in a male/female group would be heavily dominated by sexual meanings which would undermine Anderson's intentions.

Ever keen to develop her work, Anderson founded an all male company called the Featherstonehaughs, which was originally set up as a one-off project but proved so successful it has continued. Anderson's wit and ability to parody social behaviour is evident in the short dances which make up their programmes. *Clump* (1988) is reminiscent of a group of suited business men on a London tube, pressed together, they change places, wiggle their fingers, scratch their ears, move off to their destinations until one is left alone. The light-humour of the piece enables the audience to reconsider men's roles and the conformity, pressure and isolation which they experience. Lea Anderson combined the Featherstonehaughs and the Cholmondeleys for a full length work entitled *Flag* (1988) (see Figure 27).

> I wanted to explore the idea of what goes in to building a culture. Most people feel some sympathy with some kind of nationalism but when it goes too far you end up with US imperialism and the like . . . I'd always been interested in the ideas that surround nationalism, but the Olympics really pointed it up. You get situations like 'One man shames the whole of Canada' – that kind of ridiculous idea which people take seriously' (quoted in Watson, December 1988, p. 108).

Anderson mixes and matches a variety of images and styles gleaned from such diverse sources as communist and fascist propaganda posters, Scottish Highland and Spanish flamenco dance and the world competition of the Olympics in her quest to understand and question cultural confrontations. The brilliantly observed characteristic gestures of particular nations are combined with costumes which frequently mix up a number of associations. Costumes for women frequently emphasise the objectification of the dancer, which is then confirmed by the movement. The costumes Lea Anderson uses, designed by Sandy Powell, are as witty as her movement. Like the movement there are many layers of meanings from which the audience can create a variety of interpretations. In *Duet* the male/female couple wear white, satinised lycra. Her outfit is a top and skirt, his a top and tights. The partnering in the pas de deux signify ballet principals. The tennis shoes and sweatbands signify tennis stars. The net covering of the woman's skirt together with the head-dress suggest bridal couples. The costumes with such multi-layered meanings draw on references from social codes reflected in the way we dress. A subversive comment is made at the expense of our conditioned responses to stereotypes and objectification, thus subverting the social code (Adair *et al.*, 1989).

Not only does Anderson subvert objectification by her choice of dancers who do not conform to an 'ideal' body image, but also by stressing such differences in the choreography. The varied line ups and formations emphasise people's individuality and uniqueness. It is harder to objectify dancers when their individuality is so evident. Anderson usually avoids men lifting women because of the reinforcement of the dominant heterosexual imagery and sense conveyed of women being manipulated. She also emphasises the task of a movement rather than its potential for display so that rather than the extended line of an arabesque we are more likely to see the leg thrust from the body in action.

Social class is an important aspect of human society and yet is notoriously difficult to comment upon in dance. Usually we see a reinforcement of traditional class values within ballet, *Giselle* being an obvious example. In *Rabble* (see Figure 27) two sections of *Flag*, which both precede and follow *Duet*, many pertinent comments on the strengths of working class peoples are made, using an image of European peasants. The men wear trousers and boots with naked torsos and the women are dressed in cotton dresses covered with large white aprons and boots. There is a sense of unity as the group dance close together with great vigour and strength, with clenched fists, sharp turns and an impression of endless effort. The life-force communicated by this group despite the apparent hardship is effectively contrasted by the artificial, sterile pas de deux of the lycra-enclosed couple in *Duet*. Their balletic lines and lifts crumple in falls as they fail to support each other, having lost the unity and connection which the *Rabble* clearly have. The return of this group is a hopeful note as though the strength and power of working-class people will subvert the establishment and false values that the *Duet* represent.

In *Flesh and Blood* (1989), Anderson works with a seven-strong company of women who offer golden images in shimmering dresses which sweep and swirl with confined yet exacting movements. The initial solo of a high priestess, maybe from a medieval age, discloses the entrapment. If the costumes for one second suggest the garb of titillation, the giant crab-like, arched, extended stretches on the floor, revealing black tights, instantly banish such thoughts. The obsessions, fanaticisms and confinements which we experience are here laid bare. At times lying closely together in their gold foil, the performers are reminiscent of sardines; at others, they kneel touching the floor in front of them with exaggerated care, transforming domestic chores into religious rites (Adair, 1989).

Role reversal

There are a number of different approaches which women choreographers can take to male/female roles if they wish to subvert them. The most obvious is to reverse the roles, such as by women lifting men. This immediately challenges the display of women and also the assumption that women lack physical strength (however, this tactic is limited in its effectiveness; see Chapter 4). **Senta Driver**'s work is an obvious example here. As a choreographer, she is fascinated by the concept of physical power. Her use of weight presents different values in her dances, with women moving in ways which challenge gender stereotypes. She believes in sensuality and the erotic potential of movement as being part of aliveness. Her work is refreshing for the variation of roles and images which it offers for women. There have been dances in which women carry men much heavier than themselves and her work has been described as athletic, even bizarre. Driver also has a clear stance against the image of the ideal dancer. She has deliberately sought dancers for her company whose physicality does not match the much sought-after ideal. Driver is very interested in working with large variations in dancers' sizes and with momentum. When she was told that women were not strong enough for momentum lifting with men she took it as a challenge and proved the comment wrong (Lewis, 1982). One of the results was *Missing Persons* (1981). Her resolution to break with the traditions of men lifting women was formed during her time with the Paul Taylor Company when the lifts were always tried out first with the biggest man lifting the smallest women. As a consequence the tallest women had less practice and were blamed for any difficulties in lifting. Driver said, 'After they said that to me enough, I thought the hell with this, I'll do the lifting myself' (in Daly, 1987/1988, p. 90). As she points out, lifting is little to do with sheer strength and everything to do with timing and co-operation.

She views gender construction as a prison resulting in 'real men' and 'real women' which has to be fought against (Daly, 1987/1988). Driver shares some values with the early modern dancers of the thirties such as Graham and Humphrey, with her emphasis on breaking the rules, looking for new ways of making dance, and her use of size, mass and weight which emphasise women's presence and power.

Subversion or reinforcement

Although modern dance began in Germany, the war interrupted its development. It became more established in the USA and there has been a tendency to look there for innovation. This has begun to change, however, with the work of Bausch in Germany, and the innovations of De Keersmaeker in Belgium and the thriving dance scenes in Holland and France. Many of the images these and English choreographers work with are balanced precariously between subversion and reinforcement.

Anne Teresa De Keersmaeker formed the company Rosas in 1983 after studying at Bejart's Mudra school and New York University. She, like Bausch, is searching for an authentic form of dance theatre which answers her questions. In *Hoopla* (Channel 4 television, May 1988), De Keersmaeker combines a minimalistic structure, physical energy and theatricality from her previous work to Bartók's evocative music. She is also interested in working with text in order to get away from the work being abstract. Her starting point is movement from her own practice and discoveries. The four female dancers, dressed in loose dresses and boots, create slow side steps in unison, building a wonderful sense of flow. I question some of the imagery used when one of the women drops forward exposing her white pants and crotch. A sense of young girls is created but there is an ambivalence about their innocence because this innocent image has been appropriated by pornography. De Keersmaeker may be commenting on this, but the ambivalence is problematic as it is in some of Liz Aggiss' work. There is a sensuousness and a self-contained joy as the dancers push back their hair and turn, whirling their full skirts. In contrast they stride down the space with powerful walks in their boots, creating a rhythm with stamping feet. There are skips, hops and model-like walks, a shared game between the girls. But the sense of autonomy is undermined by some of the images which border on and play with soft porn stereotypes.

Angelika Oei has a similar style to de Keersmaeker in *Oidan . . . Skroeba* (1987) she creates vibrant images of young women's rebellious, gawky, power as they make their discoveries together. Dressed in schoolgirl tunics, the three dancers stamp out dance steps, following dance manuals which they hold. The forceful steps create a maze of semi-circular pathways on the sand-covered floor. At the edge of the set are memories of childhood: small chairs, a desk, and a world globe. There is a humorous sense of play and support between the dancers and at times one manically conducts the others' movements, reflecting the ways in which women are controlled and observed within society. The energy of both the music and the dancing is full of insistent rhythms to which the dancers fling themselves into ungainly jumps, sometimes with a sense of sheer, uncontained joy.

Ausdruckstanz had a deep influence on Dutch dance. The absence of a dance tradition in Holland has been fruitful and the fringe has grown fast. It has been easier to get things going and money has been more available when compared with England.[10]

The French government has encouraged the arts, resulting in numerous projects and events. The work is comparatively well funded with companies in the regions having enough money to tour without hardship. French dance has been influenced by German dance, with Valeska Gert, Wigman and Jooss all performing in Paris. This influence was heightened with the advent of the second world war when artists fleeing Nazism arrived in France (Bonis, 1988).

A French company which use their skills to comment on gender are La P'tite Cie. They have an edge to their wit expressing many aspects of women's experience. The company of three women dancers provide a stimulating and good-humoured look at pre-judice in some of its many forms. In one image three women are dressed for the office in silky blouses fussily tied at the neck with large bows and pleated skirts. To fast folk music, they cup their breasts, jump with flat feet and skulk the stage with giant crab-like movements interweaving with each other. The power of their performance is intensified by the still moments which are particularly strong. The dancers change into slinky black dresses and highlight the relentless pressure on women to look good by gesturing to areas which are frequently referred to as 'problems', for example, their buttocks, breasts, chins etc. Their humour is evident throughout but especially when they come down to the audience and shake out three small Rambo-type dolls and proceed to blow them up. With dead-pan faces the women rock these plastic 'tough guys' back and forth, gradually increasing the force until they are jerking the dolls up and down. The dancers eventually deflate them with a superb look of satisfaction on their faces. The women are reclaiming their power and making a humourous dig at male egos at the same time.[11]

In order to be radical, choreographers and dancers need to embrace political content as well as to be aware of the problems of body image and objectification. In a world where meanings and statements are dominated by men and our culture has been constructed by men, we need to understand how this has come about. In **Yolande Snaith**'s *Lessons in Social Skills* (1988) she examines nineteenth-century girls' education and many aspects of womens' roles in society to do with domesticity, caring, nurturing, education and health institutions which depend on womens' work. (This is underlined by the use of the text from *The Young Ladies' Journal*.) By doing this she invites the audience to think about how this has shaped our culture. Her ingenious use of props and movement in this dance throw absurd social conventions into sharp relief. The main prop in the dance is a column of closets filled with chamber pots which are used as bustles, hats, musical instruments, and containers for fruit and veg. The continual re-ordering of the pots, filling them, emptying them, tidying them away reminds us of the never-ending domestic chores which both engage and confine women (Adair *et al.*, 1989).

Most of Snaith's work has either been solo or with Kathy Crick. Snaith said she deliberately chose to work with another woman as such a partnership was compatible with the ideas which she wanted to develop. In *Can Baby Jane Can Can?* (1987) (see Figure 31) a reading of a lesbian relationship is available. The two women, dressed in forties-style suits, juggling with tin cans which chaotically roll from suitcases, create a wartime scenario of rations, espionage and female solidarity. It was, Snaith says, a time when many women 'came out'.

A scenario of three women's lives was created in a television production *Step in Time Girls* (Channel 4, 1988) which was a collaboration between Snaith and the filmmaker Terry Braun. Set in a flat in Rotherhithe, images of the women's lives are presented. One woman lived there soon after the flat was built in the Victorian era, another during the second world war and the third woman is a present day occupier. The juxtaposition of the three lives creates a thread between each woman's daily experiences at home in her flat, during very different social climates.

Snaith's work shows her concern with visual impact and subverting dance categories. She deliberately uses exaggerated costume as an integral part of her pieces. In *Lessons in Social*

31 Yolande Snaith with Kathy Crick – '*Can Baby Jane Can Can?*'.

Skills (1988) there are references to historical dress fashions. As she says, 'women's clothing is tied up with the body and the different ideals for the human body have changed so much, look at paintings to see the absurd outfits women wore to fit in with the ideals of the time – it is the same with silk ballet shoes, there are gruesome feet underneath.'[12]

Similarities and differences

The issues of visual impact, body image, ways of working, and political motivations are similar in many important aspects for both white and black women but there are also significant differences. The force of racism and its adverse effects on black women choreographers and performers have been discussed in Chapter 8.

As Bryan *et al.* (1985) point out,

> Any expression by a Black woman of her cultural and political identity must be seen to represent centuries of struggle. Whatever we present and however we define ourselves comes directly from that history . . . Whether our statement is conscious, or instinctive ... it will serve to reaffirm our rejection of the dominant culture and its attempted negation of our way of life. So any act of cultural defiance or ideological independence – whether it be through song, dance, our use of language . . . testifies to our existence *outside* the roles in which British society has cast us (p. 212).

In **Beverley Glean**'s choreography for her company Irie! she consciously subverts images of women as frail and reinforces their power. Male/female duos are seldom used because of the stereo-types associated with such partnering.[13] In *Cease 'n' Settle* (1989) (see Figure 32) Glean creates characters from the black community, showing the interactions which might be seen on any inner-city street. The gestures of greetings, dismissal and arguments all seem familiar; indeed, her inspiration came from watching groups on a street near her home during a hot summer.

Most of **Jawole Willa Jo Zollar**'s Company Urban Bush Women are in their thirties and she enjoys drawing on their maturity. As she says, 'You find that when you reach your 30s it's easier to throw off society's constraints to get to the essence of your womanhood' (Griffiths, 1987, p. 48). She points out that it is a western idea to stop dancing at forty.

Zollar was at one point discouraged from dancing because her body shape did not fit the required image but she eventually realised that this was a Western aesthetic which, unfortunately, even today is required for white and black classical dancers (Griffiths, 1987).

32 Irie! – '*Cease 'n' Settle*'; choreographer Beverley Glean.

The strength of Zollar's work as in *Bitter Tongue* (1987) (see Figure 24) and *Anarchy, Wild Women and Dinah* (1986) is in the sense of voluptuous enjoyment that the performers convey, together with their obvious co-operativeness. These are loud, defiant women taking the space and reminding us of their African heritage together with their American experience.

The Indian Summer Seasons (1987–89) at The Place have provided a forum for Asian artists to present their work, some of whom have begun to explore their art forms together with Western influences. **Shobhana Jeyasingh** has had to confront racism and ignorance as she has fused ideas from East and West. For example, she says there is a misunderstanding that classicism is rooted in Italy and Greece, ignoring India. However, her work has also been widely acclaimed by the media.

Jeyasingh, like many other women in this chapter, feels she has more liberty when dancing a solo or with other women, free from the interpretations usually put upon male/female work. She also points out that ornamentation is an important part of Indian life and dance, and for her as a female dancer this includes being at ease with sensuality.[14] The stamina in her dance and the image of woman which she presents is a challenge to the sexual stereotypes of Western ballet and contemporary dance.

In *Configurations* (1989) (see Figure 33) a collaboration with the composer Michael Nyman, she combines Bharata Natyam technique with some of the methods of contemporary dance. The dance is in six parts for three female dancers, exploring a theme of alienation. The discordant rhythms of the music and dance portray the outsider's realisation that the traditional pose of the other two dancers is the perfect image, but there is no real resolution. The configurations of the last section show everyone dancing together but differently, with more exploration of space, sometimes different patterns, sometimes relating and sometimes not. The coming together at the end is very important, establishing a strength and oneness. Jeyasingh's work breaks with tradition and she presents her ideas with a clear commitment.

Women only

Innovative explorations were also central to the women only events which emerged with the Women's Movement. The emphasis on women only space was fuelled by a determination not to be defined by men and to create a positive space for women apart from the

33 Shobhana Jeyasingh Dance Company – '*Configurations*'.

male-dominated structures. Whilst women-only dance companies do not necessarily come from this consciousness, the dance practice is inevitably affected and the potential for sexism in male/female partnering is eliminated.

Johanna Boyce is able to accent differences among women in an all women company. Empathy and trust allow her to ask the women in her company to look at certain issues however, she feels that she does not know the male experience sufficiently to do that with men (Daly, 1987–8). As she says, women are allowed greater freedom with our emotions than men and she sees that as the primary reason why women were central to modern dance. She also talks about her experience of mothering, informing her work on an emotional level:

> There's something about bearing a child that really freed me up to feel myself in a way that was different from feeling myself observed, in the way that I felt defined by the masculine gaze for a lot of my experience (in Daly & Martin eds, 1988, p. 100).

Johanna Boyce talks about experiencing herself as a mother as central and powerful and about wanting to explore the female as assertive matriarch.

Françoise Sergy works both from her own experience and with direct messages around themes concerned with sexual politics, for example, rape, women and health, women as objects in a consumer society. As a soloist she avoids the traditional power relationship between men and women in the roles of choreographer/director and performer. She uses a collage format involving a variety of media which inform the audience of the message and tries to provoke an emotional engagement with the audience. Her movement vocabulary ranges from self-defence to classical ballet in her attempt to formulate a new language that expresses womens' experience. She creates laughter at the expense of the dominant aesthetic (Adair *et al.*, 1989). In *Grounds to Act* (1985) an enquiry into male violence, Sergy creates a positive statement about how self-defence can assist women to fight back; for example, as she flings herself at the wall, climbs it and bounces off it she repeatedly shouts 'No!' with authority and determination.

Women's relationships

In order to survive restrictive structures, women rely heavily on networks of friends. Indeed a woman without a best friend is very lonely. Young women chose a friend with whom they can share the new identities which they are inventing and practising (Eichenbaum & Orbach, 1987b). As they continue life's journey, women seek and find female companionship, boosting each other's confidence and helping with the emotional tussles of every day. Female friendship is a close relationship, sharing experiences, pain and challenge. Tremendous co-operation, support and pleasure is gained in these friendships.

In *Girlfriends* Jawole Willa Jo Zollar makes a playful dig at women's competitiveness and desires to be attractive and conform to a particular look. As one woman moons about in her new underwear the others exaggeratedly mime an enormous group laugh which has the effect of undermining her seriousness and the sexuality of the image, but the group are united as they all share the laugh.

In *Grace and Glitter* (1987) the dancers' discussed women who were important in their own lives, looked at photographs and read texts creating a basis from which material was gathered. An important relationship for women within the family is that of sisters. For this production two sisters wrote about their memories and impressions of each other and also about themselves. From these initial ideas and further talking, each created a movement phrase, thinking at the same time of a particular mood. The many sides of such a relationship are explored in the duo, from affection and fun, to competition with each other. There is a hand clasp on the ground, repeated when they are standing, which is both combative and supportive. The blues music played underlies the harshness and softness between the sisters. As we have seen, black women are marginalised within dance, rarely seen in classical companies and only in ones and twos in contemporary companies. In this production when the black women are together their presence is established. The importance of black women taking their rightful place in dance, or anywhere else for that matter, begins to be recognised.

In addition to co-operation, competition is also a key factor in women's relationships. We learn from an early age to compete for our mother's attention. As we grow up the competition is to find the 'right man' and the pressure on us to enter this competition is strong; 'competitive structures are embedded in our social relations' (Eichenbaum & Orbach, 1987a, p. 104). These competitive feelings come from restrictions placed on women's autonomy and visibility. They are about the desire to be separate, and to achieve our dreams but without crippling doubts and a sense of inadequacy. From our unconscious deprived feelings and a sense that we may not get our needs met, women compete with each other and feel envious. We try to hold each other back. Why? As long as we do not feel good within ourselves and are encouraged to look to others, especially men, to achieve our place in the world, we will be frightened of women's successes. If we hold each other back these feelings are kept hidden (Chernin, 1983).

Gaby Agis works with close friends in her company as she then feels closer to how they think and feel, which is important as the work is very much about the performers and begins with improvisation. She organises the overall structure but the performers are very much collaborators within that. She says, 'It's . . . wanting dancers to take responsibility for their creation within the piece' (quoted in Salvadori, 1985). She works with performers who are able to work with improvisation processes and be vulnerable which, because of society's constraints, most men find difficult. 'The whole problem about men dancers is that there's such a stigma about being seen as feminine. So they all jump as high as possible and lift the women as high as possible and act as macho as possible. They don't let the more sensitive and humble side of their dancing come through' (quoted in Salvadori, 1985). Agis is interested in the women she works with not being restricted to stereotypes. There is a sensual quality in Agis' work which lends itself to both a lesbian and a feminist interpretation (Pascal, 1988). Whilst Agis is appreciative of that she is concerned that such interpretations will limit audiences' viewing of the complexities of the work.

Close Streams (1983), a duo for Gaby Agis and Helen Rowsell, begins in darkness with the sound of boots. When the lights come up we are confronted with two women in Victorian underwear and boots, out of breath after running. The dancers are extremely aware and sensitive to each other, using the skin contact and weight to build up movement which comes gradually like a breath, from stillness. By being themselves they destroy some of the illusions about women. Agis says, 'I'm very conscious of the way women are, and how they dress, and how that changes how you stand in society, and how you're seen' (in Godliman, 1983, p. 27).

The tangible intuition which Agis began to develop in *Close Streams* is very apparent in her duo with Charlotte Zerbey *Trail* (1986). In a long gallery space with Kate Blacker's sculptures, two long strips of corrugated steel placed at each end, the two dancers advance slowly towards each other. They crawl, roll, gathering in the space, building to lifting each other, jumping and stopping and balancing. The movement comes from an inner impulse passed between them. On reaching the sculptures they stamp and jump on them creating a very satisfying metallic noise.[15]

Rosemary Lee creates equally memorable images in *Egg Dances* (1988) (see Figure 34) with a cast comprising of dancers aged from nine to seventy-five. Power shifts of children leading adults, women catching men in flying leaps, results in an empowering dance. The sense of community which many of us have lost and yet so often long for is here re-created with the fun and exhilaration of chasing games; with women and men listening, with every fibre of their beings, to the lead of the smallest member of the group and with a poignant image of a small boy perched on a man's shoulder. Both the strength and the caring, the passion and the fragility are evident in a myriad of images created. The final image of children carefully placing eggs all over the stage through which they lead the adults (eyes closed), never breaking any, creates an impression of the precariousness of our lives and yet also our ability to succeed. Lee's work is important because she has presented a range of relationships, which are often central to women's lives, within a thought-provoking context.

Ways of working

Yoshiko Chuma has created work for a cast of a hundred. Her openness to her choice of performers and making work for such large numbers is radical. Her work is very much influenced by the personal, with performers teaching and sharing experiences. She is interested in performers finding movement inspired by their own physicality and focusses on tasks when making a piece. Chuma likes to work with first-choice movements, those that flash into consciousness but are usually censored.[16] For the performance she

34 Rosemary Lee Dance Company – '*Egg Dances.*'

leaves some leeway for things to change so that the performance stays alive.

In Japan she was a political activist and she sees this as preparing her for the role of making groups work. Her impromptu, guerrilla performances are impressive.

The performances worked like this. Everyone was to bring a copy of the 'Post' arrive at the location a few minutes before the performance and be very discreet, so as not to give it away. We didn't want to let passersby notice that something was about to happen, so we tried not to congregate too much or chat or be too obvious. At the hour we all took a pose. . . . until someone (usually Chuma . . .) would yell, 'Run, stop, run, stop . . .'. The performances were essentially free-form . . . the police came at a point when everyone was shadowing one person. When the cops asked who was in charge, the lead person pointed a thumb at their own chest, and in unison, the shadows imitated the gesture. (Fleming, 1985, p. 63).

In *Five Car Pile Up*, although Chuma was using everyday movements and instituting some radical ideas, hierarchy was established by having key performers dressed in different costumes and men lifting women in keeping with tradition, thus limiting the radicalness of her work.

Women's images of men

Women concerned with gender issues have not choreographed solely for women. Many women have choreographed for both women-only companies and mixed companies and a few have choreographed solos for men or for male companies. The women above who have choreographed for mixed companies usually present men with a softer image than the usual macho stance so frequently reinforced in dance. Butcher, for example, frequently has a fluid, sensitive aspect in her work for both sexes. Anderson's work relishes a wicked quip at typical masculine postures and gestures.

Jacky Lansley choreographed *Frank* (1986) for Tim Rubidge. It is a humorous but insightful look at the pressures on men and the isolation behind the facade. An office setting provides an ideal opportunity to turn arabesques into long swoops across the stage on a revolving typist's chair. The juxtaposition of familiar everyday moves, office jargon and dance sequences combine to draw us into the competitive, pressurised world of the ambitious salesman. As he gets tired, the energetic drive recedes and we get a glimpse of the high cost of keeping up this front.

For some choreographers the form of the work is central and dancers' movements are interchangeable regardless of gender, with dancers wearing the same costumes (for example t-shirt and trousers). At times this can have a liberating effect and at others simply reinforce expected images. This is the case with **Rosemary Butcher**'s work. As with other women choreographers in England her influence and work have been largely disregarded by the establishment despite the importance of her contribution to dance. *Flying Lines* (1985) is an excellent example of Butcher's work. Performed by a mixed company, references are made to kite flying through the sustained running forwards and backwards in circular pathways with angular arm gestures. 'The complex interlacing of eight dancers, circling in space, is as spell-binding and hard to fathom logically as the sight of jugglers maintaining a whirling galaxy of clubs in the air through the apparently simple act of throwing and catching' (Crickmay, 1986, p. 10). For this work and *Touch the Earth* (1987) (see Figure 35) Butcher collaborated with musician Michael Nyman. In many of her pieces Butcher has collaborated with sculptors and for *Touch the Earth* Dieter Pietsch created the set.

In one section of *Touch the Earth*, before the end, uncharacteristically Butcher created a section for the women. The women squat in a sand circle which is part of the set. One woman supportively cradles another's head and later is in turn supported by another woman. The inspiration for this had come from a book of photographs of the Native People of America and it provided a strong image of caring between women, undermining the stereotype of women being reduced to competitors (Burt, 1988).

The process continues – conclusion

Feminism as a political practice and theory has infiltrated and influenced dance through the subversive independents. This has had rippling repercussions in mainstream dance. Slow though the process may be, with retrogressive stages on the way, the women's work discussed in this chapter has highlighted an effective range of radical practices.

Women, influenced directly or indirectly by feminism, pursuing their politics through dance policies and/or their personal lives, have with deliberate intent evolved radical processes. This has resulted in confronting notions of 'the ideal body' and 'dancers' looks', providing work which emphasises the unique individualism of each

35 Rosemary Butcher Dance Company – '*Touch the Earth*'.

of us. At the same time it is important not to lose sight of the collective actions necessary for women to define our own lives and work.

The 'personal is political' is as relevant now as when first coined in the early days of feminism. Women in dance working with 'the lived body' are constantly confronting the implications of this. But whilst there are common understandings and experiences for us as human beings we cannot ignore the specific social and historical factors which affect us. Whilst the similarities are important, so too, are the differences and we cannot progress without fully acknowledging those. The issues of race and class are always present in considerations of gender and dance and need to be addressed. The issues which are relevant to a feminist perspective of Western theatre dance, including attitudes to the body, dance training, funding policies, critical practices and the representation of women in dance, are explored in the hope that this research may be the beginning of many other studies which will highlight women's work. Women do have a very strong presence in dance but a good deal of work needs to be put into equal opportunities policies and practices in dance for women to benefit. In order for womens' perspectives to be clearly established and influential, women need to have access to positions of power and decision-making as choreographers, administrators and directors.

Dance research which takes into account social issues and social contexts will enable areas of gender, race and class to be further explored. The gradually developing dance degree courses in England, for example, are providing opportunities for students to discover the importance of some of these issues and there is a growing interest in studying dance from a political perspective. In addition, the education work of some dance companies and dance projects organised by Regional Arts Boards have focussed on gender with some beneficial results.

Women's oppression has resulted in a challenge to perceived notions of sexuality which have had repercussions for some of the dance work discussed above. With constant brilliant resourcefulness women have created numerous ways to make work from their own definitions, sometimes working alone, in duos, or in all women companies, at other times choreographing for mixed companies and, a more recent phenomenon, choreographing for male soloists and companies. Women's work which breaks the boundaries of gender clearly illustrates the inter-connectedness of dance and politics and sometimes offers us visions for the future. Whilst social transformation is highly desirable, in the words of Emma Goldman, 'If I can't dance I don't want to be part of your revolution'.[17]

Notes and References

Acknowledgements

1. Some of the ideas discussed in this book are developments of two earlier studies I completed at the Laban Centre, London: *Women and Dance* (1977) submitted for the University of London Diploma in Education with Special Reference to Movement and Dance: Feminism and Dance (1984) submitted for the CNAA MA Degree in Dance Studies.

Introduction

1. Emma Goldman was a Jewish Russian; she later emigrated to America where she toured giving talks, exposing the illusions of women's suffrage, challenging the institution of marriage, advocating birth control and speaking her libertarian vision of a society which met individual needs rather than a society based on exploitation. She also put her theories into practice which rewarded her with stays in prison and a time living underground (Goldmann, 1970; Shulman, ed., 1972).
2. I use the term Women's Movement in a historical sense as the label attached to the second wave of feminism this century which emerged in the late 1960s in the United States of America and in Europe. Black women have made a strong case for this term being exclusive when used more generally than this, because their viewpoints and experiences were largely unacknowledged at that time and, therefore, the term is misleading as it appears to encompass all women. When discussing recent issues I use the term feminism, which is more representative of the many disparate groups of women who have developed theories and practice challenging male constructions of society.
3. Several dance magazines have carried occasional articles about sexual politics and dance. For example, *New Dance* magazine had two women's issues (No. 15, Summer 1980 and No. 41, Summer 1987). *Dance Theatre Journal* has printed one or two articles on this topic (McMahon, 1988; Savage-King, 1985). More recently an issue devoted to Sexual Politics was published (Vol. 7 No. 2, Autumn 1989). *Ballett*

International printed in English and German has also published articles in this area (for example, Schmidt, 1983). In the USA *Contact Quarterly* has published articles on gender and dance (for example, Copeland, 1982). *The Drama Review* (TDR) has published articles concerned with sexual politics (for example, Daly, 1986; Hanna, 1987). *Women in Performance*, a journal of feminist theory, brought out an issue devoted to dance (Vol. 3 No. 2, 1987/88). There is a section on dance in *Grafts: Feminist Cultural Criticism* (Sheridan, ed., 1988) and Hanna, has written *Dance, Sex and Gender* (1988a).

4. I use the term Britain with reservation because it obscures the differences between the people of England, Wales, Scotland and Ireland. When possible I use the term England if the reference is specific.

5. As with the visual arts, women had difficulty obtaining access to training although women from rich families often had private music teachers in the fifteenth and sixteenth centuries. There have, however, been all-women bands, from the women's orchestras of Italy in the sixteenth century, through the women's jazz bands in America in the 1920s, to numerous bands of today.

6. For example, at the Dartington International Dance Festival of 1985 I led a seminar entitled 'What is Feminist Dance?' Two years later, at the same festival a series of seminars entitled 'Asking Questions about Dance' were organised and led by Valerie Briginshaw, Ramsay Burt and myself. In these seminars we discussed issues of social class, feminism and the construction of masculinity in relation to dance. At a conference in Leeds in 1986 entitled, 'New Dance: Critical Questions and Frames of Resistance' a paper was given on *Feminism and New Dance* by Valerie Briginshaw, Kay Lynn and myself. Also in 1986, a conference at Chisenhale Dance Space in London, organised together with the National Organisation for Dance and Mime, included a discussion of new dance and feminism.

7. Any reference to the female performer, choreographer or spectator in this book is not intended to reinforce a universal notion of women as the same. Rather, it is recognised that the differentiation between women for example by class, race or sexual orientation, will affect their responses.

8. I was also involved with two dance projects which addressed gender. The first was with Extemporary Dance Theatre in 1988–89. The second was organised by Southern Arts in 1990.

Chapter 1   Dancing hierarchies – dance in society

1. Modern dance refers to the work of the 1920s, 1930s and 1940s of which Graham was a major exponent. Contemporary dance refers to dance technique and choreography after the 1950s when choreographers were becoming less interested in the dramatic choreography of

Graham, and Cunningham developed his technique. However, modern dance is still used sometimes as an umbrella term to distinguish dance work from ballet. The term postmodern when applied to dance refers to dance work that began with the reconsideration of dance itelf in the 1960s by the performers/choreographers and artists who worked in Judson Church, New York. New dance refers to work in Britain established in the 1970s primarily by the X6 group. In the 1980s and 1990s there has been much debate about the appropriateness of the labels postmodern and new dance for recent work.

2. In Chapter 2 there is a discussion of the problems of describing the body as 'the instrument' of dance.

3. A recent example is Wendy Harpe's report, *A Question of Equity*, Women in the Arts Research, funded by Merseyside Arts (1990).

4. The term 'relatively autonomous' was originally from Louis Althusser.

5. See also Williamson's (1978) work on decoding adverts, which gives excellent examples of the way women's bodies are used in advertising.

6. See examples in 'Dance Education: a Guide to Vocational Schools and Colleges in Britain', *Dance and Dancers*, September 1983.

7. Release techniques include the work of Mabel Todd who wrote *The Thinking Body* (1975) and Lulu Sweigard (1974) who pioneered a technique called Ideokinesis which aims through visual imagery to release and activate muscles, and the Alexander technique (1975) and Feldenkrais method (1980) which both bypass traditional habitual ways of moving and aim to find new, more efficient and less harmful neuromuscular pathways (Steinman, 1986). The martial arts used included T'ai chi chuan and Aikido.

8. Michel Perreault in his paper *Changes in the Roles of Male Dancers since the 17th Century – an Initial Sociological Viewpoint* presented at the International Congress 'Dance and Research' held at Vrije Universiteit Brussels, 1989, argues that despite their position as stars women submitted to male power in dance. Whilst women have undoubtedly been the objects of male desire, the agreement suggested by the term 'submission' hides the resistances of women to their subordinate roles. Such a resistance is evident for example in the costume reforms of Sallé and Camargo, the evolution of modern, postmodern and new dance and some dance writing (for example, see issues of *New Dance* magazine and *TDR*). Perreault also obscures with such comments the economic constraints which women face in dance as discussed in this chapter.

9. Although modern dance, unlike ballet, was predominantly led by women, today many of the companies are directed by men. For example, since Dame Marie Rambert's retirement the Rambert Dance Company has been directed solely by male directors including Norman Morrice, John Chesworth, Robert North and currently Richard Alston.

10. For example, the union representative of London Contemporary Dance Theatre gave these pay figures for 1989: a new company member £115

per week gross, with touring allowance of £15 per day; wages increase approximately £10 per week every year so that a dancer with ten years' service would earn about £240 per week gross (Laurie, 1989).

11. Dancers of Rambert dance company comment on the restrictions of life within the company in Sherlock (1988).

Chapter 3   Colonised bodies – the oppression of women

1. See Wolff's (1990) discussion of the development of the private and public spheres.

2. See also comments about the stereotypical images of women in dance, the romanticised feminine ideal and the seductress (Chapters 4 and 5).

3. For details and statistics of women's access to equal rights, opportunities and pay and access to family planning, education, health care in different countries throughout the world see *New Internationalist*, No 81, July, 1980.

4. Dependence can have far-reaching and sometimes disastrous effects for women as illustrated by the campaign against rape in marriage and the documentation of child sexual abuse and domestic violence ('Women against Rape', letter *Guardian*, 3 October 1989, Campbell, Pizzey).

5. See also Coote and Campbell, 1982, p. 189.

6. Chodorow's theories are useful when applied to Western society but they are limited by their universal and essentialist stance.

7. For further description of this process see 'Margaret Thatcher is My Sister', Itzin, 1985.

8. S. Kitzinger, M. Odent *et al.*, lectures at the Active Birth Conference, October 1982, Wembley, London.

9. For example, I briefly discuss my own experience of pregnancy and birth in *New Dance* No. 27, 1983.

10. Stamp Collection a group of dancers all between 28 and 35 weeks pregnant performed *The Morning Shiknesh Lands* (1991), a dance exploring how pregnancy affects a woman's body, at Chisenhale Dance Space, London. Each dancer wore a black leotard which had a white line drawing of a life-sized foetus as it would look inside the womb.

11. See review by Sarah Green, *New Dance* No. 11, Summer, 1979, p. 6. See also descriptions of women's experiences of pregnancy and medical attitudes to pregnant women in Oakley (1981); also Susan Hiller's challenge to traditional representation of pregnant women in Rowbotham, 1989.

12. For example, the English debate of the control of pornography (Barrett, 1984).

13. See also Seymour's (1984, former principal ballerina for the Royal Ballet Company) account of her negative feelings about her body.

14. For example, see Mitchell, J., *Psychoanalysis and Feminism*, Harmondsworth, Penguin, 1975 and Baker Miller, J., *Toward a new Psychology of Women* (Harmondsworth, Penguin, 1979).

15. See also discussion of compulsive eating, S. Orbach, 1979. One of the major findings of this work has been that it is difficult for woman to experience her full power in society because of social and psychological restrictions. A form of covert resistance to her prescribed role (i.e. small body, quiet voice, spatial deference) is eating 'too much' or 'weighing too much' (Brown, 1984). Chernin (1983) discusses the desire for thinness in great depth. She suggests that compulsory thinness is a backlash to feminism and an attempt to reduce our power.

16. These groups were not therapy groups. All women participated equally. The reason for sharing the information was to change personal experiences by recognising the connections with the social structure and to find ways of improving circumstances. They were also leaderless groups. There was an emphasis on women defining our own reality. Both practical and ideological issues were discussed (Jo Freemen, 1975). See also Juliet Mitchell's discussion of some of the key issues, 1984.

Chapter 4   Viewing women – the production and reception of dance

1. For example, the advertisement for Tampax, illustrating a group of ballet dancers before the beginning of a performance. Mary Fulkerson commented on the use of such advertisements in the context of a performance which commented on womens' roles in society. Her image of a modern woman with a parachute was similar to the portrayal of another Tampax advertisement. Performance at Riverside Studios, 11 November 1984, *Real Life Adventures* see discussion of Fulkerson's work in Chapter 9 (see Figure 26).
2. See reviews in *New Dance* No. 1, p. 13, No. 3, pp. 20–23.
3. See Berger, 1972; Goffman, 1979; Millum, 1975; Tuchman *et al.*, 1978.
4. Goffman (1979) suggests that advertisers draw on conventions, style, ritual and ideal representation of how things are anyway. This same process is also apparent in dance.
5. See MacRitchie, L. 'Giselle', *Performance Magazine*, No 8, 1980, pp. 10–11.

Chapter 5   Titillating tutus – women in ballet

1. For example, see Adair, *Grace and Glitter – Insights* (1987), also Rubidge, ' Political Dance' in *Dance Theatre Journal* Vol. 7, No. 2, 1989.
2. Another example, given in Au's book *Ballet and Modern dance* (1988), is the *Ballet de la Délivrance de Renaud* (1617).
3. Cabriole – a beating step in which one leg is beaten against the other in mid-air; chassé – a sliding movement of the foot forward, backwards or

sideways; coupé – a movement to change weight from one foot to the other; entrechat – a vertical jump where the calves beat together and the feet change position; sissone – a spring off two feet landing onto one foot.
4. Refers to both female and male actors (*Oxford Dictionary*).

Chapter 6   Revolutionary women – modern dance

1. Her two children were born 1907–9 and drowned when a car they were travelling in plunged into the Seine in 1913.
2. As Franks (1965) points out, ballerinas such as Karsavina were concerned about the limitations of the use of toe-slippers.

Chapter 7   We say no – postmodern dance

1. Trisha Brown in discussion with Stephanie Jordan at Sadlers Wells (1988).

Chapter 8   Black power – black dance

1. Whilst there are cultural similarities between African-Caribbean and Asian communities in Britain, partly due to a common historical experience, there are differences in their preferences in the arts which are influenced by factors including socio-economic status, religion and gender roles (Francis, 1990).
2. For the purposes of this chapter this definition of black dance is the one with which I am working. However, I have limited the chapter to work by black American and black British artists in the Western theatre. I have not included Asian work because the traditions do not stem from the Western theatre which is the focus of this book.
3. See McDonagh's comments (1968) in his article 'Negroes in Ballet.'
4. These women executed a range of highly complex skipping routines complete with verbal repartee with their male coach goading them on.
5. See John Percival's article in *Dance and Dancers* October, 1977.
6. Interview with Beverley Glean, 6 November 1989.
7. As two dancers who danced with the Extemporary Dance Theatre made clear, there are still too few opportunities for black dancers in England and their skin is considered 'too dark for TV' (*The Voice*, 18 October 1988).

Chapter 9   Beginning again – new dance

1. The Place was the home of the London Contemporary Dance School and Company with a theatre in which public performances were held.

2. See Early's descpriptions of performances in *New Dance*, No. 40, 1987. Other dancers who danced with Strider included Dennis Greenwood, Nan Hassall and Eva Karczag.

3. Sarah Green, who had a gymnastics and visual arts background joined the Collective for a short time, but for the purposes of this study I have concentrated on the founding members.

4. Interview with Duprès 1984.

5. These performances were reviewed in *New Dance*, No. 1, 1977, p. 13 and No. 9, 1979, p. 11.

6. Review by Friend *Dancing Times*, No. 871, 1983, p. 541. Early also created *Naples*, based on the last act of *Napoli* a ballet by the nineteenth-century choreographer Bournonville, *New Dance*, No. 9, 1979, p. 11.

7. Review by Early, *New Dance*, No. 7, 1978, p. 9.

8. These issues included dance in education, dance therapy, dance in the community, feminism, the beginnings of a sociological approach to dance.

9. The list of aims summarised for the purpose of grant application were printed in *New Dance*, No. 24, 1983, p. 2. These were as follows:

   '1. To encourage new writing about dance and thus develop a new language for the discussion and analysis of dance.

   2. To review and document new work, particularly that which breaks new ground, takes risks, explores new dimensions.

   3. To consider dance in its widest sense – mass culture, esoteric art, historical phenomenon, political art, anthropological and social study of such issues.

   4. To support campaigns to better the lots of dancers, choreographers and all related artists.

   5. To interrupt oppression as it affects dance, in particular by focussing on dance in relation to people commonly oppressed within our society for example: the disabled, people of non-European origin, women and others who are treated as a minority group.

   6. To document important historical influences on the development of the present British dance scene and its international role.'

10. Interviews with Fergus Early, September 1984 and February 1990.

11. Interviews with Jacky Lansley September 1984 and March 1990.

12. See reviews of, articles about, her work in *New Dance*, Nos 2, 6, 10, 18, 21 and 44.

13. See Jordan's (1986) description of Butcher's work including instructions given to dancers.

14. Aikido is another form of movement training which is popular. For an example of different trainings affecting body shape see Anna Moszynska, 1983, pp. 22–23.

15. See also interview with Agis and discussion of *Close Streams* (1983) a duo with Helen Rowsell. This shows two women strong and in harmony without the need for a man to make them complete. They

present a contradictory image in the initial opening of the piece as they stamp around the space in heavy working boots contrasting with white 'feminine' underwear. Their togetherness accentuates their strengh.
16. See review by Early, *New Dance*, No. 21, 1982.
17. See discussion and articles in *New Dance*, Nos 1, 11, 12 and 20.

Chapter 10   The subversives – women's dance practice

1. Interview with Emilyn Claid, February 1990.
2. Whilst this may be a useful vision for her to work with in terms of transcending differences, as has been dicussed in Chapter 2, a universal view of the body supports the dominant ideology which ignores the specific social and historical factors that need to be acknowledged.
3. This choreography will be hereafter referred to as *Bluebeard*.
4. Disruption of beauty contests formed part of the early actions of the Women's Movements in England and the USA in the late 1960s and 1970s.
5. One of Miller's concerns is a general lack of awareness of children's needs and an insensitivity to their emotional pain.
6. For example, John Percival, *Dance and Dancers*, February (1987).
7. For example, Julia Pascal, the *Guardian*, 3 July 1989.
8. Discussion at Dartington International Dance Festival, 1987.
9. Interview with Lea Anderson, April 1989.
10. Discussion at The Place, London, May 1989, with Dutch artists.
11. Performances at the April in Paris Season, The Place, London, 1989.
12. Interview with Yoland Snaith, May 1989.
13. Interview with Beverley Glean, 6 November 1989.
14. Interview with Shobhana Jeyasingh, May 1989.
15. Agis worked with a mixed company in *Kin* (1987) in which she further developed her ideas.
16. Mary Fulkerson also worked with these ideas; see Chapter 9.
17. The Women's Press (1980) postcard quote.

Bibliography

Abra, J., 'The Dancer as Masochist', *Dance Research Journal*, 19/2 Winter (1987/88) 33–39.

ADMA, 'Report on the First National Conference of Dance and Movement Artists', July 18 and 19 (1981).

Adair, C., 'Body Image', *New Dance*, No. 15 (1980) 3.

Adair, C., 'From Dance to Childbirth', *New Dance*, No. 27 (1983) 20.

Adair, C., 'Emilyn Claid and Maggie Semple interviewed on their Women's Project', *New Dance*, No. 41 (1987) 17–19.

Adair, C., *Grace and Glitter – Insights* (London: Extemporary Dance Theatre, 1987).

Adair, C., 'Trisha Brown', *New Dance*, No. 43 (1988) 8–9.

Adair, C., 'Dance Umbrella: The Cholmondeleys', *Spare Rib*, Dec/Jan (1989) 52.

Adair, C., 'Dancing Hierarchies, who dominates?', *MTD*, No. 1 (1990) 24–28.

Adair, C., 'Beyond Contemporary Dance', *Everywoman*, February (1991) 16–17.

Adair, C., Briginshaw, V. & Lynn, K., 'Feminism and New Dance: A History and a Future?', *New Dance*, No. 40 (1987) 13–15.

Adair, C., Briginshaw, V. & Lynn, K., 'Dance Production and Reception: A Feminist Perspective', unpublished paper (1988).

Adair, C., Briginshaw, V. & Lynn, K., 'Viewing Women – The Second Sex', *Dance Theatre Journal*, Vol. 7 No. 2 Autumn (1989) 28–30.

Adamczyk, A. J., *Black Dance: an Annotated Bibliography* (London: Garland Pub., 1989).

Adams C., *Ordinary Lives* (London: Virago, 1982).

Adams, P., 'Versions of the Body', *M/F*, No. 11/12 (1986) 26–33.

Adshead, J. (ed.), *Choreography Principles and Practice* (University of Surrey, 1986).

Alderson, E., 'Ballet as Ideology: Giselle, Act II', *Dance Chronicle*, Vol. 10 No. 3 (1987) 290–304.

Alexander, M., 'Women, Clothes', *Feminist Art News* No. 9 (1982) 4–7.

Alexander, Z., 'Black Entertainers, 1900–1910', *FAN* Vol. 2 No. 5 (undated, *circa* 1988) 6–8.

Allen, J., and Grosz, E., 'Editorial', *Australian Feminist Studies*, No. 5 Summer (1987) vii–xi.

Allen, Z. D., 'Blacks and Ballet', *Dance Magazine*, July (1976) 65–70.

Amos, V. and Parmar, P. 'Challenging Imperial Feminism', *Feminist Review*, 17 Autumn (1984) 3–19.

Anderson, J., *Ballet and Modern Dance* (New Jersey: Princeton, 1986).

Anderson, J., *Choreography Observed* (University of Iowa Press, 1987).

Anglin, W., 'The Royal Ballet and Sadler's Wells Royal Ballet' in White, J. (ed.), *20th Century Dance in Britain* (London: Dance Books, 1985).

Ardener, S. (ed.), *Perceiving Women* (London: Malaby Press, 1975).

Ardener, S. (ed.), *Defining Females: The Nature of Women in Society* (London: Croom Helm, 1978).

Ardener, S. (ed.), *Women and Space* (London: Croom Helm, 1981).

Ardolino, E. (producer), *The Martha Graham Dance Company*, video (USA, 1976).

Arms, S., 'Immaculate Deception: A New Look at Women and Childbirth in America' in Ardener, S (ed.) *Defining Females: The Nature of Women in Society* (London: Croom Helm, 1978).

Arts Council of Great Britain Report, *The Glory of the Garden: The Development of the Arts in Britain* (1984).

Aschenbrenner, J., 'Black Dance and Dancers', *CORD Research Annual*, No. XII (New York: 1980) 33–39.

Aschenbrenner, J., 'The Critical Response', *CORD Research Annual*, No. XII (New York: 1980) 41–47.

Attille, M., and Blackwood, M., 'Black Women and Representation' in Charlotte Brunsden (ed.), *Films for Women* (London: BFI, 1986).

Au, S., *Ballet and Modern Dance* (London: Thames & Hudson, 1988).

Ayalah, D., & Weinstock, I. J., *Breasts* (New York: Summit Books, 1979).

Balsdon, A. & Kaluzynska, E., 'Hairy Story', *Spare Rib* No. 66 January (1978) 6–8.

Banes, S., *Judson Dance Theatre: Democracy's Body 1962–1964* PhD. (New York University, University Microfilms, Ann Arbor, 1980).

Banes, S., *Judson Dance Theatre 1962–1966* (Bennington College, Exhibition Catalogue, 1981).

Banes, S. 'American (Postmodern) Choreography in the 1980's' in Janet Adshead (ed.), *Choreography Principles and Practice* (University of Surrey, 1986).

Banes, S., *Terpsichore in Sneakers: Post-modern Dance* (Boston: Houghton Mifflin, 1980 and revised edition, 1987).

Banks, L. R., *The L-Shaped Room* (Harmondsworth: Penguin, 1960).

Banks, O., *Faces of Feminism* (Oxford: Martin Robertson, 1981).

Barling, M., 'To Be or Not To Be? or, And From the Darkness, Let There Be Light: Some Thoughts on Developing a Feminist Aesthetic', *Resources for Feminist Research*, Vol. 13 No. 4 December/January (1984/85) 5–6.

Barrett, M., 'Feminism and the Definition of Cultural Politics' in Brunt, R. & Rowan, C. (eds) *Feminism, Culture and Politics* (London: Lawrence and Wishart, 1982).

Barrett, M., *Women's Oppression Today* (London: Verso, 1984).

Bassnett, S., *Feminist Experiences: The Women's Movement in Four Cultures* (London: Allen and Unwin, 1986).

Baxandall, L., *Radical Perspectives in the Arts* (Harmondsworth: Pelican, 1972).

Beaumont, C., *The Complete Book of Ballets* (London: Putnam, 1956).

Beauvoir de, S., *The Second Sex* (Harmondsworth: Penguin, 1972).

Beckford, R., *Katherine Dunham* (New York: Marcel Dekker Inc., 1979).

Belotti, E. G., *Little Girls* (London: Writers and Readers Co-op, 1975).

Benjamin, M., 'Stepping into Battle', *Guardian*, January 12 (1990) 38.

Benthall, J. & Polhemus, T. (eds), *The Body as a Medium of Expression* (London: Allen Lane, 1975).

Berger, J. *Ways of Seeing* (Harmondsworth: Penguin, 1972).

Best, D., 'Symbolism and The Meaning of Movement' *CORD* Research Annual X (1979) 81–92.

Bierman, J. H., 'The Alexander Technique "Gets its directions"', *Dance Scope*, Vol. 12 No. 2 Spring/Summer (1978) 24–33.

Birdwhistell, R., *Kinesics and Context* (Harmondsworth: Penguin, 1972).

Bichovsky-Little, H., 'Look After Yourself', *New Statesman*, November 27 (1987) 22–23.

Black, M. & Coward, R. 'Linguistic, Social and Sexual Relations; A Review of Dale Spender's Man Made Language', *Screen Education*, No. 39 Summer (1981) 70–85.

Blacking, J. (ed.), *The Anthropology of the Body* (London: Academic Press, 1977).

Blair, J., 'Private Parts in Public Places: The Case of Actresses', in Ardener, S. (ed.) *Women and Space* (London: Croom Helm, 1981).

Bland, A. *The Royal Ballet: The First 50 Years* (London: Threshold Books, 1981).

Bloch, C., 'Everyday Life, Sensuality and Body Culture', *Women's Studies International Forum*, Vol. 10 No. 4 (1987) 433–42.

Boas, F., *The Function of Dance in Society* (New York: Dance Horizons, 1972).

Bonis, B. 'The Shaping of French Dance', *Ballett International*, August/September (1988) 29–34.

Bray, C., 'How do Girls and Women Learn to Move', *Resources for Feminist Research*, Vol. 16 No. 4 December (1987) 39–41.

Briginshaw, V., *Images of Women* (unpublished paper, 1984).

Briginshaw, V. '"The Wiggle Goes On": A Profile of Liz Aggiss and Billie Cowie', *New Dance* No. 44 Summer (1988) 7–11.

Briginshaw, V., & Burt, R., 'Turtle Dreams (Cabaret)', *New Dance*, 39 (1987) 11–14.

Brinson, P., *Background to European Ballet* (New York: Books for Libraries, Arnos Press, 1980).

Brinson, P., 'Should the Royal Opera House be Closed?', *Dance and Dancers and Dance Theatre Journal*, Collaborative Issue May (1983) 23–24.

Brinson, P. 'The Status of Dance', lecture at Chisenhale Dance Space, London, December (1988).

Brinson, P. & Crisp, C., *The Pan Book of Ballet and Dance* (London: Pan, 1980).

Brown, B. & Adams, P. 'The Feminine Body and Feminist Politics', *M/F*, No.3 (1979) 35–50.

Brown, L. S., 'Women, Weight and Power: A Feminist Analysis of "Eating Disorders", *Abstract from Empowerment for Women Conference* (Holland, 1984) 156.

Brown, T. & Rainer, Y., 'A Conversation about *Glacial Decoy*', *October*, No. 10 Fall (1979) 29–39.

Brunt, R., ' "An Immense Verbosity": Permissive Sexual Advice in the 1970's', in Brunt, R. & Rowan, C. (eds), *Feminism, Culture and Politics* (London: Lawrence and Wishart, 1982).

Bryan, B., Dadzie, S. & Scafe, S., *The Heart of the Race: Black Women's Lives in Britain* (London: Virago, 1985).

Buckle, R. (ed.) *Dancing for Diaghilev: The Memoirs of Lydia Sokolova* (London: John Murray, 1960).

Buckroyd, J., 'Step Lively There', *Dancing Times*, Vol. LXXVII No. 913 October (1986) 45.

Bunch, C. & Myron, N., *Class and Feminism* (Baltimore, Maryland: Diana Press, 1974).

Burgin, V., 'Man – Desire – Image' in Appignanesi, L (ed.), *Desire* (London, ICA Documents, 1984) 32–34.

Burgin, V., *The End of Art Theory* (London: Macmillan, 1986).

Burt, R., 'Finding a Language: Rosemary Butcher Speaks to Ramsay Burt about her Recent Work', *New Dance* No. 44 Summer (1988) 12–14.

Burt, R. & Huxley, M., 'Not Quite Cricket: How New Dance Doesn't Play the Establishment Game' (unpublished paper; published as, 'La Novelle danse: Comment ne pas jouer le Jeu de L'Establisment' in *La Danse Au Défi* (Montreal: Parachute, 1987).

Burton, A. Koch, J., Thomas, S., Wheeler, M., 'The Spectacle of the Body', *The Journal of Physical Education and Recreation* Vol. 49 May 5 (1978) 36–39.

Butcher, H. *et al.*, *Images of Women in the Media* (Birmingham: Centre for Contemporary Cultural Studies, University of Birmingham, 1974).

Caplan, P. (ed.), *The Cultural Construction of Sexuality* (London: Tavistock, 1987).

Carroll-Smith, S. 'Dance Brigade Raised the Roof and Cash for Rural Women', Mendocino Country Magazine, 15 May (1988) (London: Macmillan, 1988).

Case, S., *Feminism and Theatre* (London: Macmillan, 1988).

Channel 4, 'Dance Lines – Step in Time Girls', TV programme (London, 1988).

Channel 4, 'Hoopla' – de Keersmaeker, TV programme, May (London: 1989).

Channel 4, 'Breaking the Mould', TV programme (London: 1989).

Channel 4, 'Dance on Four – Fonteyn', TV programme, May (London: 1989).

Chapkis, W., *Beauty Secrets: Women and the Politics of Appearance* (Boston: South End Press 1986; also London: Women's Press, 1988).

Cheney, S. (ed.), *Isadora Duncan : The Art of Dance* (New York: Theatre Art Books, 1969).

Chenzira, A., producer, *Syvilla Fort – They Dance to Her Drum*, video (distributed London: Circles, 1979).

Chernin, K., *Womansize – The Tyranny of Slenderness* (London: The Women's Press, 1983).

Chicago, J., *The Birth Project* (Garden City, New York: Doubleday Inc., 1985).

Chisenhale Conference Day, 'Dance as Social Criticism' (1983).

Chisenhale/National Organisation for Dance and Mime, conference papers for 'Weekend to Celebrate New Dance', July 12/13 (1986).

Chodorow, N., *The Reproduction of Mothering* (University of California Press, 1978).

Citron, P., 'Women in Dance: Part 1, The Impact of Feminine Consciousness', *Dance in Canada*, No. 39 Spring (1984) 15–17.

Citron, P., 'Women in Dance: Part 2, Problems, Demands and Changes', *Dance in Canada*, No. 42 Winter (1985) 19–21.

Claid, E., *Danger! Women at Work*, Press Release (London: South Bank, 1988).

Claid, E., *Danger! Women at Work*, programme notes (London: South Bank, 1988).

Clark. B., 'How to Live in your Axis', *Theatre Papers* (Dartington, 1977) 1–15.

Clarke, M., *The Sadler's Wells Ballet* (London: A & C Black, 1955).

Clarke, M., 'Danger! Women at Work', *Guardian*, September 2 (1988) 25.

Clarke, M., 'Capriccio', *Guardian*, March 16 (1989) 25.

Clarke, M., 'Graham in 1967 – Part 2', Vol. LIV, No. 637 *Dancing Times*, May (1967) 403–05.

Clarke, M. & Crisp, C., *Ballet: an Illustrated History* (London: A & C Black, 1973).

Clarke, M. & Crisp, C., *Ballet in Art* (London: Ash & Grant, 1978).

Clarke, M. & Crisp, C., *The Ballet Goer's Guide* (London: Michael Joseph, 1981).

Clarke, M. & Crisp, C., *The History of Dance* (London, Orbis Pub., 1981).

Clarke, M. & Crisp, C., *Ballerina* (London: BBC Books, 1987).

Cohen, S. J. (ed.), *Doris Humphrey – An Artist First* (Connecticut, Wesleyan University Press, 1972).

Cohen, S. J. (ed.), *Dance as a Theatre Art* (New York: Harper & Row, 1974).

Coleman, T., 'Prima Alicia', *Guardian*, February 5 (1989) 23.

Conklin, N. F. & Patraka, V. M. (eds), 'Women's Art and Culture', *Women's Studies Curriculum Series 1* (Michigan: University Microfilms, Ann Arbor, 1977).

Constanti, S., 'Coliseum Summer', *Dance Theatre Journal*, Vol. 4 No. 3 Autumn (1986) 32–34.

Constanti, S., 'Brenda Edwards', *Artrage*, Spring (1989) 39.

Cooper, E., *The Sexual Perspective* (London: Routledge & Kegan Paul, 1986).

Coote, A. & Campbell, B,. *Sweet Freedom: The Struggle for Women's Liberation* (London: Picador, 1982).

Copeland, R. 'Why Women Dominate Modern Dance', *The New York Times*, April 18 (1982a) 6 (cont. 22).

Copeland, R., 'Towards a Sexual Politics of Contemporary Dance', *Contact Quarterly*, Vol. VII No. 3/4 (1982b) 45–51.

Copeland, R. 'Genre and Style', *Contact Quarterly*, Vol. V111 No. 2 Winter (1983) 11–16.

Copeland, R., 'The Objective Temperament', *Dance Theatre Journal*, Vol. 4 No. 3 Autumn (1986a) 6–11.

Copeland, R., 'A Curmudgeonly View of the American Dance Boom', *Dance Theatre Journal*, Vol. 4 No. 1 Spring (1986b) 10–13.

Coward, R., ' "This Novel Changes Lives": Are Women's Novels Feminist Novels?', *Feminist Review*, No. 5 (1980) 53–64.

Coward, R., 'What is Pornography', *Spare Rib* No. 119 June (1982) 52–54.

Coward, R., *Female Desire: Women's Sexuality Today* (London: Paladin, 1984).

Coward, R. *The Whole Truth*, (London: Faber & Faber, 1989).

Cowie, E., 'Women, Representation and the Image', *Screen Education*, No. 23 Summer (1977) 15–23.

Creed, B., 'From Here to Modernity: Feminism and Postmodernism, *Screen*, Vol. 28 No. 2 Spring (1987) 47–67.

Crickmay, C. L., 'The Apparently Invisible Dances of Tufnell and Greenwood', *New Dance*, No. 21 (1982) 7–8.

Crickmay, C. L., 'Dialogue with Rosemary Butcher – a Decade of Her Work', *New Dance*, No. 36 Spring (1986) 10–15.

Croce, A., *Afterimages* (New York: Alfred Knoff, 1978).

Daily Express Reporter, 'Dying Swan Ballerina's Suicide Tragedy', *Daily Express*, December 3 (1987) 21.

Dale M. (producer), 'The Rambert Company', film (London, 1976).

Daly, A. 'The Balanchine Woman', *The Drama Review* 110 Summer (1986) 8–21.

Daly, A., 'At Issue: Gender in Dance', *TDR* Vol. 31 No. 2 Spring (1987) 22–24.

Daly, A., 'Classical Ballet: A Discourse of Difference', *Women in Performance*, Vol. 3 No. 2 (1987/1988a) 57–66.

Daly, A. 'Interview with Senta Driver', *Women in Performance* Vol. 3 No. 2 (1987/1988b) 90–96.

Daly, A., & Martin, C. (eds), 'Movement and Gender: a roundtable discussion', *TDR*, Vol. 32 No. 4 Winter (1988) 82–101.

Daly, M., *Gyn/Ecology* (London: Women's Press, 1979).

Davidoff, L., 'Class and Gender in Victorian England', in Newton, J. L., Ryan, M. P. & Walkowitz, J. R. (eds), *Sex and Class in Women's History* (London: Routledge & Kegan Paul, 1983).

Davis, A., *Women, Race and Class* (London: Women's Press, 1982).

Davis, K., Dickey, J. & Sandford, T. (eds), *Out of Focus* (London: Women's Press, 1987).

Davis, L., 'Revealing The Reviews', *Dance Theatre Journal* Vol. 2 No. 1 Spring (1984).

Davy, K., 'Constructing the Spectator', *Performing Arts Journal* Vol. X No. 2 (1986) 43–52.

Dean. L., interviewed in Livet, A. (ed.), *Contemporary Dance* (New York, Abbeville Press, 1978).

Dempster, E., 'Women Writing the Body: Let's Watch a Little How She Dances', in Sheridan, S. (ed.), *Grafts: Feminist Cultural Criticism* (London: Virago, 1988).

Denby, E., *Looking at the Dance* (New York: Curtis Books, 1968).

Devlin, G., *Stepping Forward – Some Suggestions for the Development of Dance in England during the 1990s* (London: Arts Council, 1989).

Dewdney, A., Michels, D., Fernardo, K. & Orcher, P., 'More than Black and White', *Ten 8* No. 30 Autumn (1988) 62–65.

Dick-Read, G., *Childbirth Without Fear* (London: Heinemann, 1957).

Doane, M. A., 'Woman's Stake: Filming the Female Body', *October*, No. 17 Summer (1981) 23–26.

Doane, M. A., 'Theorising the Female Spectator', *Screen* Vol. 23 Nos 3/4 September/October (1982) 74–87.

Dolan, J., 'Desire Cloaked in a Trenchcoat', *TDR*, Vol. 33 No. 1 Spring (1989) 59–67.

Douglas, M., *Purity and Danger* (Harmondsworth: Penguin, 1970).

Douglas, M., *Natural Symbols* (Harmondsworth: Penguin, 1973).

Douglas, M., *Implicit Meanings* (London, Routledge & Kegan Paul, 1975).

Driver, S., (producer) *Dance Preludes*, video (New York: Dennis Diamond & Video D Studios Inc., 1986).

Druss, R. & Silverman, J., 'Body Image and Perfectionism of Ballerinas', *General Hospital Psychiatry*, July (1979) 115–21.

Duchen, C., *Feminism in France from May '68 to Mitterrand* (London: Routledge and Kegan Paul, 1986).

Duncan, I., *My Life* (New York: Liveright Pub. Corps., 1955).

Dworkin, A., *Woman Hating* (New York, E. P. Dutton, 1974).

Dwoskin S., (producer), *Ballet Black*, video (London: Arts Council, 1986).

Dyer, R. (ed.) *Gays and Film* (London: BFI, 1977).

Eagleton, T., *The Ideology of the Aesthetic* (Oxford: Basil Blackwell, 1990).

Early, F., 'Liberation Notes etc.', *New Dance*, No. 40 (1987) 10–12.

Eckler, G., *Feminist Aesthetics* (London: Women's Press, 1986).

Eichenbaum, L. & Orbach, S., *Outside in Inside Out* (London: Penguin, 1982).

Eichenbaum, L. & Orbach, S., *What Do Women Want?* (London: Fontana/Collins, 1984).

Eichenbaum, L. & Orbach, S., *Bittersweet* (London: Century Hutchinson, 1987a).

Eichenbaum, L. and Orbach, S., 'The Friendship Forum', *Guardian*, July 15 (1987b) 8.

Einstein, H., *Contemporary Feminist Thought* (London: George Allen & Unwin, 1984).

Emery, L. F., *Black Dance in the U.S.: 1619 to the Present Day* (London: Princeton Book Co., 1988).

English, R., 'Alas, Alack the Representation of the Ballerina', *New Dance*, No. 15 Summer (1980) 18.

Ernst, S. & Goodison, L., *In Our Own Hands* (London: Women's Press, 1981).

Essence reporter, 'Anna Benn Sims: Toe Dancing in the Big City', *Essence*, August (1980) 12–13.

Evans, M., (ed.), *The Woman Question* (London: Fontana, 1982).

Farnham, M., 'Slimming: Conquering the Nature in our Bodies', *Trouble and Strife*, Winter (1983) 17–22.

Fast, J., *Body Language* (London: Pan Books, 1971).

Featherstone, M., 'The Body in Consumer Society', *Theory, Culture and Society*, Vol. 1 No. 2 Autumn (1982) 18–33.

Feldenkrais, M., *Awareness Through Movement* (Harmondsworth: Penguin, 1977).

Feminist Review Editorial Collective, 'Editorial', *Feminist Review*, No. 31 (1989) 2–4.

Findlater, R., *Lilian Baylis: The Lady of the Old Vic* (London: Allen Lane, 1975).

Fine Arts Museum of San Francisco, *Bronislava Nijinska: A Dancer's Legacy* (1986).

Firestone, S., *The Dialectic of Sex* (London: Women's Press, 1979).

Fischer, L., 'The Image of Woman as Image: The Optical Politics of Dames' in Altman, R. (ed.), *Genre: The Musical* (London: BFI and Routledge & Kegan Paul, 1981) 70–85.

Fisher, S., *Body Consciousness* (London: Calder & Boyars, 1973).

Fisher, S. & Cleveland, S. E., *Body Image and Personality* (New York: Dover Pub. Inc., 1968).

Flax, J., 'Postmodernism and Gender Relations in Feminist Theory', *Signs*, Vol. 12 No. 4 (1987) 621–43.

Fleming, D., 'Yoshiko Chuma and the School of Hard Knocks', *TDR*, Vol. 29 No. 2 Summer (1985) 53–64.

Fonteyn, M., *The Magic of Dance* (London: BBC, 1980).

Forsyth, S. & Kolenda, P., 'Competition, Co-operation and Group Cohesion in the Ballet Company' in Albrecht, M. C., Barrett, J. H. & Griff, M. (eds), *Sociology of Art and Literature* (New York: Prager Pub., 1970).

Forti, S. 'Dancing as if Newborn' in Banes, S. (ed.), *Terpshichore in Sneakers* (Boston: Houghton Mifflin, 1980).

Foster, S., *Reading Dancing: Bodies and Subjects in Contemporary Dance* (University of California Press, 1986).

Foucault, M., *Discipline and Punish* (Harmondsworth: Penguin, 1977).

Foucault, M., *The History of Sexuality* (Harmondsworth: Penguin, 1981).

Fraleigh, S., *Dance and the Lived Body* (University of Pittsburgh Press, 1987).

Frame, J., *You are Now Entering the Human Heart* (London: Women's Press, 1984).

Francis, J., *Attitudes Among Britain's Black Community Towards Attendance at Arts, Cultural and Entertainment Events* (London: Arts Council, 1990).

Franks, A. H., 'Graham in London', *Dancing Times*, Vol. LIV, No. 647 October (1965) 10–14.

Freeman, J., *The Politics of Women's Liberation: A Case Sudy of Emerging Social Movement and its Relation to the Policy Process* (New York: David McKay, 1975).

Friedan, B., *The Feminine Mystique* (New York: Dell Publishing, 1963).

Frisch, R. E., 'Delayed Menarche and Amenorrhoea in Ballet Dancers', *New England Journal of Medicine*, 303 July 3 (1980) 17–19.

Fryer, P., *The History of Black People in Britain* (London: Pluto Press, 1984).

Fuirer, M., 'Toward a Feminist Ideology', *FAN* No. 6 (1982/83) 20–21.

Fulkerson, M., 'The Move to Stillness', *Theatre Papers*, Fourth Series, No. 10 (Dartington, 1982) 1–26.

Furse, A. 'From Outside In to Inside Out', *New Dance*, No. 17 (1981) 9–11.

Furse, A. & Early, F., 'White Lodge Revisited', *New Dance*, No. 10 Spring (1979) 7–11.

Furse, A. & Lansley, J., 'Off Our Toes', *Spare Rib*, No. 64 November (1977) 5–8.

Furse, A., Gilmor, S., Lansley, J. & O'Brien, M., 'Up Front in Edge', *New Dance* No. 9 New Year (1979) 14.

Gallagher, C. & Lacqueur, T. (eds), *The Making of the Modern Body, Sexuality and Society in the Nineteenth Century* (Berkeley: University of California Press, 1987).

Gamman, L., 'Watching the Detectives' in Gamman, L. & Marshment, M. (eds), *The Female Gaze* (London: Women's Press, 1988).

Gamman, L., and Marshment, M. (eds), *The Female Gaze* (London: Women's Press, 1988).

Garner, D. M., Garfinkel, P. E., Schwartz, D., & Thompson, M., 'Cultural Expectations of Thinness in Women', *Psychological Reports*, 47 (1980) 483–91.

Gautier, T., 'Fanny Elssler in *La Tempête*', in Copeland, R. & Cohen, M. (eds), *What is Dance?* (Oxford University Press, 1983) 431–34.

Gautier, T., 'Revival of "La Sylphide", in Copeland, R. & Cohen, M. (eds), *What is Dance?* (Oxford University Press, 1983) 434–37.

Gautier, T., 'Fanny Elssler (1810–1884)' in Steinberg, C. (ed.), *The Dance Anthology* (London: New American Library, 1980).

Geertz, C., *The Interpretation of Cultures* (London: Hutchinson, 1975).

Gieve, K., 'Rethinking Feminist Attitudes towards Motherhood', *Feminist Review*, No. 25 Spring (1987) 38–45.

Gieve, K., (ed.) *Balancing Acts* (London: Virago, 1989).

Goffman, E., *Gender Advertisements* (London: Macmillan, 1979).

Goffman, E., *Relations in Public* (Harmondsworth: Penguin, 1972).

Godliman, J., 'Gabrielle Agis talks to Johanna Godliman about her new work "Close Streams" in *New Dance* No. 25 Summer (1983) 26–27.

Goldberg, M., 'She Who is Possessed No. Longer Exists Outside: Martha Graham's Rite of Spring', *Women and Performance*, Vol. 3 No. 1 Issue 5 (1986) 17–27.

Goldberg, M., 'Trisha Brown: "All of the Person's Person Arriving"', *TDR*, Vol. 30 No. 1 Spring (1986) 149–70.

Goldberg, M. & Cooper Albright, A., 'Roundtable Interview: Post-Modernism and Feminism in Dance', *TDR*, Vol. 3 No. 2 (1987/88) 41–56.

Goldman, E., *The Traffic in Women and Other Essays on Feminism* (Washington: Times Change Press, 1970).

Gordon, C., (ed.), *Power and Knowledge: Selected Interviews and Other Writings 1972–77, (by) Michel Foucault* (Brighton: Harvester Press, 1980).

Gottschild, H., 'Late Awakening: The Re-Emergence of German Dance', *Ballett International*, March (1985) 12–14.

Gracyk, T. A., 'Pornography as Representation: Aesthetic Considerations', *Journal of Aesthetic Education*, Vol. 21 No. 4 Winter (1987) 103–21.

Graham, M., *The Notebooks of Martha Graham* (New York: Harcourt Brace Jovanovich Inc., 1973).

Graydon, J., 'But it's more than a Game. It's an Institution: Feminist Perspectives on Sport' *Feminist Review*, Spring (1983) 5–16.

Green, M. D., *Black Women Composers* (Boston, Mass.: Twayne, 1983).

Green, S., 'Review of *Making a Baby*', *New Dance*, No. 11 (1979) 11.

Greer, G., *The Female Eunuch* (London: Paladin, 1971).

Greer, G., *The Obstacle Race*, (London: Book Club Associates, 1980).

Greer, G., *Sex and Destiny* (New York: Harper & Row, 1984).

Greškovic, R., 'Armitagean Physics or The Shoes of the Ballerina', *Ballet Review*, 13:2 Summer (1985) 73–89.

Grewal, S., Kay, J., Landor, L., Lewis, G. & Parmar, P. (eds), *Charting The Journey* (London: Sheba, 1988).

Greig, C., 'Big Women', *Women's Review*, No. 5 March (1986) 10–11.

Griffiths, L., 'Reclaiming the Dance', *The Voice*, October 2 (1987) 48.

Griffiths, L., 'Beneath the Exotic Umbrella of Dance', *The Voice*, 18 (1988) 32–33.

Griffen, S., *Pornography and Silence* (London: Women's Press, 1981).

Griffen, S., *Made From this Earth* (London: Women's Press, 1982).

Grigoriev, S. L., *Diaghilev Ballet 1909–1929* (Harmondsworth: Penguin, 1960).

Grosz, E., 'Notes towards a Corporeal Feminism', *Australian Feminist Studies*, No. 5 Summer (1987) 1–16.

Guest, I., *The Dancer's Heritage* (Harmondsworth: Penguin, 1962).

Guest, I., *The Romantic Ballet in England* (London: Pitman, 1972).

Guest, I., *The Romantic Ballet in Paris* (London: Dance Books, 1980).

Gunew, S., 'Authenticity and the Writing Cure' in Sheridan, S. (ed.), *Grafts: Feminist Cultural Criticism* (London: Virago, 1988).

Hall, E., *The Hidden Dimension* (New York: Anchor Books, 1969).

Hall, S., Hobson, D., Lowe A. & Willis, P., (eds), *Culture, Media, Language*, (London: Hutchinson in association with the Centre for Contemporary Cultural Studies, University of Birmingham, 1980).

Halprin, A., 'Planetary Dance', *TDR*, Vol. 33 No. 2 Summer (1989) 60–74.

Hamilton, W., 'The Best Body for Ballet', *Dance Magazine*, October (1982) 82–83.

Hanna, J. L., *The Performer and Audience Connection* (Austin: University of Texas Press, 1983).

Hanna, J. L., 'Patterns of Dominance', *TDR* 113 (1987a) 22–47.

Hanna, J. L., 'Gender "Language" onstage: Moves, New Moves and Countermoves', *Journal of the Washington Academy of Sciences*, Vol. 77 March 1 (1987b) 18-26.

Hanna, J. L., *Dance, Sex and Gender* (Chicago and London: The University of Chicago Press, 1988a).

Hanna, J. L., 'Do We Teach Sex Roles Through Dance', *Dance Teacher Now*, September (1988b) 36–41.

Hanna, J. L., 'Dance Politics and National Identity', *Ballett International*, 2 (1989) 21-24.

Harding, E., *Women's Mysteries* (London: Rider, 1982).

Hargreaves, J. A., 'Social Production of Gender Relations in and through Sport' *Theory, Culture and Society*, Vol. 3 No. 1 (1986) 109–19.

Harpe, W., *A Question of Equity* (Merseyside Arts Report, 1990).

Harrison, J. F. C., *The Common People* (London: Fontana, 1984).

Harrison, M., 'Notes on Feminist Art in Britain 1970–77', *Studio International*, Vol. 193 No. 987 March (1977) 212–20.

Hartmann, R., 'Talking with Anna Halprin', *Dancescope*, Fall/Winter (1977/78) 57–66.

Haskell, A., *Diaghileff* (London: Victor Gollanz, 1955).

Haskell, A., *Ballet Russe* (London: Weidenfeld & Nicolson, 1968).

Hearn, J., *The Gender of Oppression* (Brighton: Wheatsheaf Books, 1987).

Hebidge, D., *Subculture: The Meaning of Style* (London: Methuen, 1979).

Hebidge, D., 'A Report on the Western Front: Postmodernism and Politics of Style', *Block*, Vol. 12 (1986/87) 4–26.

Heinemann, S., 'Inside/Out a Return to my Body', *Heresies*, Vol. 1 No. 2 May (1977) 12–15.

Henley, N., *Body Politics* (New Jersey: Prentice-Hall inc., 1977).

Heron, L. (ed.), *Truth, Dare or Promise: Growing up in the Fifties* (London: Virago, 1985).

Hess, T. & Nochlin, L., *Art and Sexual Politics* (New York: Macmillan, Collier Books, 1973).

Heymann, J. L., 'Dance in the Depression', *Dance Scope*, Spring/Summer Vol. 9 No. 2 (1975) 29–41.

Heidensohn, F., *Women and Crime* (London: Macmillan, 1985).

Holland, A. (ed.), *British Theatre Directory* (London: Richmond House Pub. Co. Ltd. 1987–8).

Howard, S. N., *Ballet Basics* (University of Arizona: Mayfield Publishing Co., 1974).

Howard, B. & O'Connor, P., *Josephine Baker* (London: Cape, 1988).

Howe, D., *Manifestations of the German Expressionist Aesthetic as presented in the Drama and Art in the Dance and Writings of Mary Wigman*, Phd. thesis, University of Wisconsin in Madison (Ann Arbor UMI, 1985).

Hughes, D., 'Dance Away the Frontier', *Performance*, No. 58 (1989) 68–75.

Humphrey, D., *The Art of Making Dances* (New York: Grove Press, 1959).
Humphrey, D., *The Collected Works Vol. 1* (New York; Dance Notation Bureau, 1978).
Hutchinson, A., 'What is Balletmakers?', *Dancing Times*, Vol. LVII, No. 679 April (1967) 360–61.
Hutchinson, R., *The Politics of the Arts Council* (London: Sinclair Browne, 1982).
Huxley, M., 'Invisibility, Hegemony and the Identity of New Dance', *New Dance*, No. 26 (1983) 16–17.
Imray, L., 'Heterosexual Feminist to Political Lesbian', *Women's Studies International Forum*, Vol. 7 No. 1 (1984) 39–41.
Itzin, C., 'Margaret Thatcher is my Sister', *Women's Studies International Forum*, Vol. 8 No. 1 (1985) 73–83.
Jackson, G., 'The Political Ballet', *Dance Scope*, Vol. 5 No. 2 Spring (1971) 37–39.
Jacobs, E. W., 'Why everybody suddenly Loves Dance', *Arts in Society*, Vol. 13 No. 2 Summer/Fall (1976) 266–70.
Jakins, T. & Smith, H., 'Fat Lib', *Spare Rib*, No. 182 September (1987) 14–21.
Jameson, F., 'Postmodernism or the Cultural Logic of late Capitalism', *New Left Review*, 146 July/August (1984) 53–92.
Jessel, C., *Life at the Royal Ballet School* (London: Methuen, 1985).
Jeyasingh, S., 'Bharatha Natyam', *New Dance*, No. 23 Autumn (1982) 3–5.
Jeyasingh, S., 'Conservative Steps', *Guardian*, December 2 (1988) 26.
Johnstone, J., *Marmalade Me* (New York: E. P. Dutton, 1971).
Jordan, S., 'Dartington International Dance Festival', *Dancing Times*, July (1981) 791–93.
Jordan, S., 'R. Butcher: Two Workshops' in Adshead, J. (ed), *Choreography Principles and Practice* (University of Surrey, 1986).
Jowitt, D., 'Post-Judson Dance', *Art in America*, 59 September/October (1971) 81–87.
Jowitt, D., *Dance Beat* (New York: Marcel Dekker, 1977).
Jowitt, D., 'Abandoning the Ivory Tower', *The Village Voice*, January 7–13 (1981) 55.
Jowitt, D., *Time and the Dancing Image* (New York: William Morrow and Company Inc., 1988).
Kane, A., 'Royal Ballet', Guardian, October 9 (1989) 37.
Kaplan, A., *Women and Film, Both Sides of the Camera* (London: Methuen, 1983).
Kaplan, J. L., 'Pina Bausch: Dancing Around the Issue', *Ballet Review*, Spring (1987) 74–77.
Katz Rothman, B., *In Labour: Women and Power in the Birth Place* (London: Junction Books, 1982).
Keersmaeker de, A., 'Valeska Gert', *TDR*, Vol. 25 No. 3 Fall (1981) 55–66.
Kelly, M. 'Woman – Desire – Image' in Appignanesi, L. (ed.), *Desire* (London: ICA Documents, 1984) 30–31.
Kendall, E., *Where She Danced* (New York: Alfred Knopf, 1979).
Kerensky, O., *Anna Pavlova* (London: Hamish Hamilton, 1975).

Kern, S., *Anatomy and Destiny: a Cultural History of the Human Body* (Indianapolis: Bobbs-Merrill, 1975).

Kertess, K., 'Dancing with Carmen', *Art in America*, April (1987) 180–83.

Khan, N., *The Arts Britain Ignores* (London: Committee for Racial Equality, 1976).

Kirkland, G., *Dancing on my Grave* (London: Hamish Hamilton, 1986).

Kirstein, L., *Dance: A Short History of Classic Theatrical Dancing* (New York: Dance Horizons, 1935).

Kitzinger, S., *The Experience of Childbirth* (Harmondsworth: Penguin, 1981).

Kitzinger, S. 'When giving birth feels degrading', *Independent* August 29 (1989) 13.

Klett, R., 'In Rehearsal with Pina Bausch', *Heresies*, Vol. 5 No. 1 (1984) 13–16.

Koegler, H., *The Concise Oxford Dictionary of Ballet* (London: Oxford University Press, 1982).

Koreweg, A. (ed.), *Go Dutch* (Amsterdam: Netherlands Theatre Institute, 1989).

Kraus, R. & Chapman, S., *History of the Dance in Art and Education* (New Jersey: Prentice-Hall Inc., 1981).

Kreemer, C., *Further Steps* (New York: Harper and Row, 1987).

Kroker, A. & M., (eds) *Body Invaders: Sexuality and the Postmodern Condition* (London: Macmillan, 1988).

Krzowski, S., & Land, P. (eds), *In Our Experience* (London: Women's Press, 1988).

Kuhn, A., *Women's Pictures, Feminism and Cinema* (London: Routledge & Kegan Paul, 1982).

Kuhn, A., *The Power of the Image* (London: Routledge & Kegan Paul, 1985).

Kuhn, A., 'Other Observers', *Women's Review*, No. 13 November (1986) 23–25.

Kuhn, A., 'The Body and Cinema', in Sheridan, S. (ed.), *Grafts* (London: Verso, 1988).

Kunzle, D., *Fashion and Fetishism* (New Jersey, Totowa: Rousman & Littlefield 1982).

Laban, R., *Modern Dance* (London: Macdonald & Evans, 1963).

Langer, S., *Feeling and Form* (London: Routledge & Kegan Paul, 1973).

Lansley, J., 'Writing', *New Dance*, No. 1 New Year (1977) 3.

Lansley, J. talks to Middleton, M., 'A Ballerina's Revenge', *Spare Rib*, 99 November (1980) 41.

Lansley, J., 'Womanless Ceremony', *Performance* No. 13, September/October (1981a) 4.

Lansley, J., 'Claire Hayes and Anna Furse at the Women's Arts Alliance', *New Dance*, No. 17 (1981b) 18.

Lansley, J. interviewed by Solway, A., *New Dance* No. 39 (1987) 18–20.

Lansley, J., 'The Centre Line', *New Dance*, No. 43 (1988) 10–11.

Laurie, H., *Women and Dance* (Essex University, Sociology project 3rd Year, 1989).

Lawson, J., *A History of Ballet and Its Makers* (London: Pitman, 1973).

Lawson, J., *The Principles of the Classic Dance* (London: Charles Black, 1979).

Layson, J., 'Isadora Duncan: Her Life-art, Choreographic and Performance Style of an Early Modern Dance Pioneer' in Adshead, J. (ed.), *Choreography Principles and Practice* (University of Surrey, 1986).

Layson, J., *Isadora Duncan: Her Life, Work and Contribution to Western Theatre Dance* (PhD. thesis, University of Leeds, 1987).

Lazarre, J., *The Mother Knot* (Boston: Beacon Press, 1986).

Leboyer, F., *Birth Without Violence* (Norwich: Fontana/Collins, 1982).

Lee, R., 'Resisting Amnesia: Feminism, Painting and Postmodernism', *Feminist Review* No. 26 July (1987) 5–28.

Lessing, D., *The Golden Notebooks* (Harmondsworth: Penguin, 1962).

Levinson, A., 'Marie Taglioni' in Steinberg, C. (ed.), *The Dance Anthology* (London: New American Library, 1980).

Lewis, J., 'Senta Driver and the Erotic Potential', *Dance Magazine*, May (1982) 134–7.

Lewis Williams, J., 'Black Dance: A Diverse Unity', *Dance Scope*, Vol. 14 No. 2 (1980) 54–62.

Lippard, L., *From the Center* (New York: E. P. Dutton, 1976).

Lippard, L., *Contribution of Feminism to Art of the 1970's* (New York: E. P. Dutton, 1984) 149–58.

Livet, A. (ed.), *Contemporary Dance* (New York: Abbeville Press, 1978).

Lloyd, M., *The Borzoi Book of Modern Dance* (New York: Dance Horizons, 1949).

Lomax, A., *Folk Song, Style and Culture* (New Brunswick: Transaction Books, 1978).

Lorde, A., *Uses of the Erotic: the Erotic as Power* (New York: Out and Out Books, 1978).

Luger, E. R. & Laine, B., 'When Choreography Becomes Female: a Talk with Anna Halpin', *Dancers' Workshop, San Francisco*, December (1978) 63–66.

Lyotard, J. F., *The Postmodern Condition* (University of Manchester Press, 1984).

McCarren, F., 'Isadora Duncan', *Women's Review*, 12 (1986) 46–47.

McConnell, J., *Ballet as Body Language* (New York: Harper & Row, 1977).

McDonagh, D., 'Negroes in Ballet', *New Republic*, 159 November 2 (1968) 41–44.

McDonagh, D., *The Rise and Fall of Modern Dance* (New York: Dutton and Co., 1970).

McDonagh, D., *The Complete Guide to Modern Dance* (New York: Doubleday & Company, 1976).

Mackrell, J., 'The Role of the Critic', *Dancing Times*, Vol. LXXIII, No. 866 November (1982) 113–14.

Mackrell, J., 'Words, Words, Words', *Dance Theatre Journal*, Vol. 3 No. 1 Spring (1985) 32–35.

Mackrell, J., 'A dance with a Turtle called Proton: Interview with Meredith Monk', *Independent*, October 16 (1986) 12.

Mackrell, J., 'A war Dance in Underpants', *Independent*, February 16 (1987) 11.

Mackrell, J., 'Should New Dance Be Ugly?', *Independent*, March 3 (1988) 15.

Mackrell, J., 'The Proud Body-Builders of Ballet', *Independent*, September 4 (1989) 16.

McMahon, D., 'The Dancers and The Dance: Ballerinas in Print', *Dance Theatre Journal*, Vol. 5 No. 4 Spring (1988) 26–30.

MacRitchie, L., 'I Giselle', *Performance*, No. 8 (1980) 10–11.

McRobbie, A., 'Dance and Social Fantasy' in McRobbie, A. & Nava, M. (eds), *Gender and Generation*, (London: Macmillan, 1984).

McRobbie, A., 'Fashion and Sexuality', *Women's Review*, No. 13 November (1986) 13–14.

McRobbie, A., 'Women and the Arts into the 1990s', *Alba*, Vol. 1 No. 2 April/May 1991.

Maitland, S., *Very Heaven: Looking Back at the 1960s* (London: Virago, 1988).

Maldoom, R., 'Dance as Social Criticism', Chisenhale Conference Day (1988).

Malecka, M., 'Royal Opportunites', *New Dance*, No. 9 New Year (1977) 20-21.

Mann, J., 'Ballet Rambert' in White, J. (ed.), *20th Century Dance in Britian* (London: Dance Books, 1988).

Manning, S., 'From Modernism to Facism: the Evolution of Wigman's Choreography', *Ballet Review*, Vol. 14 No. 4 Winter (1987) 87–98.

Manning, S., 'An American Perspective on Tanztheater', *TDR*, 110 Summer (1986) 57–79.

Marks, E., & Courtivron de I. (eds), *The New French Feminisms* (Brighton: Harvester Press, 1985).

Martin, C. 'Johanna Boyce: An Interview', *Dance Scope*, Vol. 14 No. 4 (1980) 35–46.

Martin, J., *America Dancing* (New York: Dance Horizons, 1968).

Mauss, M., 'Techniques of the Body', *Economy and Society*, Vol. 2, February (1973) 70–88.

Mazo, J. H., *Prime Movers* (London: Charles Black, 1977).

Mead, M., *Male and Female* (Harmondsworth: Penguin, 1970).

Meade-King, M., 'A Sound Vision: Women in T.V.', *The Guardian* August 18 (1987) 8.

Meisner, N., 'Modern Women Step out to Find their Form', *Sunday Times*, September 4 (1988) C8.

Mille de, A., *Dance to the Piper* (London: Hamish Hamilton, 1951).

Mille de, A., *To a Young Dancer: A Handbook for Dance Students, Parents and Teachers* (London: Putnam, 1963).

Miller, A., *Thou Shalt Not Be Aware* (London: Pluto Press, 1985).

Miller, J. B., *Psychoanalysis and Women* (Harmondsworth: Penguin, 1974).

Millet, K., *Sexual Politics* (London: Sphere, 1971).

Millum, T., *Images of Women: Advertising in Women's Magazines* (London: Chatto & Windus, 1975).

Mitchell, J., *Women: The Longest Revolution* (London: Virago, 1984).

Mitchell, J. & Oakley, A. (eds), *What is Feminism?* (Oxford: Basil Blackwell, 1986)

Moi, T., *Sexual Textual Politics* (London: Methuen, 1985).

Moi, T., 'Vive La Difference', *Women's Review*, April 6 (1986) 30–31.

Montagu, A., *Touching* (New York: Harper & Row, 1978).

Montague, S., *The Ballerina* (New York: Universe Books, 1980).

Moore, L., 'Graham in 1967', *Dancing Times*, Vol. LVII, No. 680 June (1967) 460–61.

Moore, W., 'Reflections and Perceptions on Black Dance', *The Western Journal of Black Studies*, No. 4 December (1977) 276–77.

Morgan, R., *The Anatomy of Freedom* (Oxford: Martin Robertson, 1983).

Morris, S. & Prince, K., 'Calling the Tune', *Spare Rib*, No. 172 November (1986) 38–42.

Morrison Brown, J., *The Vision of Modern Dance* (London: Dance Books, 1980).

Moss, J., 'The Body as Spectacle', *Women and Performance*, Vol. 3 No. 1, Issue 5 (1986) 5–15.

Moszynska, A., 'The New American Woman', *Performance*, No. 25 August/September (1983) 22–23.

Mottram, E., *The Algebra of Need* (London: M. Boyars, 1977).

Müller, H., 'Mary Wigman and the Third Reich', *Ballett International*, November (1986) 18–24.

Mulvey, L., 'Visual Pleasure and Narrative Cinema', *Screen*, Vol. 16 No. 3 Autumn (1975) 6–18.

Mulvey, L., 'On Duel in the Sun', *Framework* No. 15, (1981) 12–15.

Mulvey, L., 'The Image and Desire', in Appignanesi, L. (ed.), *Desire* (London: ICA Documents, 1984) 28–29.

Murdin, L., 'Arts and Money', *Sunday Correspondent, Guide to the Arts*, Part 1 (1990) 26–27.

Murray, J., *Dance Now* (Harmondsworth: Penguin, 1979).

Mutnick, D., 'Crowsfeet: A "Motherlode" of Stimulating Dance', *Guardian*, New York, March 30 (1988) 18.

Myers, K., 'Pasting Over the Cracks', in Appignanesi, L. (ed.), *Desire* (London: ICA Documents, 1984) 35–38.

Naess, J. L., 'Books/The Dancer's Body', *Dancescope* Vol. 15, No. 2 (1981) 52–56.

Nettleford, R., 'Jamaican Dance Theatre', *Dancing Times*, Vol. LIV, No. 646 September (1965) 617–19.

Nettleford, R., 'Understanding Black Dance', lecture (London: Salut! at the South Bank, August 2, 1989).

Neuls-Bates, C. *Women in Music*, (New York: Harper Row, 1982).

Neustatter, A., 'An Everyday Guide to Mysogyny', *Guardian* April 18 (1989) 17.

Newton, J. & Rosenfelt, D., (eds) *Feminist Criticism and Social Change: Sex, Class and Race in Literature and Culture* (London: Methuen, 1985).

Noverre, J., *Letters on Dancing and Ballet* (New York: Dance Horizons, 1968).

O'Brien, L., 'Starring Role', *Guardian*, September 27 (1989) 21.

Oakley, A., *Subject Women* (Great Britain: Fontana, (1981).

Odent, M., *Entering the World: the De-medicalization of Childbirth* (London: Boyars, 1984).

Odom, S. K., 'Wigman at Hellerau', *Ballet Review*, Summer (1986) 41–55.

Oglesby, C. A., *Women and Sport* (Philadelphia: Lea & Febiger, 1978).

Onwurah, C., 'Black Fire', *Guardian*, July 12 (1986) 13.

Orbach, S., *Fat is a Feminist Issue* (London: Hamlyn, 1979).

Orbach, S., 'From mother to daughter', *New Stateman*, March 29 (1985) 26–29.

Orbach, S., 'Why Women Deny their Bodies' *New Statesman*, February 14 (1986) 22–24.

Orloff, K., 'Women in Performance Art', *Heresies*, No. 17 (1984) 36–40.

Ortner, S. 'Is Female to Male as Nature is to Culture?', in Rosaldo, Z. M. and Lamphere, L. (eds), *Women, Culture and Society* (California: Stamford University Press, 1974).

Outram, D., *The Body and the French Revolution* (London: Yale University Press, 1989).

Owens, C., 'The Discourse of Others: Feminists and Postmodernism', in Foster, H. (ed.), *Post-Modern Culture* (London: Pluto Press, 1985).

Padgette, P., (ed.), *The Dance Writings of Carl Van Vechten* (New York, Dance Horizons, 1974).

Parker, J., 'The Image as Given', *Radiance*, Spring (1987) 26–28.

Parker, R. & Pollock, G. (eds), *Framing Feminism* (London: Pandora, 1987).

Parker, R., 'Art, of course, has No Sex but Artists do', *Spare Rib*, No. 25 July (1975) 34–35.

Parmar, P., 'Transitory Movements', *Spectrum Women's Photography Festival Exhibition Catalogue* (London, 1988).

Parry, J., 'Women Beware', *Observer*, September 4 (1988) 38.

Partington, A., 'Conditions of Feminist Art Practice' *FAN*, Vol. 2 No. 4 (undated, circa 1987).

Partsh-Bergsohn, I., 'Dance Theatre form Rudolf Laban to Pina Bausch', *Dance Theatre Journal*, Vol. 6 No. 2 Summer (1988) 37–39.

Pascal, J., 'Prima Ballerina Assoluta' in Heron, L. (ed.), *Truth, Dare or Promise: Growing up in the fifties* (London: Virago, 1985).

Pascal, J. 'Beautiful Dreamer', *City Limits*, May 26 – June 3 (1988) 22.

Pascal, J., 'Star and the Tsar', *Guardian*, June 26 (1989) 36.

Paxton, S., 'Contact Improvisation Views', *Contact Quarterly*, Fall (1981) 33.

Paxton, S., 'Contact Improvisation', *Theatre Papers*, Fourth Series, No. 5 (1982).

Paxton, S., 'The Grand Union', *TDR*, Vol. 16 No. 3 (1972) 128–41.

Pennebaker Associates, Jane Balfour Films Ltd. (producers), *Dance Black America*, video, (USA, 1985).

Pepper, K., 'Pina Bausch's Bluebeard', *New Dance*, No. 33 (1985) 26.

Peppiatt, A., 'Funding Dance', *Dance Theatre Journal*, Vol. 2 No. 2 Summer (1984a) 10–11.

Peppiatt, A., 'Sickled Feet, Scrunched Shoulders and Sexual Stereotypes', *Dance Theatre Journal* Vol. 2 No. 4 Winter (1984b) 8–10.

Peppiatt, A. & Tolley, J., 'Ugly Ducklings', *Dance Theatre Journal*, Vol. 4 No. 3 August (1986) 12–13.

Percival J., 'An Endangered Species', *Dance and Dancers*, January (1987) 19–23.

Perreault, M., 'Changes in the Roles of Male Dancers since the Seventeenth Century', International Congress 'Dance and Research' (Brussels: Vrije Universiteit Brussels, 1989) 1–12.

Perron, W. & Woodward, S., 'When a Woman Dances Nobody Cares', *Village Voice*, March 1 (1976) 61–62.

Petty, M. 'Royal Baby Doctor', *Today*, August 2 (1988) 20–21.

Pierpoint, M., 'Dancing for the Mother-to-Be', *Dance Magazine*, March (1981) 86.

Pistill, J. A., *Stereotyped Perceptions of Women as a Function of Menstrual Cycle Phase and Physical Function*, PhD. thesis (Kent State University, 1975).

Polhemus, T. (ed.), *Social Aspects of the Human Body* (Harmondsworth: Penguin, 1978).

Pollock, G., 'What's Wrong with Images of Women', *Screen Education*, No. 24 Autumn (1977) 25–33.

Pollock, G., 'The Politics of Art or an Aesthetic for Women', *FAN*, No. 5 (undated, circa 1981) 15–18.

Pollock, G., 'Vision, Voice and Power', *Block* 6 (1982) 2–21.

Poovey, M., 'Scenes of an Indelicate Character: The Medical Treatment of Victorian Women' in Gallagher, C. and Lacqueur, T. (eds), *The Making of the Modern Body, Sexuality and Society in the Nineteenth Century* (Berkeley: University of California Press, 1987).

Poster, M., *Foucault, Marxism and History* (Cambridge: Polity Press, 1984).

Potter, S., 'Women and Performance in the U.K.', *Studio International*, No. 982 July/August (1976) 33–34.

Powell N., ' The Soul Power in Modern Dance', *Wall Street Journal*, February (1987).

Prestidge, M., Theatre Paper, unpublished paper (*circa* 1983).

Preston-Dunlop, V., 'Laban and the Nazis', *Dance Theatre Journal*, Vol. 6 No. 2 (1988) 5–7.

Pritchard, M., & Pritchard, K., 'Politics and Contact', *Contact Quarterly*, Vol. V11 No. 1 Fall (1981) 34–38.

Puretz, S. L., 'Modern Dance's Effect on the Body Image, *International Journal of Sport Psychology*, Vol. 13 No. 3 (1982) 176-186.

Radcliffe Richards, J., *The Sceptical Feminist* (Harmondsworth: Penguin, 1982).

Rainer. Y., *Work 1961–73*, (Halifax, Canada, Press of the Nova Scotia College of Art & Design, 1974).

Reagan, N., 'A Home of One's Own: Women's Bodies in Recent Women's Fiction', *Journal of Popular Culture*, Vol. II September (1978) 772–88.

Reed, E., *Woman's Evolution* (New York: Pathfinder Press, 1975).

Reeves Sanday, P., *Female Power and Male Dominance and the Origins of Sexual Inequality* (Cambridge University Press, 1981).

Reich, W., *The Function of the Orgasm* (London: Souvenir, 1973).

Retallick, M., 'The Wallflower Order Dance Collective: Dancing the Revolution', *New Age* November (1981) 31.

Rhode, H., "You Have to Discover Your Own Beauty", *Ballett International*, January (1986) 28.

Rich, A., *Of Woman Born* (London: Virago, 1984).

Rigby, C., 'The Dancer Who Became Herself', *Dance and Dancers*, May (1988) 22–26.

Ritchie, M., *Women's Studies: a Checklist of Bibliographies* (London: Mansell, 1980).

Roberts, H. (ed.) *Doing Feminist Research* (London: Routledge & Kegan Paul, 1981).

Roberts, N., *The Frontline: Women in the Sex Industry Speak Out* (London: Grafton Books, 1986).

Rodgers, R., 'For the Celebration of Our Blackness', *Dance Scope*, Spring (1967) 7–11.

Rodgers, S., 'Women's Space in a Men's House: The British House of Commons, in Ardener, S. (ed.), *Women and Space* (London: Croom Helm, 1981).

Roslavleva, N., *Era of Russian Ballet* (London: Victor Gollanz, 1966).

Root, A,. 'Woman to Woman', *New Internationalist*, No. 149 (1985) 7–9.

Roth, M. (ed.), *The Amazing Decade: Women's Performance Art in America* (Los Angeles: Asto Artz, 1983).

Rowbotham, S., *Woman's Consciousness, Man's World* (Harmondsworth: Penguin, 1973).

Rowbotham, S., 'To Be or Not to Be: the Dilemmas of Mothering', *Feminist Review*, No. 31 Spring (1989) 82–93.

Royce, A., *The Anthropology of Dance* (Bloomington: Indiana University Press, 1977).

Rubidge, S., 'Steps in Time', *Dance Theatre Journal*, Vol. 6 No. 1 Summer (1988) 15–17.

Rubidge, S., 'Dance Umbrella and New Dance', *Dance Theatre Journal*, Vol. 6 No. 3 (1988) 6–9.

Rust, F., *Dance in Society* (London: Routledge & Kegan Paul, 1969).

Sabbage, M., 'Body Language', *Guardian*, March 28, (1987) 12.

Sachs, C. *The World History of the Dance* (New York: Norton Library, 1963).

Salmon, M., 'Ethnic, Minority and Black Arts Policies in Britain and their Influence on the Development of Black Dance since the 1940s' (B.A. dissertation, Roehampton Institute of H.E., 1987).

Salvadori, H., 'Gaby's Out Loud Debut', *Guardian*, August 30 (1985) 11.

Santora, S. 'Censored', *Spare Rib*, No. 54 January (1977) 43–45.

Savage-King, C., 'The Women – Feminism, Dance and Gaby Agis', *Dance Theatre Journal*, Vol. 3 No. 4 Winter (1985a) 12–14.

Savage-King, C., 'Classical Muscle', *Women's Review*, No. 2, December (1985b) 28–29.

Sayers, J., *Biology and Theories of Contemporary Feminism* (London: Tavistock, 1982).

Sayers, J., *Sexual Contradictions* (London: Tavistock Publications, (1986).

Sayers, L. A., *A Study in the Development of Twentieth Century British Dance Criticism*, M.Phil. thesis (Laban Centre in collaboration with the Victoria and Albert Theatre Museum, 1987).

Sayers, L. A., 'The Smaller British Dance Companies 1989–1990' in Schoenberg, B., (ed.), *World Ballet and Dance* (London: Dance Books, 1989) 72–77.

Schechner, R., 'Race Free, Gender Free, Body-Type Free, Age Free Casting', *TDR*, Vol. 33 No. 1 Spring (1989) 4–11.

Schmidt, J., 'From Fanny Elssler to Pina Bausch or From Female Other: Directedness to Self-Determination in Ballet', *Ballett International*, Vol. 5, No. 1, January (1983) 17–19.

Schmidt, J., 'Theatre of Paradise Wuppertal Dance Theatre's Retrospect on Pina Bausch', *Ballett International*, No. 11 November (1987) 28–29.

Segal, L., *Is the Future Female?* (London: Virago, 1987).

Seager, J. & Olson, A., *An International Atlas of Women in the World*, (London: Pan Books, 1986).

Semple, M., 'Black Dance', unpublished paper (Sussex University, 1985).

Sergy, F., 'Feminism and Dance', *Spare Rib*, February (1984) 6–7.

Servos, N., *Pina Bausch – Wuppertal Dance Theater or the The Art of Training Goldfish*, (Köln: Ballett-Bühen-Verlag, 1987).

Seymour, L. with Paul Gardner, *Autobiography of Lynne Seymour* (London: Granada, 1984).

Shaw, L., *Where are the Women in Ballet Today?* (Middlesex Polytechnic: BACS 111 Study, 1989).

Sheets-Johnstone, M., *The Phenomenology of Dance* (London: Dance Books, 1979).

Sheets-Johnstone, M., 'Thinking in Movement', *JAAC*, Vol. 34 No. 4, Summmer (1981) 399-407.

Sheridan, A. (ed.), *Michel Foucault: The Will to Truth* (London: Tavistock Pub., 1980).

Sheridan, S. (ed.), *Grafts: Feminist Cultural Criticism* (London: Verso, 1988).

Sherlock, J., *The Cultural Production of Dance in Britain*, PhD thesis (Laban Centre, 1988).

Shipman, M., *A Sociological Perspective of Dance* (Association of Teachers in Colleges and Departments of Education, Dance Section, 1973) 1–6.

Shorter, E., *A History of Women's Bodies* (Middlesex: Pelican, 1984).

Shulman, A. (ed.), *Red Emma Speaks: Selected Writings and Speeches by Emma Goldman* (New York: Vintage Books, 1972).

Shuttle, P. & Redgrove, P., *The Wise Wound: Menstruation and Every Woman*, (London: Victor Gollanz, 1978).

Shutz, A., *The Phenomenology of the Social World* (London: Heinemann, 1980).

Siegel, M., *At the Vanishing Point* (New York: Saturday Review Press, 1972).

Siegel, M., 'Dance is a Human Art', *Arts in Society*, No. 10 Spring/ Summer, (1973) 106-110.
Siegel, M., *Watching the Dance Go By* (Boston: Houghton Mifflin Co., 1977).
Siegel, M., 'Love Isn't All We Need', *The Soho News*, December 17, (1980) 30.
Siegel, M., *The Shapes of Change* (New York: Avon Books, 1981).
Siegel, M., 'Evolutionary Dreams: Meredith Monk', *Dance Theatre Journal*, Vol. 4 No. 3 Autumn (1986) 2–5.
Siegfried, C. H., 'Feminist Aesthetics and Marginality', *RFR/DRF*, Vol. 16 No. 4 December (1987) 10–15.
Silverstein, B., 'The Role of the Mass Media in Promoting a Thin Standard of Bodily Attractiveness for Women', *Sex Roles*, Vol. 14 Nos 9/10 (1986) 519–32.
Simons, P., 'Women in Frames: the Gaze, the Eye, the Profile in Renaissance Portraiture', *History Workshop*, No. 25 Spring (1988) 4–30.
Smith, A. 'Autobiography and the Avant-Garde', *Dance Magazine*, January (1985) 50–53.
Smith, B., 'Towards a Black Feminist Criticism', in Showalter, E. (ed.), *The New Feminist Criticism* (London: Virago, 1986).
Smith, J., *The Genesis of Misogynies* (London: Faber & Faber, 1989).
Sorell, W., *The Dance Has Many Faces* (New York: Columbia University Press, 1966).
Sorell, W., *Hanya Holm* (Middletown: Wesleyan University Press, 1969).
Sorell, W., *Dance in its Time* (New York: Anchor Press Doubleday, 1981).
Spalding, F., 'Postmodernism', *Women's Review*, September 11 (1986) 25–27.
Spelman, E. V., 'Woman as Body: Ancient and Contemporary Views', *Feminist Studies*, Vol. 8, No. 1, Spring (1982) 108–30.
Spence, J., 'What Do People Do All Day?', *Screen Education*, No. 29 Winter (1978/79) 29–45.
Spencer, P., *Society and the Dance* (Cambridge University Press, 1986).
Spender, D., *Man Made Language* (London: Routledge & Kegan Paul, 1980).
Spender, D., *Women of Ideas* (London: Ark, 1983).
Spender, D., *Time and Tide Wait for No Man* (London: Pandora, 1984).
Stacey, J., 'Desperately Seeking Difference', in Gamman, L. & Marshment, M. (eds), *The Female Gaze* (London: Women's Press, 1988).
Steinburg, C. (ed.), *The Dance Anthology* (New York: New American Library, 1980).
Steinman, L., *The Knowing Body* (London: Shambala, 1986).
Stephenson, J., *Women in Nazi Society* (London: Croom Helm, 1975).
Stodelle, E., *The Dance Technique of Doris Humphrey and Its Creative Potential*, (Princetown: Princetown Book Co., 1978).
Stone, L., *The Family, Sex and Marriage in England 1500–1800* (London: Weidenfeld and Nicolson, 1977).
Straker, C., 'Breaking the Mould', Channel 4 Television, TV Programme, (1989).

Sullivan, L., 'Les Noces: the American Premier', *Dance Research Journal*, 14 (1981/82) 3–14.

Sweigard, L., *Human Movement Potential: Its Ideokinetic Facilitation* (London: Harper & Row, 1974).

Tawn, D. 'Reconstructing Representation of Female Imagery in visual Arts and Dance' (West Sussex Institute, dissertation, 3rd year, 1989).

Taylor, D. (ed.), 'Living Images', *New Internationalist*, 98 April (1981).

Taylor, D. (ed.), 'Women: the Facts', *New Internationalist*, No. 89, July (1980) 10–11, No. 90 August, (1980) 10–11, No. 150 August, (1985a) 10–11.

Taylor, D. (ed.), 'The Culture Club', *New Internationalist*, No. 144 February (1985b) 10–11.

Taylor, D. (ed.), 'Woman to Woman: A World Report', *New Internationalist*, No. 149 July (1985c) 7–29.

Tickner, L., 'Notes on Feminism, Femininity and Women's Art', *Lip*, Vol. 8, (1984) 14–18.

Thomas, H., untitled, a discussion of the body as a medium of expression (unpublished paper, mimeo, 1982a).

Thomas, H., untitled, a discussion of Nancy Henley's book *Body Politics* (unpublished paper, mimeo, 1982b).

Thomas, H., *Movement, Modernism and Contemporary Culture* (PhD. thesis, London University, Goldsmiths' College, 1986).

Thorpe, E., *Black Dance* (London: Chatto & Windus, 1989).

Tobias, T., 'In Praise of Older Women', *Dance Magazine* November (1982) 55–58.

Todd, M. E., *The Thinking Body* (New York: Dance Horizons, 1975).

Torres, F., 'Dance troupe puts struggles on stage', *Lanley Tower*, California, November 13, (1986), 6.

Tuchman, G. (ed) *et al.*, *Hearth and Home: Images of Women in the Mass Media* (New York: Oxford University Press, 1978).

Turner, B. S. *The Body and Society* (Oxford: Basil Blackwell, 1984).

Turner, J. (ed.), 'Talking of Gender', *MTD* Summer (1990) 36–44.

United Nations Report (1980), postcard quote (London: Women's Press).

Valois de N., *Invitation to the Ballet* (London: John Lane, The Bodley Head, 1937).

Valois de N., *Come Dance With Me* (London: Hamish Hamilton, 1957).

Valois de N., *Step By Step* (London: W. H. Allen, 1977).

Vincent, L. M., *Competing with the Sylph* (New York: Andrews & McMeel, 1979).

Walker, J. A., *Art in the Age of Mass Media* (London: Pluto Press, 1983).

Walters, M., *The Nude Male* (London: Paddington Press, 1978).

Walum, Richardson, L., *The Dynamics of Sex and Gender, a Sociological Perspective* (Chicago: Rand McNally College Pub. Co., 1977).

Wandor, M., 'The Impact of Feminism on the Theatre', *Feminist Review*, No. 18 Winter (1984) 77–91.

Wandor, M., *Carry on Understudies* (London: Routledge & Kegan Paul, 1986).

Warner, M., *Monuments and Maidens: The Allegory of the Female Form* (London: Weidenfeld & Nicolson, 1985).

Warwicke, Z., 'Diabolic Steroids', *Guardian*, 7 June (1988) 16.

Watson, K., 'Shapes of the Nation', *Hampstead and Highgate Express*, December 16 (1988) 108.

Watts, J., 'Can All Art be Completely Sexless?', *Observer*, August 20 (1978) 25.

Weeks, J., *Sex, Politics and Society* (London: Longman, 1981).

Weideger, P., *Female Cycles* (London: Women's Press, 1975).

Weil, M., 'Dance in Early America' in Weil, M. & Hartley, D. (eds), *The Sociology of the Arts* (Illinois: Interstate Printers and Publishers, 1975a) 37–50.

Weil, M. 'Isadora Duncan and the New Feminism' in Weil, M. & Hartley, D. (eds), *The Sociology of the Arts* (Illinois: Interstate Printers and Publishers, 1975b) 27–31.

Weinbaum, B., 'Music, Dance and Song: Women's Cultural Resistance in Making their own Music', *Heresies*, Vol. 6 No. 2 Issue 22 (1987) 18–21.

Weiss, A., 'A Queer Feeling When I Look At You', lecture, *National Film Theatre, Third Lesbian and Gay Film Festival* (London, October, 1988).

Wex, M., *Let's Take Back Our Space: Female and Male Body Language as a Result of Patriarchal Structures* (Shaftesbury: Element Books, 1979).

White, J. (ed.), *20th Century Dance in Britain* (London: Dance Books, 1985).

Whitfield, M., 'Royal Ballet Dancers Vote to Accept 15% Rise', *Independent* January 27 (1990) 8.

Wigman, M., 'The Dance and the Modern Woman', *Dancing Times*, November (1927) 162–63.

Williams, A., 'Re-Viewing The Look: Photography and the Female Gaze', *Ten 8*, No. 25 (1987) 4–11.

Williams, J. L., 'Black Dance a Diverse Unity', *Dance Scope*, Vol. 14 No. 2 (1980) 55–63.

Williams, R., *The Long Revolution* (Harmondsworth: Pelican, 1961).

Williams, R., *Culture* (London: Fontana, 1989).

Williamson, J., *Decoding Adverts* (London: Marion Boyars, 1978).

Williamson, J., *Consuming Passions: The Dynamics of Popular Culture* (London: Marion Boyars, 1986).

Willis, P. E., 'Performance and Meaning: A Socio-cultural View of Women in Sport', *Centre for Contemporary Cultural Studies, Women Series* (University of Birmingham, SP No. 19 March, 1974).

Wilson A., 'Fit for What?', *Trouble and Strife*, No. 10 Spring (1987) 16–17.

Wilson, E., *Women and the Welfare State* (London: Tavistock, 1977).

Wilson, E., *Adorned in Dreams* (London: Virago, 1985).

Winship, J., 'Sexuality for Sale', in Hall, S. *et al.* (eds), *Culture, Media, Language* (London: Hutchinson, 1980).

Wolff, J., *The Social Production of Art* (London: Macmillan, 1982).

Wolff, J., *Aesthetics and the Sociology of Art* (London: George & Allen Unwin, 1983).

Wolff, J., *Feminine Sentences* (Cambridge, Polity Press, 1991).

Wollstonecraft, M., *Vindication of the Rights of Women* (1891), in Krammick (ed.) (Harmondsworth: Penguin, 1975).

Woolf, V., *A Room of One's Own* (London: Panther Books, 1977).

Woodcock. S., 'Margaret Rolfe's Memoirs of Marie Taglioni: Part 1', *Dance Research*, Vol. V11 No. 1 Spring (1989) 3–19.

Wooley, O. W., Wooley, S.C. & Dyrenforth, S. R., 'Obesity and Women – II: A Neglected Feminist Topic', *Women's Studies International Forum*, Vol. 2 (1972) 81–92.

Youngerman, S., 'Curt Sachs and His Heritage: A Critical Review of World History of the Dance with a Survey of Recent Studies that Perpetuate His Ideas', *Cord News*, Vol. 6 No. 2 (1974) 6–17.

Zimmer, E., 'Parallels in Black', *Dance Theatre Journal*, Vol. 5 No. 1 Spring (1987) 5–7.

Index